Contents

A Post-Elton Foreword

This book is a re-issue of Management of Disruptive Pupil Behaviour in Schools with a modified title and a different cover. More significantly, printing technology has made it possible for this additional foreword to be included following the publication of the Elton Report (1989) on Discipline in Schools. The analysis of the problem and many of the major recommendations contained in the Report were anticipated by the contributors to the book. This is as we would have expected it to be, as it is unlikely that discipline in schools has changed dramatically in the last three years and, what is more, all the contributors were specialists in their respective fields with an extensive combined knowledge of the issues. In fact, some of the contributors made submissions to the Committee of Enquiry. One of the strengths of this book is that it provides an excellent companion volume to the Report in that it expands on many of its recommendations with supportive research from a wide field of interests.

Both book and report focus on a whole-school approach to discipline and reject the view that cause and cure rest entirely with the individual pupil. The following chapters acknowledge the complexity of the problem but, like Elton, accept that, 'Reducing bad behaviour is a realistic aim. Eliminating it completely is not' (Elton, p. 65). This realism is an acceptance of the fact that schooling by its nature and organisation is a contributory element in the problem of pupil misbehaviour, and disruptive behaviour and absenteeism are the two main expressions of pupil disaffection. In chapter one McGuiness and Craggs analyse the pathogenic effect in schools — 'the process by which an organisation ostensibly designed to enhance the potential of young people in fact stunts that potential, leaving the victims bewildered, resentful, and hostile towards the source of their frustration'. They then proceed to outline ways which will reduce the pathogenic effect through a developmental pastoral care programme which emphasizes the importance of interpersonal skills of teachers in their daily interactions with pupils in a range of contexts and situations. Elton too places the quality of teacher-pupil relations at the centre of its analysis:

> 'The most central of these influences is the relationship between teacher and pupils. When a teacher sees misbehaviour, judges it to be unacceptable and intervenes to

371.93   Disruptive
          Pupil Management

DIS

MA

DI

David Fulton Publishers
London

David Fulton Publishers Ltd
2 Barbon Close, London WC1N 3JX

First published in Great Britain by John Wiley 1986
David Fulton Publishers 1989

British Library Cataloguing in Publication Data

[Management of disruptive pupil behaviour in schools]
  Disruptive pupil management.
  1. Schools. Disruptive students
  371.8'1

  ISBN 1 85346 133 4

Printed in Great Britain

stop it, it is the relationship between the teacher and the pupils or pupils involved which will determine the success of that intervention' (p. 64).

Schools are complex organisations and pupil indiscipline is a complicated expression of deviant behaviour on a continuum of severity. Therefore, our responses to the problem must also be varied and multi-faceted, progressing from crisis-management to interventionist strategies and on towards a' preventive, whole-school policy on discipline. In fact, the Committee of Enquiry was set up by the Secretary of State for Education in March 1988, following growing expressions of concern by the teacher unions responding to survey results which indicated that an increasing number of teachers were subjected to physical and verbal abuse. Elsewhere (Tattum, 1989), I have made a detailed review and critique of two decades of surveys and reports on discipline in schools from Teacher Unions, Government and Local Authorities, and individual and local surveys. The Elton Report makes particular reference to the results of the Professional Association of Teacher's survey which was in part instrumental in the setting up of the Enquiry. The survey was conducted in Autumn 1987 in conjunction with the Daily Express. Members were invited to complete a questionnaire in their professional journal and from the responses of 1,500 teachers to the question, 'Have you ever been subjected to a physical attack by a pupil?' a disturbing 32 per cent answered in the affirmative.

From a similarly worded question in an NOP survey of a controlled sample of nearly 500 NUT members only 5 per cent replied that they had been physically assaulted or threatened (Teacher, 1988). Consideration of the wide discrepancy in the percentages highlights the research problems and, more importantly, will determine the nature of the profession's response to indiscipline. Faced with these and other inconsistencies the Committee commissioned its own survey from Sheffield University's Educational Research Centre. The research involved a nationally representative survey of just under 4,400 secondary and primary teachers and also interviews of 100 teachers in 10 inner city secondary schools not covered by the survey. Just over two per cent of teachers reported some form of 'physical aggression' towards themselves, either in the classroom and/or about the school. The main problem reported was the 'continuous stream of relatively minor disruptions', such as, talking out of turn, bickering and jostling, hindering other pupils and calculated idleness or work avoidance. As Lord Elton said, "The picture is not one of crisis, but one of continual draining stress on teachers". To perceive of the problem thus is not to underestimate its frustrating and debilitating effect on teachers, rather it recognises the nature of the problem and points us towards positive strategies.

Within the present climate it is probably necessary that schools and local authorities devise a series of approaches to cope with difficult pupils. The most violent and aggressive may need to be sent to special units for the benefit of everyone; but where units do exist we would do well to consider the review made by ILEA of its extensive support provision (Chapter 12). Their recommendations are that where units continue to function they should be bigger and cover a wider catchment area. This would enable them to offer a broader curriculum and reduce the sense of isolation experienced by staff. Most interestingly, the writers propose that there needs to be a change in the way we view support units within the wider concept of children with special needs, and they suggest that larger units may become centres of alternative education. The positive aim must be to convince pupils and parents that what is offered is worthwhile in educational terms.

An even more constructive approach to crisis provision is provided by Lane (Chapter 7). In addition to receiving very difficult children at the Educational Guidance Centre the centre's staff also provide interventionist support for individual teachers and whole schools. Several other contributors describe how other professionals may provide context intervention which is collaborative, that is, educational psychologists (Chapter 2) and educational psychiatrists (Chapter 11) may work alongside the teacher in the classroom.

Finally, the main thrust of the book is towards a whole school discipline policy which is proactive rather than reactive in its practice. No self-respecting school would be without a whole school curriculum policy but, as we have learned from the Elton survey, teachers experience a series of minor disturbances which are both frustrating and challenging. It is therefore necessary to look at discipline in a broadly-based way and regard it as integral to the entire teaching function involving curriculum, personal and social education, class management, teacher-pupil and teacher-parent relations and so on. In its 138 recommendations Elton covers all the above named areas of schooling — and others; and in this book the contributors too offer practical advice and guidance on all these key concerns. Its trend is to progress from individualizing blame to understanding the school as an institution which, by its policies and practices can, either, create a climate of dissension and disaffection, or a positive ethos of whole school concern for mutual respect, high expectations, and an orderly community.

References

Elton Report (1989) Discipline in Schools. HMSO, London.
Tattum, D. P. (1989) Violent, Aggressive and Disruptive Behaviour. In N. Jones (ed.) Special Educational Needs Review, Vol. I. Falmer Press, London.

List of Contributors

ANTHONY BOLGER Senior Lecturer in the Department of Sociology, Social Anthropology and Social Work, University of Keele

ANTHONY BOWERS Tutor in Psychology and Special Education, Cambridge Institute of Education

BARRIE J. BROWN Senior Lecturer in Psychology, Institute of Psychiatry, The Maudsley Hospital, London

Present Address
District Psychologist, Bloomsbury Health Authority, National Temperance Hospital, London

MAURICE CHAZAN Emeritus Professor of Education, University College of Swansea

DENISE CRAGGS Teacher in Felstead Special School, Sunderland

JEAN DAVIES Senior Research Officer, Research and Statistics Branch, ILEA

DANIEL L. DUKE Professor of Educational Administration, Lewis and Clark College, Oregon, USA

VERNON F. JONES Professor of Education, Lewis and Clark College, Oregon, USA

ALICE F. LAING Senior Lecturer in Education, University College of Swansea

DAVID A. LANE Director, Islington Educational Guidance Centre, ILEA

JEAN LAWRENCE Principal Lecturer in Education, University of London Goldsmiths' College

JOHN McGUINESS   Lecturer in Education, University of Durham

ANDREW POLLARD   Reader in Education, Bristol Polytechnic

DAVID STEED   Senior Lecturer in Education, University of London Goldsmiths' College

DEREK STEINBERG   Consultant Psychiatrist, Department of Child and Adolescent Psychiatry, The Bethlem Royal and the Maudsley Hospitals, London

DELWYN P. TATTUM   Principal Lecturer in Education, South Glamorgan Institute of Higher Education, Cardiff

KEITH TOPPING   Educational Psychologist, Kirklees Psychological Service, Huddersfield

ANDREAS VARLAAM   Deputy Director, Research and Statistics Branch, ILEA

ANNE WEST   Senior Research Officer, Research and Statistics Branch, ILEA

PAMELA YOUNG   Lecturer in Educational Administration, University of London Institute of Education

Preface

Disruptive pupil behaviour is a major concern in many advanced industrial societies. The aim of this book is to offer practical advice and guidance on the management of problem behaviour to teachers, students in training, educational administrators, teacher trainers, and others involved in education. Throughout, the emphasis is on preventing problems from becoming crises.

The problems associated with the management of disruptive behaviour are approached in four different ways.

(1) The book draws upon the expertise of a wide range of disciplines, professions, and approaches. The contributors cover the problem from the perspectives of psychology, sociology, social administration, and philosophy, and there are contributions from an educational psychologist, a clinical psychologist, a psychiatrist, a counsellor, educational researchers, and a teacher in a special school.

(2) The book covers management on a large scale through to working with individual pupils, and includes organizational change and changing the behaviours of classroom teachers.

(3) Whilst the problem of disruptive behaviour is concentrated in the secondary schools, many contributions are equally relevant for primary school teachers, and certain chapters are written with particular reference to young children in infant and junior schools.

(4) Evidence from other countries is included in order to widen the debate, and these contributions offer constructive examples of other national management initiatives.

All chapters have been written specially for this book and many draw upon original material. They are written by contributors who are experts in their respective fields, and have considerable experience in writing academic texts. The emphasis is on organizational management and person management, rather than on management of knowledge through the curriculum. This is a deliberate decision, as disruptive pupils represent a much larger body of disaffected youngsters who express their dissatisfaction with school fare either by opting out or by switching off. The growth in the knowledge of person management is considerable, and one of our concerns must be to bring it to the attention of teachers, students in training, teacher trainers, advisors, and administrators. There is no single solution to the problem; the multidisciplinary perspectives will help us better understand pupils' problem behaviour, and to draw upon the particular approaches which best suit individual needs and preferences.

As editor, I wish to express my thanks to all the authors who gave of their valuable time to write contributions to this book, and for the many ways in which they cooperated to ease my task.

The publishers also thank Allyn & Bacon, Inc., for permission to include copyright material from *Comprehensive Classroom Management* by Vernon F. Jones and Louise S. Jones, 1985.

Delwyn P. Tattum

Management of Disruptive Pupil Behaviour in Schools
Edited by D. P. Tattum
©1986 John Wiley & Sons Ltd

Introduction

Delwyn P. Tattum

The aim of this book is to be pragmatic and practical. It is pragmatic in that it starts from the acknowledgement that indiscipline is a fact of school life with which teachers, to a greater or lesser degree, will have to cope; also, that to focus on the pupil alone is to ignore the interactive nature of human relationships and the very special social context that exists in schools and classrooms. The quality of relationships and the nature of the social context created are vital elements in the whole process of control and discipline. The book is practical in that it examines a variety of ways by which the profession can respond to the problem of indiscipline, and in so doing it looks to offer practical advice and guidance at a number of different levels—local authorities, schools, and classrooms. The contributors do not claim to have all the answers, and the book does not attempt to cover every conceivable approach.

We may be criticized for appearing to accept the social situation and failing to give due attention to the wider social and economic problems which impinge on school order. Factors such as unemployment, depressed job opportunities, poor housing, decaying inner cities and racial tensions undoubtedly have a disruptive impact on families and communities. But these are aspects of society over which teachers have no control—although they are deeply concerned and affected by them, and even if teachers did have some direct influence we may question their right of involvement. On the other hand, teachers do have professional influence over what goes on in schools, and the recent rise in interest in the effects schools have on their pupils places schools in a more important position than was thought to be the case from earlier research. Changing schools as organizations, and changing teacher behaviour, are therefore major focuses of the book; together with approaches which not only seek to contain but, more importantly, to prevent problem behaviour from arising and escalating into confrontation.

In this introduction I have tried to avoid the temptation to review the problem of disruptive pupils that has emerged over the last two decades; this has been done effectively in a number of books on the topic published during the 1980s. If anyone has doubts that concern for the problem of indiscipline in schools has escalated in recent years (which is quite different from offering evidence of an increase in its incidence) then a review of the range of books and articles devoted to the subject would soon dispel them. Instead, I shall address myself to two issues. Firstly, I shall attempt to locate the growth in the provision for disruptive pupils in a wider educational context, and to consider some of the management problems associated with a crisis management response. Secondly, I wish to examine the effects that indiscipline can have on teachers at a time when large sections of the education service are being undermined and attacked. Concern for teachers is one of the major reasons for this book, and all the contributors offer ways which give help, guidance, and support in the management of disruptive pupil behaviour.

Disruptive pupils and some management problems

Discussion of the growth in provision for children with special educational needs can be approached in a variety of ways. One could examine the rapid growth in the number of places available for the different categories of pupils, or one could discuss the increase in the categories of pupils designated as in need of special provision. And as the approaches to this management problem are clearly related, so we can consider both aspects through the recent advent of that new special category—the disruptive pupil.

In a recent article, Swann (1985) challenges the view that the Education Service is positively responding to the integration recommended in the Warnock Report (1978) and promoted in the 1981 Education Act. He demonstrates that between 1978 and 1982 the proportion of pupils of secondary school age with behaviour and learning difficulties (ESN(M), ESN(S), and maladjusted) increased by 13.5, 8.5 and 10.0 per cent respectively. But the maladjusted constitute only a small proportion of the total population of pupils variously labelled as disruptive, disturbed, disaffected, or having behaviour problems. This particular group does not appear in the Department of Education and Science Statistics of Education (Schools) as a special education category as the children are not designated, and remain on the registers of their parent schools. These are among the lost statistics of special education needs, and are difficult to quantify because of the fluid state of the population and provision. When discussing this group, Swann speculates on their increased prevalence, and questions whether they are the product of a 'greater incidence in problem behaviour, a decline in the tolerance of ordinary schools, changes in ascertainment practices or a combination of these'. To his proposed explanations we need to add the existence (and extent) of local authority provision, local pressure groups, and the present educational–political climate.

The emergence of the disruptive pupil must therefore be discussed against the increased ability of the teaching profession, aided by educational psychologists, to identify more children who, on the grounds of 'defect, dullness, handicap or special need', have to be segregated from normal schools. It is also necessary to review briefly the ill-conceived and *ad hoc* way in which local authorities set about swiftly making special provision for disruptive pupils.

The growth of special education provision over the last century (Tomlinson, 1982; Ford *et al.*, 1982) demonstrates not only the power of vested interests but also the use of the provision as a method of social control. By facilitating the separating out of the defective and troublesome, special education has served the smooth running of ordinary schools. Whilst we would argue that the segregation of children into special schools enables the concentration of expertise and resources, it is also true to say that defective and troublesome pupils make extra demands on the school management and create extra problems for teachers. But the transfer to a special facility raises certain fundamental questions about the nature and quality of education provided. (See Ghodsian and Calnan, 1977, and Galloway and Goodwin, 1979.) The HMI (1978) report on the provision available in special units for disruptive pupils is also disquieting, for it is critical of the quality of some premises, the lack of facilities and resources, and the narrow curriculum available to secondary age pupils.

Illustrations of the massive expansion in special education provision can be seen in the figures for those ascertained as maladjusted or educationally sub-normal. In 1950 there were 587 pupils in schools for the maladjusted, but by 1979 the figure had risen to 22 402 in England and Wales. The figures representing ESN(M) showed an increase from 15 173 in 1950 to 32 815 in 1960, and when the figures for ESN(S) and ESN(M) were combined in 1970 the total increased to 51 769—and to 119 005 in 1979. From these figures it would seem evident that teachers in ordinary schools have been able to identify more and more children who are in need of special education and who should therefore be transferred to special schools. It was against this backcloth of expanding demand for more places to which to transfer the defective and troublesome from the normal school that the Warnock Report was published. The report, particularly in an attempt to stem, and even reverse, the flow of problem children from the 'normal' schools, recommended that more children should be integrated into mainstream schooling. The implication of this recommendation is that the *problem* of catering for children with special needs will fall upon teachers working in classes in ordinary schools.

The identification of a category of pupils who exhibit social and conduct disorders is consistent with our general preoccupation to sift out more and more children who do not fit into the model of the normal child in the ordinary school. By definition, their behaviour is the problem of management and control. They disrupt the legitimate activities of schools and classrooms, and interrupt the learning opportunities of other pupils as well as their own.

The speed of growth of special provision for disruptive pupils is no less dramatic than that for maladjusted and ESN pupils. The peak year for the setting up of special units was 1974; and in a survey in the summer of 1977 the DES found that 69 of the 96 English local education authorities (LEAS) had one or more units, giving a total of 239 units providing places for 3962 pupils (HMI, 1978). Further expansion in the 1970s was corroborated by the ACE Survey (1980) which indicated the existence of units in Scotland, Wales, the Isle of Man, and the Channel Islands. The numbers identified by the Inspectorate were markedly increased in 1979 when the Inner London Education Authority (ILEA) approved 240 support centres to accommodate 2280 pupils; and according to the latest survey by the Social Education Research Project (SERP) there has been a further increase of 140 per cent in off-site units compared with the number quoted in the Inspectorate's returns (Ling, 1984). From Lawrence, Steed, and Young (chapter 14 of this book) and other sources we learn that the United Kingdom is one of the very few countries to adopt segregation as an attempted solution to in-school behaviour problems. Most other countries have initiated schemes to tackle the problem where it occurs, in the school and classroom.

Our pattern of response to disruptive pupils has been mainly one of crisis management and, though understandable, it has been negative and reactive. Many schemes have been hastily conceived, with little regard for aims and objectives, or for the philosophical and educational issues implicit in the segregation of a new category of pupil from mainstream schooling. Research and educational thinking about indiscipline and related issues have progressed since the mid 1970s, and the contributors to this book adopt a more proactive, preventive approach to disruptive behaviour. In the main, their thesis is that schools and teachers in classrooms are contributory factors in the equation of pupil misbehaviour. They move beyond the popular 'medical model' which locates both cause and cure in the individual, for whom an appropriate course of treatment is prescribed as necessary to effect a recovery to a 'normal' state. For

concentration on the social pathology of the individual permits us to ignore deficiencies in the system. To look beyond the pupil takes us into the school and classroom, and requires us to consider whether the nature of the organisation places constraints and controls on the pupil which are themselves problematic. What is more, that the attitudes and expectations of teachers can create confrontational situations for pupils who lack the social skills of 'pleasing teacher'. (Tattum 1985)

That is, the pupils lack the ability to give acceptable reasons for their behaviour and to express themselves in acceptable language. They also fail to adopt the correct demeanour and attitudinal responses. If this is the case, then their handicap is social and not medical.

Disruptive pupils are by definition different from other categories of special needs children in that their handicap is not constitutional. They are not, by designation, physically handicapped nor mentally deficient, neither are they emotionally disturbed or distressed—rather, it is that aspects of their behaviour are socially unacceptable to certain adults in a particular kind of organization. This does not mean that that same behaviour would not be disapproved of elsewhere and by other adults. Social behaviour is learned, and it is relative and situational. These pupils are aware of their excesses and their unacceptability—they have learned in their years of schooling what teacher expects (Tattum, 1982). One problem is that in most societies there are conflicting social norms, attitudes, and values; and the value system of schools conflicts in many ways with the prevailing values and styles of adolescent subcultures. School delays their entry into adulthood, and much of what is taught they regard as irrelevant to their needs. In their disillusionment with school many turn to troublemaking.

The persistent theme of this book is that of examining ways by which schools in general and class teachers in particular can be helped to prevent disruptive behaviour from occurring, and when it does happen, as it inevitably will, how individuals can best cope with the problem behaviours confronting them. The writers recognize that there will be some children who need special help and that provision needs to be made to isolate the extreme cases, but in the main the support is directed towards schools managing their own problem pupils.

Evidence of progress from crisis management to more preventive approaches is to be found in the ILEA review of its extensive support centre provision (see chapter 12 of this book). It recommends (ILEA 5042 and 5141) that there should be a major reduction in off-site units; and, where they continue to function, they should cover a wider catchment area and so be large enough to offer a broader curriculum for pupils over 14 years. Larger units will help to reduce the feeling of professional isolation that many teachers who work in them experience. Units with more than three teachers will also ease release for attendance on in-service courses, casestudy meetings, visits to schools and homes, and work with pupils away from the centre. There is a need to change the concept of where units actually fit into a local authority's provision for children with special needs, and larger units can become centres of alternative education within state provision. The aim must be to convince pupils and parents that what is offered is worthwhile in educational terms.

The ILEA reports also recommend an expansion of on-site unit provision for reasons developed in Tattum (1982) and touched on in chapter 12. But most interestingly, they recommend the setting up of peripatetic teams in each division. The teams will be trained to provide classroom support for teachers. The teachers appointed will have to have broad-based and balanced skills and expertise, covering interpersonal and organizational knowledge, as well as subject and teaching skills. The teams will also need to have support from other professionals, such as psychologists and psychiatrists. (See chapter 7, by Lane, for he, with his Division 3 team, are involved in the emerging programme.)

One of the difficult management problems associated with segregating children into special units is that of reintegration into mainstream schooling (West, Davies, and Varlaam, in chapter 12, touch on some of the reasons). And although there is a growing body of literature on units the only published study of this important question is by ILEA (1985). ILEA claims 30 per cent completely successful and 40 per cent partially successful returns for the spring and summer terms 1982, when 331 pupils aged 11–14 left off-site units. The most important management factor related to the success of reintegration was the efforts made by the school staff to support the pupil through what is a testing time for all parties.

> Pupils assessed by staff as being 'completely successful' at reintegrating back into school were likely to have been made the subject of some kind of special arrangement (such as gradual reintegration, special meetings with staff or a special timetable) just prior to, or immediately on, their return. The deliberate policy of giving the pupil 'a fresh start' without the benefit of any special arrangements appeared to be somewhat less effective. The more successful group also tended, on average, to have a higher number of school staff, particularly form and subject teachers, involved actively in the reintegration programmes. Thus it appears that the efforts of the school staff were making a significant contribution to the success of the pupils' reintegration back into school. (ILEA, 1985)

In Tattum (1982) the procedures for successful reintegration are dealt with in detail.

Teacher stress and disruptive pupil behaviour

The 'battered teacher' syndrome is a concern that we cannot ignore in the present educational climate. Morale in the profession is low; teachers are suffering shell-shock from attacks on their professional competence and commitment. They are made scapegoats, by government spokespersons, for football hooliganism, use of drugs, pornography, violence and contempt for authority. Government financial policies have resulted in a deterioration in their physical work conditions and their professional resources. Their sense of personal worth is diminished as they have experienced a decline in their relative income and hence their family's standard of living. It is against this catalogue that they are expected to cope with the consequences of falling pupil rolls, professional accountability (and, no doubt, in the near future, personal assessment), and the demands from a range of curricular and examination innovations and reforms. The collective spirit in staffrooms is under strain; and this year, for the first time in my career as a teacher trainer, my students returned from teaching practice in secondary schools with their idealism and enthusiasm for their chosen profession tarnished. As PGCE students they were reluctant to enter the job market rather than, as has been the case in previous years, fired by the prospect of their first teaching appointment. From colleagues in other teacher-training institutions I have learned that my experience is not unique. This mood of despondency cannot be healthy for the profession, and if it is evident to students it will not have escaped the notice and experiences of pupils.

Concern has developed about the evidence of a growth in stress in teachers arising from increasing and conflicting demands on their time and energy (NUT, 1985). Kyriacou and Sutcliffe (1978), concentrating on medium-sized, mixed comprehensive schools, reported that 20 per cent of the 257 teacher respondents in a self-report questionnaire found teaching to be either very stressful or extremely stressful. They identified four items as sources of stress — pupil misbehaviour, poor working conditions, time pressures, and poor school ethos. But, as the authors observe, the causes of stress are multi-dimensional and interactive. From his extensive research and in-service work with teachers, Dunham (1984) presents a comparable list which includes organizational and curricular changes, role conflict and role ambiguity, difficult working conditions, and children's behaviour and attitudes. The symptoms of stress manifest themselves in a variety of ways — excitement, anxiety, frustration, anger, fear, and irritability — conditions which will affect a person's ability to cope, and have harmful and debilitating effects on inter-personal relations. In addition to the conflictive aspects of pupil behaviour, such as rowdyism, abuse and threats of violence, foul language, defiance, and refusing to accept teacher's authority, there are the much more complex inner states of uncertainty and confusion. Dunham writes about teachers who are distressed by exhibitions of 'raw emotion' by pupils.

For teachers whose personal values and experience have led them to believe that the right way to deal with angry feelings is to 'swallow' and hide them, it can be a frightening experience to be faced with children and young adults who do not seem to share their inhibitions . . . and, therefore, another major source of stress in teaching disruptive children is insecurity which is increased by the unpredictability of the pupils' behaviour. (Dunham, 1984)

When faced with open defiance or anger teachers are unsure of how to respond, as it is unlikely that their training or previous experience has prepared them for such behaviour. (Several of this book's contributors address themselves directly to this problem — amongst them are Bowers, Pollard, Laing and Chazan.) Another source of professional stress arises from the teacher's increased involvement in pupils' social and personal education through pastoral care and other related innovatory courses on guidance and counselling of young people in a range of interpersonal matters. Involvement in pupils' problems can result in a sense of frustration and helplessness at being unable to change the conditions within the family and, more pertinently, within the school itself. (This aspect of the problem is dealt with by McGuiness and Craggs, Tattum, and Bolger.) The feeling of inadequacy at not being able to help the child can be compounded by communication difficulties within the school's disciplinary structure (see Tattum, 1982), and with interprofessional contacts (Dunham, 1984). If the internal mechanisms for dealing swiftly and effectively with indiscipline are inadequately worked out then teachers can feel isolated in dealing with the problem. Teachers at the 'chalk-face' need to feel that they have the support of senior management when in a confrontational situation. Evidence of support extends to a more open discussion of discipline problems, which will bring about a sharing of staff expertise in dealing with them; there is a need for in-service courses on class and pupil management in addition to courses on curriculum development; and wider support is required from professional workers such as educational psychologists, social workers, psychiatrists, and others. In very different ways Topping, Jones, Lane, and Steinberg address these points directly, although most contributors have something to offer on the need to support teachers in the classroom.

In concluding his chapter on the pressures created by pupil behaviour, Dunham (1984) observes, 'The interaction between disruptive pupil behaviour and stress in teaching is a two-way process: the former can be either a cause or an effect of the latter.' But the problem is much more complex, because the other factors noted in this section on teacher stress will contribute to an individual's ability or inability to function effectively in the classroom, and to respond appropriately when faced with disruptive pupil behaviour. We cannot isolate pupil behaviour from other adverse factors, nor can we ignore the fact that the behaviour is also affected by the conditions the pupils experience and suffer in schools and classrooms—a point developed by all of the contributors to this book.

The original plan for this book divided the contributions into sections dealing with school approaches, classroom management, and helping individual pupils, but as the manuscripts arrived on my desk it became evident that, although a contribution may focus on one aspect, rigid demarcation was meaningless. The interactive nature of the various contextual and personal elements is the strength of the analysis throughout the book. Progression from school management to programmes with individual pupils remains, but more as a convenience than a necessity.

The contributors cover a wide range of specialisms, and write as experts in their fields, with extensive experience in the area of dealing with problems of disruptive and aggressive behaviour. Together they offer perspectives and insights which will stimulate discussion and ideas in pre-service and in-service courses for teachers and others involved in the education service.

In the first chapter, McGuiness and Craggs examine critically the pathogenic effects of schools, and advocate that pastoral care systems should adopt what they call a 'developmental' view instead of the prevalent 'crisis management' approach. From their Schools Council sponsored research on helping young teachers expand their classroom management skills, they concentrate on self theory and theories of relationship skills in the promotion of teachers as both task and social leaders in classroom interaction.

Education has given little thought to the role of consultants as change agents, and both Topping (chapter 2) and Steinberg (chapter 11) demonstrate how the educational psychologist and the educational psychiatrist respectively can enhance the skills of the teacher and the resources of a school. Topping focuses on work with pupils, parents, and teachers, and provides an invaluable list of recent resource information which is available to students and teachers.

Disruptive pupils complain about being 'picked on', and there is some evidence to support their belief that they are discriminated against. In an attempt to bring more even-handed treatment into teacher–pupil relations, I recommend in chapter 3 several ways whereby schools' management teams can bring greater consistency among teachers in the handling of indiscipline, also how class teachers can reduce inconsistency in their management of their classrooms. It is a move towards reducing pupil disillusionment with a system that has in-built preferences and prejudices.

Jones (chapter 4) examines 20 years of research and prescription in classroom management in the USA. It is an excellent review and many of the points highlighted are enlarged upon in subsequent chapters. He demonstrates the progression from the corrective approach to indiscipline

.o a preventive one, and his concluding points are very topical in the light of recent developments in the UK.

Early childhood is a time of considerable social learning, and Laing and Chazan (chapter 5) deal with children aged 3-7 years. Young children assert themselves as a result of growing self-awareness and independence, and when this behaviour is seen in play and games it is natural and socially acceptable. But the authors are concerned with early manifestations of over-reactive, hostile, and antisocial behaviour, which is seen to be maladaptive, and they deal with identification and prevalence, principles of measurement, and management strategies for teachers of young children.

Pollard (chapter 6) turns his attention to conflict and stress in the primary school classroom. He is critical of quantified approaches to teacher–pupil relationships, and offers a qualitative approach to the processes of social interaction and the subjective perspectives of the participants. He analyses the interests and concerns of teachers and pupils and the strategies each adopts to maximize them. Like Laing and Chazan, he advocates that teachers become more observant, analytic, and reflective as they assess and diagnose pupil behaviour, and adopt what is termed 'practical theorizing'.

Collaborative intervention, involving the individual pupil, the family, and the school, is the triangular approach which Lane (chapter 7) optimistically recommends to bring about positive classroom behaviour. He, too, stresses the importance of schools analysing their own problems rather than importing solutions, and, from extensive personal experience gained while working from the Islington Educational Guidance Centre, he advocates the setting up of peripatetic advisory teams and offers a model of practical advice and assistance.

As the quality of relationships is vital to creating an effective learning environment, Bowers (chapter 8) argues that teachers need to develop their interpersonal skills. He presents conflict as a process (not an incident) which pervades every aspect of human interaction—it is different from confrontation which is an open challenge. The ability to cope successfully with conflict is an important social skill, and he gives us five styles of management to reduce or resolve conflictive situations. They are self-management styles which can be learned and applied.

Bolger (chapter 9) offers a model that can be usefully followed when counselling disruptive pupils, the affective-cognitive-behavioural approach. It is a client-centred approach, appropriate to all kinds of pupil needs, and can be used in both formal and informal settings. His model will be most valuable to pastoral care tutors, and to those in mid-management positions who spend a disproportionate amount of their time dealing with (and counselling) a small minority of difficult youngsters. Teachers working in special units can usefully adopt his recommendations. His message for class teachers is contained in the term 'unconditional positive regard'—a pupil-centred rather than a subject-centred approach to teaching.

In many respects the contribution by Brown (chapter 10) follows on naturally from Bolger's, as he deals with analysis and modification through the learning of more appropriate social behaviour. He discusses how teachers can change behaviours which can adversely affect class and individual pupil behaviour, and how they can change unwanted social behaviour in pupils by the use of reinforcers. He discusses the efficacy for teachers of a wide range of social learning approaches, including continguent reinforcement techniques—both teacher-managed and self-managed—plus other approaches aimed at developing greater self-control in the child.

There is a spectrum of degrees of psychiatric intervention in the management of behaviour problems—consultative, collaborative, and clinical approaches. In chapter 11, Steinberg commits himself to the consultative approach, which makes full use of the skills and experience of teachers, augmented by psychiatrists' specialist and technical knowledge and understanding. He deals, in summary, with psychotherapy, family therapy, casework, and behavioural therapies; and though he identifies the range of psychiatric and physical health disorders he concentrates on those most likely to be encountered in schools, namely conduct disorders, hyperactivity, and drug abuse.

West, Davies, and Varlaam (chapter 12) distinguish between the different forms of support centres to which exceptionally disruptive pupils may be sent. From their extensive research into the provision made in ILEA they deal with the social characteristics of pupils who attend centres and the reasons for referral, and evaluate the success of special units from the viewpoints of pupils, staff, and headteachers. Finally, they draw out a series of implications which need to be considered by local authorities concerning the management of support centres and similar provision.

School discipline has been a national concern in America for the last two decades, and in the 'quest for order' in their schools American educators have tried a range of measures. Duke (chapter 13) briefly reviews their changing methods of dealing with indiscipline and then concentrates on one of the more recent developments, namely, the formalizing of comprehensive school and classroom rule systems and the consequences for breaking them. As an organizational response to indiscipline three of every four schools have some form of school discipline plan, in an effort to achieve a greater measure of concensus and consistency in student, parent, and teacher behaviour.

The final chapter (14) provides us with a valuable insight into the different ways in which other Western European countries tackle disruptive pupil behaviour. It may be of some comfort to teachers in the UK to know that colleagues in many other countries face similar problems, for, in addition to the countries dealt with by the authors, the problem of disruptive pupil behaviour is experienced in Canada, Australia, New Zealand, Finland, and Japan, to give a worldwide sample. The authors provide cameos from Holland, Belgium, Austria, France, and Denmark, and the examples they have selected range from a scheme with nursery age children to schemes with primary and secondary school pupils; there is also an example of in-service training for teachers. None of the countries listed has adopted the special unit approach described by West, Davies, and Varlaam; rather, they have chosen to work in the schools with teachers and pupils, which is the substance of what is recommended by all the contributors to this book.

References

ACE Survey (1980) Disruptive units, *Where*, **158**, 6–7.

Dunham, J. (1984) *Stress in Teaching*. Croom Helm, London.

Ford, J., Morgan, D., and Whelan, M. (1982) *Special Education and Social Control.* Routledge & Kegan Paul, London.

Galloway, D. M., and Goodwin, C. (1979) *Educating Slow-learning and Maladjusted Children: Integration or Segregation?* Longman, London.

Ghodsian, M., and Calnan, M. (1977) A comparative longitudinal analysis of special education groups, *British Journal of Educational Psychology*, **47**, 162–174.

HMI (1978) *Behavioural Units: A Survey of Special Units for Pupils with Behavioural Problems.* DES, London.

ILEA (1985) School support programme: the reintegration of pupils into mainstream schools. RS 968/85.

Kyriacou, C., and Sutcliffe, J. (1978) Teacher stress: prevalence, sources and symptoms, *British Journal of Educational Psychology*, **48**, 159–167.

Ling, R. (1984) SERP survey of off-site units in England and Wales (excluding ILEA), *Journal of the National Organisation for Initiatives in Social Education*, **3** (1), 5–11.

NUT (1985) *Today's Teachers* NUT, London.

Swann, W. (1985) Is the integration of children with special needs happening? An analysis of recent statistics of pupils in special schools, *Oxford Review of Education*, **11** (1), 3–18.

Tattum, D. P. (1982) *Disruptive Pupils in Schools and Units.* Wiley, Chichester.

Tattum, D. P. (1985) Disruptive pupil behaviour: a sociological perspective, *Maladjustment and Therapeutic Education*, special edition, **3** (2), 12–18.

Tomlinson, S. (1982) *A Sociology of Special Education*. Routledge & Kegan Paul, London.

Warnock Report (1978) *Special Educational Needs. Report of the Committee of Enquiry into the Education of Handicapped Children and Young People*. HMSO, London.

Management of Disruptive Pupil Behaviour in Schools
Edited by D. P. Tattum

_____*1*___

Disruption as a school-generated problem

John McGuiness and Denise Craggs

If a group of psychologists, expert in attitude formation, were invited to devise a situation and create a series of experiences specifically to provoke young people into disruptive, hostile, or aggressive behaviour, they could well come up with something uncomfortably close to what is experienced by large numbers of pupils in many British secondary schools. The surprise is not that we do face an increasing incidence of disruptive behaviour in our classes—it is rather that we face relatively little of it. One of the authors has written elsewhere (in Coffield and Goodings, 1983):

> These children are invited day after day for fifteen thousand hours to contemplate their worthlessness in terms of what their teachers and school evidently prize most highly. Those pupils who learn the lesson of docility must carry away from school as indelible impression of their inadequacy and inferiority. Others who have a more resilient attachment to their sense of personal worth reject school as an inauthentic commentator on their personal worth, by truancy or disruption—these we label deviant. (pp. 175–197)

It is as much for the sake of those accepting non-disruptives who yield to the pressure that they are of little worth, as for the disruptives who reject such a label, that the profession needs to review the destructive effect of much of the schooling experienced by many of our pupils. We are already in a situation where the children mentioned in R. D. Laing's (1967) doleful prophecy are leaving school with 'a ten-times greater chance of being admitted to a mental hospital than to a university'—a pathogenic effect with a vengeance. It cannot be ethical to leave any stone unturned, any sensitive spot unprobed in such a situation. It is in such a spirit, then, that this chapter will argue the existence of a widespread pathogenic effect in school. We

13

will make an analysis of the mechanics of that effect—the process by which an organization ostensibly designed to enhance the potential of young people in fact stunts that potential, leaving the victims bewildered, resentful, and hostile towards the source of their frustration. The final section will outline ways in which the authors have found it possible to use the analysis of the mechanics of the pathogenic effect to produce positive results.

The evidence

The problem of disruptive behaviour in school children, then, has been increasingly researched in recent years. The initial emphasis of the literature has been to link the problem with factors outside the school. Thus we have a range of theories which see some personal inadequacy in the child or his family as causative.

These psychological and sociogenic analyses of disruptive behaviour have had the professionally reassuring consequences of pushing blame firmly away from school. We propose to outline the literature which raises a new, challenging possibility—the existence of the child-damaging or 'pathogenic' school.

By the late 1960s Power *et al.* (1967) had carried out a study of delinquency rates in Tower Hamlet schools. They broadened the discussion of causes of this particular problem to include not only the child and his home but also the school as a further possible contributory factor. One of their conclusions was that factors did exist *within the school* which influenced delinquency rates. The research clearly suggested that some schools responded more effectively to the pupils' need for social development than others, and that, further, some schools had a detrimental effect on their pupils. Power did offer suggestions for further research into the variable ways in which schools respond to the broad development of pupils, but his valuable contribution to the opening of the discussion on school generation of behaviour problems was lost in the methodological criticism of his work.

Reynolds in 1976 did see the importance of this earlier work and decided to follow the lines of investigation to which Power initially drew attention. He concludes that 'some schools are sending out into life pupils whose chances of success in that life appear disturbingly poor'. He stresses that it is not possible to attribute children's success or failure merely to some personality or environmental factor. Reynolds again directs our attention to in-school factors which lead to different responses in children who come from similar home backgrounds. Rutter (1979) reinforced the findings outlined above in a study of twelve comprehensive schools in London. He, too, came to the conclusion that 'the results carry the strong implication that schools can do much to foster good behaviour and attainment and that even in a disadvantaged area schools can be a force for good' (p. 205).

Among the increasing number of researches into this issue Grunsell (1980), Bird *et al.* (1980), Galloway *et al.* (1982), and Tattum (1982) re-emphasize the earlier finding that problems of behaviour are firmly set within the social context of the school. They reveal schools to be creators of anti-authority identities in young people and argue powerfully that school ethos is a major contributory influence on pupil behaviour.

Several recent investigations in this field have looked critically at school effect on pupils. Schostak (1982) carried out more than one hundred interviews while looking into reasons why children truant from school. His findings have evident applications beyond truancy to other behavioural problems. He acknowledges the effect of unemployment and other social factors, but concentrates on in-school effects, identifying a number of areas of pressure which 'affect the quality of experience at school'. Such factors as the quality of relationships within school, the possibility of pupils taking initiatives, and the issues of autonomy are identified as meriting further investigation and reinforce some of Rutter's findings.

Steed *et al.* (1983) put forward a yet more critical view of school influence. These researchers describe the attribution of blame to the pupils as 'scapegoating'. Steed's team suggest that the tendency to divert attention away from the teacher denies the interactive process between teacher and pupil. The teacher's role in this interaction has not been fully investigated, suggests Steed *et al.*, 'presumably because it seems easier to modify the pupils' behaviour than the teacher's'.

Vaughan (1983) argues forcefully that the fatalistic view of some teachers that nothing can be done is not borne out by research. The possibility of taking away from large numbers of children the burden of patronizing, rejecting, failure-rich relationships and replacing them with the kind of valuing, safe experiences identified by Schostak is real for the individual teacher and his school.

The clear conclusions from a wide range of research that schools do affect pupil behaviour in identifiable ways led to the establishment of a Schools Council funded research project in Durham University, designed to use those findings which had already been made to help young teachers to avoid pathogenic effects. The results of this investigation are not yet published, but the initial data suggest that the negative effects outlined so powerfully by Power, Reynolds, Rutter, Schostak, and Steed can be counteracted by skilled, carefully analysed teaching.

As phrases like 'the pathogenic school' (Hargreaves, 1976), 'the betrayal of youth' (Hemmings, 1980), and 'maladjusted schools' (Schostak, 1982) begin to sprinkle the educational literature, it has become increasingly difficult to close our eyes to the idea that the effect of school on pupils is a crucial factor in the generation of disruptive behaviour.

The next section outlines how the work in Durham tried to use available research on the *mechanics* of the pathogenic effect to help young teachers to develop a wider repertoire of responses, grounded in greater self-confidence and more perceptive sensitivity to young people's views of the classroom, in order to eliminate or reduce the destructive elements of the school's influence.

Like all human behaviour, disruptive behaviour in the classroom is a product of complex, interacting influences which are difficult to isolate. On the project, then, we chose, somewhat arbitrarily, to focus on two theoretical inputs—self theory and theories of relationship skills. The justification for choosing these two was our experience that they do in fact help teachers to expand their classroom management skill. A complete account of the training *process* we used on the Durham project will appear at a later date.[1]

The self: teacher and pupil

McGuiness (1982) likens the child's experience of education to being tossed into a large sieve at the age of 5. For the next 10 years teachers and schools shake that sieve around in a limited grading and selecting process, which neglects many areas of human potential in its rigid cleaving to exams, and disgorges half its pupils damaged in some way at the end of the process. The problem seems to be that all pupils are exposed to a curriculum which, despite periodic tinkering, remains dedicated to the academic development of about 20 per cent of its clients. It is not our task in this chapter to debate the appropriateness of the curriculum—this has been challengingly done by McMullen (1978), Donaldson (1978), Hemmings (1980) and Hargreaves (1982, 1984). It is our intention to look at the effect this curriculum has on pupil behaviour, particularly from the point of view of self theory.

Significantly, self theory (Burns, 1982, 1979; Thomas, 1973; Snygg and Combs, 1959; Rogers, 1965, 1967) has had limited influence on British pedagogy. It is beginning to find a place on teacher-training syllabuses, but although some signs of change are appearing, students are still much more likely to be asked questions on cognitive psychology or learning theory in their educational psychology examinations. If, as Snygg & Combs (1959) argue, the maintenance and enhancement of the self is 'the all-inclusive human need which motivates all behaviour, at all times, in all places', then we might well argue that self theory merits a more central consideration, at both initial training and post-experience level. When we move from a general consideration of the central importance that a feeling of self-worth has for the individual and look at the situation of the teacher and the pupil in the classroom, we begin to acquire an insight into one way in which the pathogenic school effect works.

The vast majority of us are fortunate enough to arrive at the end of the first 5 years of our lives with growing self-esteem—a sound psychological state of affairs. Of course, some children even at that early stage have their self-esteem damaged, and they require special responses beyond the scope of this chapter. Part of the difficulty is the temptation to consign all children to the category of 'home-damaged' rather than 'school-damaged', thus again absolving ourselves of blame—and even of the need to intervene. The majority, though, have learned at home that they are lovable, talented, worthwhile, nice to be with: a clear self-image. They pick up messages, too, about their selfishness and failings, but in broad terms they are cuddled, caressed and stroked—psychologically and physically (see Figure 1.1).

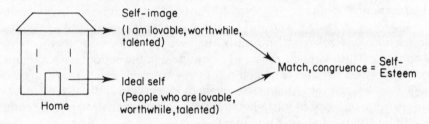

FIGURE 1.1   Constructing a sense of self-worth (home)

We all form two mental constructs: a picture of ourselves, *a self-image*; and a clear perception of the kind of person who is valued, admired, imitated in our environment, *an ideal self*. The basis of these two perceptions is the feedback that pours from the environment to the individual. I tell a joke, people laugh, I learn that I am witty; I help with the washing up, people compliment me, I learn that I am helpful; I paint a picture, people admire it, I learn that I am talented—and so it goes on. I hear admiring comments made of Mother Theresa, Eric Clapton, Luther Blisset, and I learn about what is valued in my family. The key issue is that self-esteem, that all-embracing human need, appears to be a correlate of the self-image and the ideal self of an individual. To the extent to which I see myself as being like these people who are valued in my environment I will have self-esteem.

Since we all exist in more than one environment as we grow up, we emerge from the safety of home to meet the challenge of new environments in which our sense of personal worth may well vary. My peer group, my professional group, my religious group will all feed in different information to *my self-image*, and offer different views of *an ideal self*. If an adult joins, say, a tennis club in which the valued individual is a John McEnroe clone, and if he constantly overhears snatches of conversation in the changing rooms about himself—'God! Have you seen Bob's serve, it's pathetic. He looks as if he's dusting Dresden china'—it is unlikely that he will stay on to suffer further damage to his self-esteem. The self-image and ideal self fail to match. Bob is lucky. He can quietly disappear from the tennis club and take up flower arranging. In addition, unlike the pupil at school, Bob will probably have a range of other solid esteem bases, for example at work, at home or in other leisure pursuits. He is not locked for 15 000 hours in the tennis club.

The pupil in school lacks an easy escape route. We can see the problem in Figure 1.2. Many pupils, like Bob at the tennis club, will pick up constant feedback on their lack of talent in those areas that school patently values. They will develop a self-image which will include items like 'I am non-academic, barely worth bothering with, lacking in talent', as a result of the environmental feedback—Bob's overheard locker-room gems. Taylor (1976) has given us an insight into the ideal self of the schools as valued by the profession; his research indicates that we tend to value conforming academics. Thus, large numbers of our pupils, in the school environment, make a forlorn attempt to match self-image to ideal self, fail, and protect fragile adolescent self-esteem assertively by disruption (Tattum, 1982, p. 97). This is not a defence of misbehaviour—it is one explanation of why some of it may occur. How might we respond?

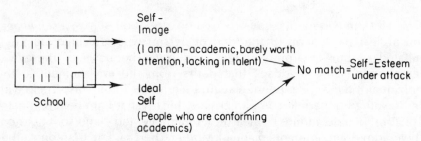

FIGURE 1.2   Constructing a sense of self-worth (school)

As the review of the literature at the beginning of this chapter suggested, schools signal values very clearly to their clients and it is these signals, this hidden curriculum, that merit careful attention. Quite simply, we need to measure our curriculum in terms of the effect it has on our pupils' dignity. Is it a daily insult to them, a regular slap in the face? The answers at this level lie in broadening our concept of talent dramatically, and by signalling that change by altering the resourcing, the rewards, the structures. It is still the case in schools that the status of the teacher who takes four pupils through Russian scholarship papers is higher than that of the 'remedial' or 'pastoral' teacher whose work is singularly more demanding. That is perceived clearly by teachers and pupils alike, both groups registering it as part of a generally projected 'ideal self'.

The explanation of the above issue (McMullen, 1978; Hemmings, 1980; McGuiness, 1982, 1983) raises the interesting point that most systems of guidance in English and Welsh schools are set up and operated as repair shops, dealing with damage done at least partly by the narrow, academic focus of the curriculum. The Inspectorate's exhortation (DES, 1977) that social objectives, including good behaviour, 'must be realised through the nature of the personal relationships in the classroom . . . and through the daily example of all the adults with whom the pupils are in contact', was found not to have been achieved by the 1979 Secondary School Survey (DES, 1979). In that analysis, the Inspectorate expressed disappointment that only a small minority of schools were able to use the academic curriculum for anything other than academic purposes. In an ideal world we would not need guidance systems because we would have got the curriculum right. Given the imperfect world in which we carry out our professional duties we are forced to ask how guidance services or pastoral care might help to create a community in which productive mutual respect is the norm.

There is now a large body of literature on pastoral care in schools (Best, Jarvis and Ribbins, 1980; Best *et al.*, 1983; McGuiness, 1982). A chapter of this length can do little more than identify some of the key practical issues in the discussion.

One such issue pertinent to the problem of disruption in school is the 'developmental' versus the 'crisis management' view of pastoral care and the consequences of the outcome of that debate for both the initial and in-service training of teachers. As a head or as a teacher, I can usefully ask whether my pastoral resources are deployed primarily to pick up and respond to deficiency, inadequacy, and underfunctioning, or whether they are deployed with a more positive focus to contribute to the social and emotional development of the pupils. Figure 1.3 illustrates the problem.

To leave unexamined the 'pathogenic' effects of what the Newsom Report (1963) described as 'unsuitable programmes and teaching methods, which led to difficulty, frustration, apathy and rebelliousness', with a consequent 'wastage, economically and humanly speaking', would verge on the unprofessional. There can be no excuse for not subjecting the curriculum to the closest scrutiny, looking for its *total* effect, not merely its academic outcomes for our more able pupils. Pastoral specialists (those teachers who have a special interest, expertise, and responsibility for the social and emotional wellbeing of pupils) must be involved in such considerations, but in the final analysis this is a whole-school responsibility. It involves not only preparation of teachers with sound tutorial skills, but also a greatly increased awareness among the profession of its effect beyond and in

Pastoral Care

Developmental	Crisis management
Involves all staff	Involves some staff
Focuses on all pupils	Focus on 'deficient' pupils
Attention given to:	Attention given to problems:
Socio-emotional effect	Disciplinary incidents
of the curricum	Results of domestic problems,
Developing specific	bereavements, divorce, prison;
objectives in tutorial time	often involves referral to
Concern with school ethos	outside agency

The better we perform the developmental
role, the less will be the pressure on
the crisis management response

FIGURE 1.3   Perceptions of pastoral care

addition to the academic development of pupils. This we explore in the next section.

Given an organizational division—heads of subject departments and heads of year or house with their separate empires—there is an inevitable narrowness in the decision making of both groups. Thus the major concern must be the establishment of the closest possible liaison between the two groups. Decisions made by subject department heads on purely academic grounds will lack roundness, and may simply produce more damaged children for the attention of the pastoral staff. Equally, the pastoral staff will benefit from close planning contact with the subject specialists. Only by means of the closest liaison in the planning stage will it be possible to move away from the 'safety net' view of guidance, a wasteful model in that it is merely a rescue service. Resources are better deployed on prevention rather than on cure. A persuasive argument could be made that at the moment we use academic groups to 'plan' the failure of large numbers of pupils, safe in the knowledge that our pastoral rescue service will pick up the pieces via counselling, remedial work—even caning. A more proper use of guidance is as a monitoring device to examine the whole-school ethos for negative effects.

Interpersonal skills

The pathogenic effect of school ethos can be intensified by the lack of interpersonal skills in individual teachers: thus a whole-school effect is consolidated by the daily interaction between pupil and teacher. In 7 years of detailed work with young teachers in their classrooms, the Durham group has come to realize that they are reluctant to seek help from anyone who is seen to be a 'judge' of their professional competence. This raises questions about the way in which the probation of teachers ought to be managed—an issue of particular importance as the profession feels its way towards a new career and salary structure. Headteachers, heads of departments, senior colleagues, and advisors seem to provoke a defensive, self-protective response. The young teachers will often endure lonely humiliation to keep a veneer of competence when facing the judges. They seem to be looking for and to respond to *peer* support groups, with outside non-judgemental consultancy. Not only is this more effective in terms of enhancing the pedagogical skills of young teachers, it is also professionally more appropriate that they feel secure enough to take a large measure of responsibility for their development as teachers. There is a real danger that, despite the best of intentions, the latest DES initiatives to improve the quality of teaching will provoke a defensive stance on the part of teachers, who will display safe control strategies, with minimal facilitation of learning for the pupils. The reality is that we can always *control* in the final analysis. Physical restraints (handcuffs, straitjackets) are still used in special situations, tranquillizers are administered to children whose disruptive behaviour is re-labelled hyperactive. The cane, sarcasm, verbal lashings lie at one end of a continuum, and at the other end are control strategies like reasoning, discussion, negotiating, and counselling. The issue is not one of control, it is the creation of environments which enhance our pupils—all of them.

One of the opening exercises on a BEd Guidance and Counselling option invites the students to list, for private meditation and consumption, 'all those personal inadequacies, quirks of character and limitations which will diminish my effectiveness as a teacher'. It is a salutary exercise and, as participants are assured of privacy, the lists tend to be long, detailed, and perceptive. They are invited (great emphasis is placed on their total freedom to decline) to share with a partner some of the components of the list, and to plan ways to diminish their effects. One student's comment at the end of the session was very illuminating: 'This is my final year in teacher training. It's amazing that this is the first time I've been invited to look specifically at myself. I've looked at children, materials, curricula, and teaching skills, but never just at me—yet I must be a key factor in the classroom equation.' Egan (1982), speaking of counsellor training, refers to the importance of trainee counsellors coming to terms with 'the problematic' in themselves.

No less can be expected of teachers. We need to come to terms openly with the problematic in our interpersonal skills, and that involves a degree of self-awareness and self-analysis which we rarely have an opportunity to pursue. The difficulty is that, try as we might to escape, we are still locked into content rather than process. Our major concern is knowledge, not psychosocial development, despite the indication from a growing body of research that the key to adult success is psychosocial development and not academic development (Kohlberg, 1977; Heath, 1977; Nicholson, 1970).

The student's comment was, of course, accurate. The teacher is a key factor in the classroom equation and, as such, needs to be the object of careful study. The discussion earlier of self-esteem as the factor that motivates all human behaviour was applied to our pupils. It has significance no less for the teacher. Like his pupils, he receives, via feedback from senior staff and colleagues, information which helps him to form a self-image. He, too, takes in the 'ideal self' projected by his school—and, like his pupils, he lays one next to the other, trying continually to attain that level of congruence between the two which will leave him with self-esteem intact or even enhanced.

An important difference is that an adult's self-esteem is less fragile than that of the adolescent; it has more contexts, as we saw with Bob and his tennis club; it also tends to become more internalized, less and less dependent on others and more related to one's own perceptions of self-worth. We are in other words resilient—or we should be. That is a normal, adult, developmental step forward—a more secure sense of self. Nevertheless, there are pressures which can reduce self-esteem, with all the damaging effects identified previously in pupils appearing as well in their teachers.

We have tried two approaches in Durham to help develop the self of teachers. The first occurs when a peer support group explores the range of worries, problems, issues, and challenges which the participants bring. Its use is that teachers feel less lonely, less uniquely incompetent once they learn to share, seeing teaching as a collaborative venture. They speak of the collapse of confidence they experience when, after carefully plucking up courage, they ask in the staffroom, '3X are giving me a bit of bother at the moment. Does anyone else find them a handful?' How depressingly insensitive they find the (feigned?) 'No—they seem a nice bunch really.' No one is willing to admit publicly to control difficulties since the ability to control is so integral to the 'ideal self' of the profession.

More taxing, and requiring skilled leadership, is a range of sensitivity training which is increasingly used in industry and is beginning to appear in education. The growing awareness that skilled social leadership enhances task performance has led industry to make intensive use of organizations like the Tavistock Institute and the Grubb Institute as a means of developing self-esteem, leadership, and interpersonal skills in their managers. We plod on in education hoping that gifted amateurism will win the day. It never could, and we certainly face such increased expectations on the part of our employers that amateurism is dead. We need to develop the same professional approach to interpersonal and management skills as our colleagues in industry and commerce.

There is now clear evidence that many young teachers feel unprepared to cope with discipline problems in the classroom (HMI, 1982). Their teacher-training tutors refer them to wide reading lists, exhort them to prepare lessons meticulously, teach them to philosophize about autonomy, discipline, punishment, intrinsic, and extrinsic controls—then send them out each September, a band of well-read, earnest, philosophically competent neophytes, woefully underskilled in classroom management. Again, the teachers themselves thrust the lessons under the noses of the theorists. A letter recently received by a university department of education was sent by a former student about to fail his probationary year.

He wrote 'without any sense of acrimony' but in the hope that his insight might help future students. He wanted to draw attention to the fact that the focus of his training had been a *subject*, not a *process*. His central consideration during teacher training had been geography, not teaching. He knew his geography well—the textbooks, the schemes, the strategies, the approaches—but he had never done anything on the practice of classroom management. To his horror, he had discovered that he could not create a learning environment in his room. He perceptively commented that people never failed probation because they did not know enough French or Chemistry or Maths or Geography. They invariably failed because of faults in classroom management—yet he had had nothing on *skill development* in that area. It is sadly still the case that while a chemistry graduate will receive financial help from his LEA to do an MSc to extend his chemistry competence, a request to do an MA in Guidance and Counselling will lead a puzzled LEA administrator to ask why a chemist needs to work on relationship skills.

The Durham project was deliberately given the ambiguous title 'Whose classroom is it anyway?' to emphasize the shared responsibility and interactive nature of the classroom reality. There can only be one answer to the question: 'Ours!' It drew voluntary participation from young teachers across the whole of the curriculum, all of them experiencing some level of anxiety about their classroom management skills. The organizers argued that the cost of training these young teachers made it important that the profession did not lose expensively trained personnel because of avoidable skill deficiency. In addition, there was growing evidence that some teachers survived in the classroom by adopting strategies which were costly in terms of personal wellbeing, and counterproductive in educational terms. How wasteful it is to have highly skilled mathematicians and physicists leave the profession because of faulty management skills. The aim of the course, then, was to develop the personally enhancing, effective interpersonal skills which are the hallmark of good managers in industry, commerce—or education.

Drawing extensively on the work of Argyle (1972, 1981) and Trower *et al.* (1978), we explored in theory and practice the intimate interactions of groups. To learn how groups work, we had to become aware participants in our own group process, experiencing the same thrill, support, threat, insecurity, aggression, and safety that all groups offer their members.

One of the first exercises was to invite the participants to define 'love' in ten words or less. The groups invariably set to with a will, usually coming up with an impressive definition. At this point we would confess our subterfuge, admitting that the task, defining love, had been a blind, and that we had been observing (sometimes televising) the group process. Who took charge as soon as the task was given? Why him or her? Who said nothing or little? Did they have nothing worthwhile to say? What blocked them? Who showed concern about the social climate of the group? So the analysis went on. We were working towards an awareness of a fundamental aspect of group functioning—the role of leaders. We could, of course, have referred the participants to a wide literature on the topic, but were fascinated to find that time and again they arrived experientially at three important insights.

The group observed that even though they started without an obvious leader, they invariably created (or accepted a self-appointed) one. There was a lot of discussion about the way this occurred, why some individuals emerged as leaders after as little as 10 seconds of interaction. The young teachers found it easy to apply this insight to their own classrooms. Groups need leaders—if I fail to lead, the class will throw up its own challenger for leadership. A badly prepared lesson will lead to one of the class donning the mantle of leadership the teacher has failed to put on.

A little further analysis led them to see that that was too simple. The geographer mentioned earlier prepared well; he knew his geography, wanted to lead—but things went wrong. We went back to our 'love definition' subterfuge. On reflection and re-analysis the group members could see two kinds of leadership in the group—both necessary, both open to challenge. Thus, the well-prepared lesson is a characteristic of *task* leadership: 'Let's get this done', 'Here's the way we're going to proceed', 'I'm familiar with the terrain around here, and I'll guide you'. Most teachers, like our geography friend, do this well; it is rarely a major cause of ill-disciplined classes. Much less adverted to is *social* leadership, characterized by unspoken messages which communicate to the group 'You're safe with me', 'I'll not show you up', 'I value you as a person and member of this group'. As teachers (indeed as lecturers, headmasters, and anything else) we are often much less at home with social leadership skills—but skills they are, and they can be learned. The geographer had learned a lot of task leadership skills, but was practically devoid of social leadership skills.

Argyle's research (1972, 1975) has given classroom practitioners an invaluable analytical tool for checking levels of skill in group behaviour. He suggests that all our group behaviour is rooted in certain intentions we bring to the group. In a classroom, at a party, at a conference, our behaviour in social group terms has access to a wide repertoire of possibilities. Some of us choose deliberately to stick with a limited selection of group behaviours, but each member of the group can select from the following intentions when interacting with the rest of the group.

(1) Task focus—an intention to get things done.
(2) Dependency—ensuring help and guidance.
(3) Affiliation—emphasizing social contact and comfort.
(4) Dominance—taking control of others.
(5) Sex—Awareness of the sexuality of another.
(6) Aggression—needing, wanting to strike out at others in the group.
(7) Self-esteem—establishing one's sense of worth in the group.

By analysing group behaviour, the participants became increasingly aware cognitively, and increasingly able at performance level, to analyse their own and their pupils' social behaviour. Their assessment of pupil behaviour, for example, used a much finer filter than previously—crude leaping to conclusions about pupil intention gave way to a judicious willingness to suspend judgement. The growing realization that apparently aggressive behaviour on the part of a pupil may in fact be a desperate bid for self-esteem shed new light on old problems. Of course, if there is aggressive behaviour it must be responded to. But what response will the teacher select? Will he show aggression too? Dominance? Dependency? Creative use can be made of the full repertoire, as we practised in role play. We analysed, for example, the use of dependency as a means of defusing awkward situations, without surrendering self-esteem.

We also found in Argyle a means of analysing the signalling of social intent in great detail. How do we *know* if someone is intending to be aggressive, sexual, dependent, and so on. Of course, individuals can say, 'I'm going to bash you' (aggressive intent?), or 'I will not have that kind of behaviour in my class' (Dominant intent), but the research suggests that a much more potent communicator of intent is non-verbal—so much so, that the teacher who *speaks* dominant messages, but *non-verbally* communicates dependency, will in fact signal to his group his dependency and fear. We often found this incongruence between spoken messages and non-verbal messages. Thus skills in non-verbal signalling also had to be worked on, despite initial resistance to the idea of 'teacher-as-actor'. Gradually, and to varying degrees, the teachers explored the non-verbal possibilities open to them. For example:

Body contact—how can I use it aggressively (caning?), affiliatively (ruffling hair? shaking hands?), dependently (can you give an old man a hand down the ladder?). The range is inexhaustible—a hand placed on a shoulder while working with a pupil at his desk can be used to signal dominance or affiliation, and so on.

Proximity—how can I use the physical closeness I have to members of the group to send out accurate messages about my intent. I can hide behind my desk, get in among my pupils. Pupils themselves send non-verbal messages to teachers, e.g. by arranging desks so that a small group of them are inaccessible—a no-go area for the teacher. As observers, we watched young teachers being 'psyched' in that way. Once their analytical skills had developed they were into the no-go area—no verbal confrontation, an affiliative jocular, breaking down of the barricade.

Orientation—what difference does it make if I sit with, stand beside, stand behind a pupil? We experimented ourselves. How different did we feel? A new tool entered the repertoire.

And so on. *Posture, gesture, eye contact, head movement, facial expression, physical appearance, grooming, and voice quality*—all were seen to add an initially imperceptible layer of meaning to the interaction within groups, until eventually the signal went out.

The final piece in the jig-saw was a gradual moving away from wanting to be *dominant* in the class. Once they had practised dominant behaviour they saw how blunt a weapon these behaviours are. Good teachers are subtle, they keep pupils (nicely!) on the hop, they range along a wide repertoire of behaviour. Thus Argyle's suggestion that purely dominant behaviour—e.g. prodding a forefinger into a group member's chest, standing up close to him, having a fixed, unsmiling expression, with unwavering eye contact—may achieve control, but it will be seen as a continual threat to the group. It may effectively lead the group to a task, but it is more likely to provoke counter behaviour from the group to protect itself. It will search for a social leader, someone who will say to the group, 'You are safe here', 'I value you', 'I will not make a fool of you'. However, if the teacher can be both task and social leader, then classroom management is on the way to success. In Argyle's terms, this involves combining dominant behaviour with affiliative behaviour, so that the strength of the former is not seen as a threat by the group, because of the warmth and acceptance of the latter. An example illustrates this.

A physics teacher was having difficulty with one third-year group, despite his comfortable control of his other groups. We observed and checked with him. Very highly visible dominant behaviour was leading to self-protective resistance from some of his group. We worked on affiliative behaviours and were delighted to see them practised skilfully and effectively as follows. During a lesson on states of matter with his 'problem' group, a couple of girls in the group crowded round his demonstration bench and began to misbehave. He stopped, looked fiercely, fixedly, unsmilingly for a few seconds and asked in a firm voice, 'How many ice-cubes did you have in your dish?' 'Three, sir,' came the rather cowed reply to his dominant behaviour. The look continued momentarily and then melted into a hint of a wink and a smile as he said, 'OK, just checking you're keeping up with me.' The subtle switch from dominant to affiliative behaviour was almost surely unconscious, but practised many times previously in safe, studio conditions, it came easily in the 'real' situation.

Of course, it would be foolish to offer patterns of behaviour to young teachers — this is the way to manage classes effectively. What we can do and have done is to help them to explore and develop greater awareness of their own interpersonal skills, and a more confident and creative use of those skills. It is important to emphasize the idea that since classroom control is about interpersonal skill and style, it needs to be developed — and practised — in an idiosyncratic way by each teacher. What is needed is not a model, but a support system within which young teachers can develop their individual style.

Thus our key intentions when working on interpersonal skills met with a measure of success. We removed the problem of classroom management away from a judgement context to a support context, in a way which succeeded in encouraging young teachers to identify, own, and analyse management failure. They developed, in a support context, the confidence to plan and practise more creative responses to taxing classroom incidents; by sharing experience and insight with a group of peers, they developed a broader repertoire of responses — and had an opportunity to practise these responses in role play and simulation. They had an awareness of their potential as pathogenic influences in the classroom and confidently worked towards acquiring highly developed pedagogical skills which would permit them to be enhancers of their pupils' self-esteem and not destroyers. They are, of course, aware of the larger issues which also promote the pathogenic curriculum — university requirements, parents, credentialism, and so on — but they have firmly rejected that lack of self-awareness and sensitivity which oozes so destructively into too many classrooms. This work must become central to professional development, not an optional extra.

Note

1. It will be published by the School of Education, University of Durham.

References

Argyle, M. (1972) *The Psychology of Interpersonal Behaviour.* Penguin, Harmondsworth, Middx.

Argyle, M. (1975) *Bodily Communication.* Methuen, London.

Argyle, M. (ed) (1981) *Social Skills and Health.* Methuen, London.

Best, R., Jarvis, C., and Ribbins, P. (1980) *Perspectives on Pastoral Care,* Heinemann, London.

Best, R., Ribbins, P., Jarvis, C., and Oddy, D. (1983) *Education and Care.* Heinemann, London.

Bird, C., Chessum, R., Furlong, J., and Johnson, D. (1980) *Disaffected pupils.* A report to the DES by Education Studies Unit, Brunel University.

Burns, R. B. (1979) *The Self Concept: Theory Measurement, Development and Behaviour.* Longman, London.

Burns, R. B. (1982) *Self Concept Development and Education.* Holt, Rinehart, & Winston, New York.

Coffield, F. J., and Goodings, R. (1983) *Sacred Cows in Education: Essays in Reassessment.* Edinburgh University Press.

DES (1977) *Curriculum 11–16.* HMSO, London.

DES (1979) *Aspects of Secondary Education in England.* HMSO, London.

Donaldson, M. (1978) *Children's Minds.* Fontana, London.

Egan, G. (1982) *The Skilled Helper.* Brookes Cole, Monterey, California.

Galloway, D., Ball, T., Blomfield, D., and Seyd, R. (1982) *Schools and Disruptive Pupils.* Longman, London.

Grunsell, R. (1980) *Beyond Control? Schools and Suspension.* Writers & Readers, London.

Hargreaves, D. H. (1976) *The real battle for the class-room, New Society,* 29 January '1976'.

Hargreaves, D. H. (1982) *The Challenge for the Comprehensive School: Culture, Curriculum and Community.* Routledge & Kegan Paul, London.

Hargreaves, D. H. *Improving Secondary Schools.* ILEA, London.

Heath, D. H. (1977) *Maturity and Competence.* Gardner, New York.

Hemmings, J. (1980) *The Betrayal of Youth: Secondary Education Must Change.* Marion Boyars, London.

HMI (1982) *The New Teacher in School.* Matters for Discussion, no. 15.

Jones, N. J. (1975) Emotionally disturbed children in ordinary schools, *British Journal of Guidance and Counselling,* July, **1975,** 146.

Kohlberg, L. (1977) Moral development, ego development and psycho-educational practices. In *Developmental Theory* (ed. D. Miller). Department of Education, Minnesota.

Laing, R. D. (1967)

Lowenstein, L. F. (1975) *Violent and Disruptive Behaviour in School.* NAS Pub., New York.

McGuiness, J. B. (1982) *Planned Pastoral Care: A Guide for Teachers.* McGraw-Hill, New York.

McGuiness, J. B. (1983) Secondary education for all? In *Sacred Cows in Education: Essays in Reassessment* (ed. F. Coffield and R. Goodings). Edinburgh University Press, 175–197.

McMullen, J. (1978) *Innovative Practices in Secondary Education.* OECD, Luxembourg.

Newsom Report (1963) *Half our Future.* HMSO, London.

Nicholson, E. (1970) Success and admission criteria for potentially successful risks. Project Report. Brown University Providence RI and Ford Foundation.

Power, M. J., Alderson, M. R., and Phillipson, C. M. (1967) Delinquent schools? *New Society,* 19 October **1967**, 542–543.

Reynolds, D. (1976) Schools do make a difference. *New Society,* 29 July **1976**, 223–225.

Rogers, C. R. (1965) *Client-centred Therapy.* Constable, London.

Rogers, C. R. (1967) *On Being a Person.* Constable, London.

Rutter, M., Maugham, B., Mortimore, P., and Ouston, J. (1979) *Fifteen Thousand Hours: Secondary School and the Effect on Children.* Open Books, London.

Schostak, J. (1982) Black side of school, *TES,* 25 June **1982**, 23.

Snygg, A. W. and Combs, D. (1959) *Individual Behaviour.* Harper & Row, New York.

Steed, D., Lawrence, J., and Young, P. (1983) Beyond the naughty child, *TES,* 28 October **1983**.

Tattum, D. (1982) *Disruptive pupils in schools and units.* Wiley, Chichester.

Taylor, M. T. (1976) Teacher perceptions of pupils, *Research in education,* November **1976**, 25–35.

Thomas, J. B. (1973) *Self Concept in Psychology and Education: A Review of Research.* NFER.

Trower, P., Bryant, B., Argyle, M., and Marzillier, J. (1978) *Social Skills and Mental Health.* Methuen, London.

Vaughan, M. (1983) Disruptive teachers? *TES,* 28 October **1983**.

Wedge, P., and Prosser, H. (1973) *Born to Fail.* Arrow Books, London.

Management of Disruptive Pupil Behaviour in Schools
Edited by D. P. Tattum
©1986 John Wiley & Sons Ltd

2

Consultative enhancement of school-based action

Keith Topping[1]

Consultants who try to work with schools to resolve problems presented by children behaving disruptively are themselves on a hiding to nothing. For one thing, of all the different types of difficulty encountered in schools, disruptive behaviour creates the most immediate threat to the teacher and arouses much greater emotional reaction in the adults involved. So the external consultant often has an uphill struggle to introduce some objectivity, to develop any sort of consensus perception of the nature of the problem, and to work towards a possible solution which is enough of a compromise to be widely acceptable yet not so watered down as to be totally ineffective.

Secondly, something of a catch-22 situation pertains regarding the advice given by a consultant, who can rarely bring any external pressure to bear to ensure that her[2] advice is taken, and thus has to rely on a majority of the consultees already having adequate intrinsic motivation to solve the problem. If the advice given refers to general principles of action, on the assumption that the consultees themselves are best equipped to relate these to their own environment, the consultant runs the risk of being dismissed as vague, airy-fairy and theoretical — i.e. not practical. If, on the other hand, the advice given is fully elaborated, very specific, and minutely detailed, it may be dismissed as too time consuming to implement, and irrelevant to the environment in question — i.e. not practical.

Another hurdle in the consultative process may be the tenacity with which the clients cling to a 'medical model' of causation, i.e. the assumption that the problem child's behaviour is caused by some defect or ailment within the 'black box' of the child's mind. Brain surgery is not usually a favoured intervention amongst educational consultants, so resolution of the problem must perforce be in terms of adjusting the *environment* to better meet the

31

child's needs. However, so long as the clients continue to clamour for the problem child to be taken away, 'diagnosed', 'cured' and returned only when certified free from infection, the consultant will find it very difficult to persuade them to scrutinize the environment they provide for the problem child in the search for mal-adjustments. This is perhaps particularly true where the consultant is an educational psychologist, of whom expectations tend to be paramedical (Freeman and Topping, 1976).

The fourth major factor influencing the consultant's success or failure is undoubtedly the existing patterns of relationship, communication, and organization within the problem child's environments—school as well as domestic. A school riven by antagonism between certain staff members, where communication is fragmentary and inconsistent, and where organizational structure is slack, haphazard, and self-contradictory, is not a place for a lone consultant to venture. In such a situation, the probability of consultancy succeeding is negligible, and a choice must be made between flooding the school with consultative input backed up by authoritarian punishments and rewards (explicit or implicit), or deploying those consultants to benefit far more children elsewhere. To put it another way, consultation is a relatively 'light' intervention, and to expect it to work miracles is to force the consultant into a blind alley where failure and associated loss of credibility become automatic.

Consultative input may be undertaken by educational psychologists, LEA advisors, peripatetic support teachers, or workers from institutes of higher education. Of these, LEA advisors may have the advantage of access to curriculum development monies, but the uncertainty in schools about their role and function and their frequent lack of a specific knowledge base relevant to the problems of disruptive behaviour are major handicaps. Educational psychologists (EPs) also have an expectancy problem—they suffer from inappropriate rather than conflicting expectations—but they certainly have a relevant knowledge base. The credibility and perceived weight of EP input will vary from person to person and LEA to LEA, but not least according to the confidence of the psychologist in what psychology has to offer. Support teachers, provided they are experienced and especially able (which implies high pay), link into appropriate knowledge bases and use well-articulated strategies and problem-solving techniques, are part of a stable and self-supporting team, and are otherwise accredited with high status and credibility by the LEA, seem particularly well-placed to offer consultative service to schools and families (Topping, 1983). University and other higher education (HE) workers are likely to find that their distance from the minutiae of LEA concerns results in their consultative input being made to schools which can most readily and easily benefit therefrom, and which often will have themselves invited the input.

Whatever the administrative or institutional background of the consultant, it is to be hoped that a problem-solving model of operation will be followed. Any fool can ask questions; the trick is, to ask questions which can be answered. Thus, the stages in problem solving can be set out as in Figure 2.1. While the employment of this 'scientific' model of process may not give instant 'cures' to 'crises', it greatly increases the chances of worthwhile improvements enduring and generalizing. The use of this model helps to explicate 'ownership' of the problem, facilitates joint working amongst ill-assorted agents of action, and renders the clinical concept of identification of the primary client largely irrelevant. It also makes people stand up and be counted.

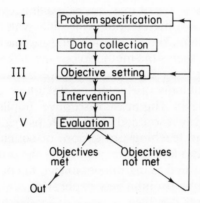

FIGURE 2.1   Stages in problem solving

Does consultation work?

The sceptical reader may have construed the introductory section of this chapter as an apologia for consultants. It is true that the evaluation evidence on the effectiveness of consultants is far from uniformly reassuring. Studies by Iscoe *et al.* (1967) and Pierce-Jones *et al.* (1968) suggested that the amount of consultation sought about a child bore little relationship to the objective severity of the problem, and that the main requirement teachers had of consultation was confirmation of decisions already made. During the process of consultation, relationships between consultants and consultees improved, but few other positive results were evident. This finding is echoed in a UK study (Topping, 1978), where 60 per cent of the teachers involved felt they had had some advice from the consultant, 45 per cent considered it practical, 35 per cent followed it, and only 20 per cent reported a positive outcome which could be attributed to the consultative input. Yet the teachers overwhelmingly reported feeling that the consultants were nice people, and 50 per cent reported feeling more confident and less worried as a result of the consultation. In the consultative process, good relationships appear to have some of the same features as money—you can't do much without them, but it's no use having them if you can't do something constructive with them. They are certainly not a satisfactory end in themselves.

Other studies shed further light on the parameters of effective consultation (Topping, 1983). Consultation with teachers individually is an expensive process, and there is evidence that consultation in groups is no less effective, is often preferred by teachers, and is considerably cheaper. Consultation must be well thought through and clearly structured and organized if it is to have any impact. This feature, when coupled with intensity of input in terms of man-hours, maximizes outcomes. However, pouring in more consultative hours willy-nilly with no clear objectives is ineffective and wasteful. The problem-solving approach within a behavioural analysis framework seems the methodology most likely to result in the best outcomes. However, it is clear that consultation by itself cannot be expected to solve all the problems presented by disruptive pupils, particularly at secondary school level. The most 'disruptive' pupils in an LEA are likely to need a more heavily resourced input, perhaps involving some additional direct teaching. The teaching profession, of course, tends to see extra provision of this latter kind as the solution to the problems of all children who might be construed as disruptive. In fact, of course, it isn't, and even if it were, it would be prohibitively expensive.

Consultative inputs can have a range of foci and methodology. In the rest of the chapter, we shall consider, in turn, consultation involving direct work with children, direct work with parents, in-service training for teachers, and organizational development in schools.

Direct work with children

Educational psychologists and peripatetic support teachers spend a considerably greater proportion of their time dealing with individual cases than do LEA Advisors or HE workers. For educational psychologists, individual casework occupies between 40 and 80 per cent of their time (Topping *et al.*, 1981).

At its simplest, this might involve the consultant in some direct counselling with the child or young person. However, there is very little evidence that counselling by adults has any effect on children presenting behaviour problems, particularly if the behaviour is of the acting-out, aggressive type and the child is of secondary school age (Topping, 1983). There is some evidence that *group* counselling with secondary age pupils can improve academic performance, but only one significant study has reported an associated reduction in disruptive behaviour (Kolvin *et al.*, 1981).

On the whole, directive and behavioural counselling which focuses immediately on the objectives of the exercise has proved more valuable (Henry and Killman, 1979), but in all cases volunteers respond better than the forcibly drafted. In any event, the danger is that purely verbal input in the counselling process will result only in verbal changes in the children—who will still be just as disruptive, but will be better able to explain why this is so. Using peers as counsellors for disruptive pupils has also been tried, sometimes involving training programmes and payment for the 'peer counsellors'. There is some evidence of the effectiveness of this approach with shy, withdrawn children, but little with reference to disruptive children.

Social skills training is an area of work which is attracting increasing interest, but here again successful results are easier to obtain with shy, withdrawn pupils than with acting-out 'disruptives'. Generalization and durability of behavioural gains have been demonstrated by a minority of studies. The more elaborately structured programmes involving behaviourally defined target skills, direct instruction, modelling, prompting, role playing, interpersonal and video feedback, shaping, continued practice and transfer of training via reinforcement tend to show better outcomes with disruptive pupils. Again, other children can prove to be as good at training as adults (Goldstein *et al.*, 1980), and training in groups can be as effective as training individually, with concomitant cost benefits.

For those interested in this area, the books by Sarason and Sarason (1974), Goldstein *et al.* (1980), Cartledge and Milburn (1980), Spence (1980), Ellis and Whittington (1981), and Hopson and Scally (1981) are all valuable in their different ways. The Hopson and Scally work is particularly related to integrating social skills training in the school curriculum. As we get better at social skills training, more positive evaluation results should accumulate. There is already a considerable body of work documenting the effectiveness of the technique with delinquents (Minkin *et al.*, 1976; Cooke and Apolloni, 1976; Maloney *et al.*, 1976; Spence and Marzillier, 1981), and if the technique can crack nuts of this degree of toughness, there must be every hope for its usefulness with disruptive pupils in schools. At least, this will be true in so far as disruptive behaviour results from a lack of social skills. Some pupils will undoubtedly lack the skills to cope with potentially stressful social situations in the classroom (as will some teachers), and this may precipitate disruptive behaviour. Other pupils, however, may already possess these skills, but choose not to use them because disruptive behaviour has become, to them, rewarding in itself. In these cases, social skills training alone will do little to remedy the situation.

A related area of work centres on teaching difficult pupils problem-solving skills (as per Figure 2.1). Again, if this has any effect at all, it is only likely to reduce disruptive behaviour in those pupils who perceive their disruptive behaviour to be a problem and wish to use the techniques to reduce it. The obverse is possible, wherein some children use the problem-solving conceptual structure to facilitate their becoming more effectively and scientifically disruptive. However, as long ago as 1974 Spivack and Shure presented some evidence that training in problem solving could have an enduring impact on the behaviour of young children. This work is further developed in Spivack *et al.* (1976), which will be of interest to teachers. In the UK, Thacker (1982) has produced a useful package for teaching problem-solving skills to 11–13-year-old children with difficulties, and it is available commercially.

In the USA, similar work has attracted the label of training in 'decision-making skills', and details of this may be found in Russell and Thoresen (1976) and Russell and Roberts (1979). A further extension of this is the notion of training in self-control, often using techniques such as self-verbalization to inhibit impulsivity. Schneider and Robin (1976) report the successful use of the 'Turtle Technique' as part of a programme of such training for highly over-reactive children, wherein the children were trained to deal with their own over-reaction by curling up and 'counting ten' while they considered a strategy for solving the presenting problem. This whole area is ably reviewed by Thoresen and Coates (1976), while in the UK McNamara (1979a) offers a brief and useful review of more 'ordinary' means of developing 'pupil self-management' in the secondary school.

Related to behaviourally oriented social skills training programmes are systems of training pupils in self-recording, which have the advantage of requiring much less adult time input. While self-recording is of little use in teaching new behaviour, it does provide a useful way of supporting and confirming positive behaviours known to be in the pupil's repertoire, but currently under-used. Many secondary schools have 'report card' schemes for children whose behaviour has been bad, the card being signed by each class teacher, who may add written comments. Developments of this scheme include orienting it to highlight good behaviour rather than bad, having teachers give ratings or points for behaviour rather than make nebulous comments, having the card taken home to be inspected and signed by parents, and having parents contract to apply domestic rewards and punishments on the basis of carded pupil performance. The system can include academic output as well as disruptive behaviour.

Self-recording is a fairly obvious development from these schemes, and may be used as a 'lighter' intervention than the traditional form of reporting, either for an experimental period, or as a way of 'phasing out' support for a child who has been on a full report card system. Clearly, the pupil must have some intrinsic motivation to cooperate, but teachers should not under-estimate the children's ability to utilize the procedure constructively. Children as young as 7 years old have effectively used quite complex forms of self-recording to improve their behaviour in a variety of classroom environments (Lovitt, 1973). Success with the technique by 8–11-year-old and 14-year-old disruptive pupils is reported by Gallagher (1972) and Broden *et al.* (1971) respectively. McNamara and Heard (1976) and McNamara (1979a, and 1979b) document the effectiveness of the technique with whole classes of difficult pupils, and both these latter papers are commended to teachers as practical and simple expositions of procedure.

This section on direct work with children would not be complete without some reference to the effectiveness of training other children to modify the disruptive behaviour of target children. A large number of studies testifying to the impact of this method are reviewed in Topping (1983). Utilizing peer group pressure by arranging a system of rewards for the whole class, earned by improved behaviour in target pupil(s), is one possibility. Success has also been achieved by acquiring peer cooperation in ceasing to reinforce disruptive behaviour in target pupils. This latter is particularly easy where the cooperation of a few high-status peers can be won. Peers can be asked to record the frequency of occurrence of disruptive behaviour in target pupils, a task at which they are more effective than adults, since they more often have the target pupil in their sight. Peers (particularly of high status) can be asked to model appropriate positive behaviours for the benefit of target pupils. Some workers have used peers to dispense reinforcement to target pupils showing improvement. Although this idea might seem alarming to teachers, it has been proved effective with 5-year-olds dispensing reinforcement to 3-year-olds. It is reassuring that there is no evidence that using peer 'volunteers' in this way results in any detriment to them, and indeed there is some evidence that the volunteers gain something from their involvement. For those interested in exploring this field further, Rosenthal (1976) provides a review of the use of peer modelling, and McGee *et al.* (1977) offer a useful review of the whole field of using children as 'therapeutic change agents'.

Having reviewed the major methods of direct consultative training input to children presenting disruptive behaviour in schools, consultative impact upon the mediators between the child and his various environments must now be explored. The most significant of these mediators are the parents.

Direct work with parents

A token genuflection is often made towards involving parents in discussion of the special needs of their children, but relatively rarely does this have a specific purposive structure and well-articulated strategies for mobilizing parental influence. It is well documented that parents and home circumstances generally have a greater impact on children than does school. Even with children who present as disruptive, the facile assumption that if the school has lost control of the child, the parents will have done likewise, needs substantiating factually in every individual case. A number of workers report difficulty in involving parents, but this is perhaps merely a reflection of how ill-developed this area of professional skill seems to be, and how large the gulf of alienation between school and home.

But many successes have been achieved, and indeed some workers report better effectiveness via direct work with parents than via direct work with children or both combined (D'Angelo and Walsh, 1967; Lisle, 1968; Glavin and Quay, 1969). Results from a consultative social work input to parents and teachers concerning disruptive adolescents have proved disappointing (Kolvin *et al.*, 1981), but much greater encouragement comes from studies based on behavioural methodology. Johnson and Katz (1973) provide a useful review of many successful studies of training parents to modify their children's behaviour. The papers by Rinn *et al.* (1975) and Patterson (1975) are particularly impressive. An up-to-date review by the current author (Topping, 1986) discusses evaluative evidence from parent training schemes addressing a great variety of presenting problems.'

Practitioners will require more details of the content and organization of these schemes than it is possible to give here. A useful summary of Patterson's methods is available in Horne and Patterson (1980). A classic work worth consulting in its entirety is that of Tharp and Wetzel (1969), since few UK professional agencies are yet anywhere near the level of development reported therein so long ago. The work of Rinn *et al.* (1975) is equally breath-taking by UK standards. Their Positive Parent Training Course was offered to *all* parents referred to a child guidance clinic. Both parents were required to attend, and pay a 30-dollar fee for the privilege. A refund of 10 dollars was made if the parents attended punctually and did their homework. Of the clinic referrals, 36 per cent refused to take the course. However 1128 parents of 639 children aged up to 18 completed it!

The course consisted of five 2-hour sessions. 'Homework' involved demonstrating mastery of five operations: (1) specifying behaviour, (2) measuring baseline behaviour and setting targets, (3) identifying rewards and punishments, (4) developing a behaviour modification programme, and (5) evaluating the programme. A random sample of parents who had completed the course was followed up between 6 and 36 months later. At the end of the course, 90 per cent of these parents had rated their problem children as 'much improved', but at long-term follow-up this proportion had fallen to 54 per cent. Nevertheless, a further 30 per cent of parents reported their children to be 'moderately improved', and the total 'improvement' rate of 84 per cent over a mean follow-up time of 17.3 months is impressive. The training course, considerably more effective than traditional clinic procedures, required about a quarter of the professional man-hours necessitated by traditional procedures, and cost one-third as much.

The potency of well-organized group training is emphasized by Kolvitz (1976), who systematically compared group and individual training. Teaching methods for the parents included talks, video modelling, discussion, reading programmed texts, and homework, followed by practice of analysis and programming on video examples and case studies. Parents contracted to attend, be punctual, complete tasks, etc., during the 6 weeks of the course. All parents had the same 'curriculum', except some had it in groups and some individually.

The results showed that skills could be taught in this way and transferred by the parents to ameliorate behavioural problems in the home. The group training was just as effective as the individual training, but of course was much less time consuming. The individual training was in turn at least as effective as the more informal, lengthy 'guidance' offered traditionally — which was yet more time consuming.

Interesting as this may be, the practical implications for a harassed teacher may not be immediately clear. An even briefer intervention procedure, readily adaptable to individual problems, has been termed 'behavioural contracting'. An early but nevertheless noteworthy example is the work of Stuart (1971), combining behavioural psychology with a systems analysis approach to family therapy with the families of delinquents. Contracts structure reciprocal exchanges by specifying who is to do what, for whom, in what circumstances. Put another way, contracts are a way of scheduling, and thereby reciprocally balancing, the exchange of positive (and sometimes negative) reinforcements between two or more persons.

For each party to the contract, the contract details the privileges which each expects to gain *after* fulfilling his or her responsibilities. The responsibilities themselves are also delineated, and their discharge should be monitorable. The contract may also specify a system of sanctions (or response costs) for failure to meet responsibilities. 'Bonus' clauses may serve to ensure that the major emphasis is kept on the positive. Feedback systems are laid down in the contract so that all parties are assured of receiving information on their performance. These considerations apply to *all* parties to the contract, be they child or adult. Further details and materials may be scrutinized in Stuart (1971), although no large-scale evaluation results are cited.

Another programme of action, one with a more 'homely' feel, is 'Responsive Parenting', which is an approach to teaching single parents parenting skills and is currently being delivered by educational psychologists in various parts of the USA as an integral part of psychological services for the community (Hall and Nelson, 1981). The 'Responsive Parenting' training is based on an applied behaviour analysis approach, and consists of ten weekly sessions of 2 hours each. A manual for parents is available, sectioned into sessional modules. Each weekly session begins with a large group meeting (25–40 parents) for instruction in basic concepts as in the manual, presented in a lecture, demonstration, and/or discussion format (including slide and film presentations). Then the participants divide into smaller groups (5–12 parents) in which a parent serves as group leader. Individual questions, concerns, and feedback are dealt with, especially concerning the progress of the Behaviour Change Project which each parent is implementing as 'homework' to practise the techniques learned in each session. The 'curriculum' followed includes the usual elements of behavioural training: definition of problem behaviour, recording, reinforcement, modelling, shaping, and fading. Other areas covered are: how to give instructions, punishment, time-out, correction and over-correction. Diplomas are awarded for successful course completion.

Parents who have taken the course are subsequently enlisted to help train other parents. Through further training and involvement parents may assist at four different levels: as apprentice group leaders, group leaders, apprentice programme directors, or programme directors. An attrition rate of 25 per cent is reported, which compares very favourably with rates of teacher drop-out from many in-service courses. Later courses have grouped participants according to the age range of the children in question. The main programme requires a fairly high level of reading and verbal skills and has not proved applicable to parents with low literacy and linguistic abilities. A modified programme is therefore being developed which depends less on reading skills and more on modelling, imitation, and rehearsal, with specific instructions, prompts, and immediate feedback during small group sessions. The level of parental assumption of the didactic role is likely to be lower in this modified programme.

This kind of structured work with parents is by no means purely an American phenomenon. Sanders and Glynn (1981) report an interesting initiative in New Zealand, again based on behavioural methodology, but incorporating a large element of self-management training. In other words, the parents were trained to apply behavioural methods to themselves in order to change their own behaviour to help change their children's behaviour. Evaluation results with a small number of cases suggest that the Self-management Training component is effective in producing generalization across settings in the community for both children and parents. The effects persisted at 3 months follow-up.

The maintenance of treatment effects is, of course, a constant topic of concern for the 'helping professions'. Patterson and Fleischmann (1979) have addressed themselves to the question of whether changes in the family *system* are necessary to ensure long-term improvement. They conclude that some effective single interventions do have the result of radically reshaping the family system, whether this was intended or not. However, some treatment effects persist without apparently having changed the family 'system'. The inevitable conclusion is that 'more research is needed'.

These issues are also explored by Forehand *et al.* (1979), who note that improved behaviour at home following a parent-training programme by no means automatically generalizes to school behaviour. So a school which has taken the time and trouble to advise or train parents about the management of problem children in the home may well never see a resulting improvement in behaviour at school.

In many schools, of course, neither expertise nor manpower exists for any elaborate parent-training scheme, and here the external consultant should be able to offer a fall-back resource. But of immediate relevance to teachers are the various behavioural systems of linking home and school referred to earlier. Almost by definition, schools have few rewards and/or punishments which impinge upon the disruptive pupil, but reinforcers of some power may exist in the home environment. A simple system of recording child behaviour at school and communicating this in a fail-safe manner to the parents, who contract to apply reinforcers at home as appropriate, has been demonstrated to be effective with disruptive pupils by a number of workers. Atkeson and Forehand (1976) and Broughton *et al.* (1981) provide useful reviews of these studies. For teachers, Walker (1979) provides a brief and readable summary of the area, while Schumaker *et al.* (1977), on the basis of their own highly successful work in the area, have produced a manual giving step-by-step instructions and detailed practical guidelines for the development of such schemes.

Having considered the potential impact of training children and training parents, it is clearly time to turn to the role of the external consultant in training the third party in the eternal triangle of disruptive behaviour — teachers.

In-service training for teachers

Pre-service training for teachers rarely inludes any work on managing disruptive children, although all children are potentially disruptive. This lack must perforce be made good via in-service training. Educational psychologists make a greater contribution to this latter than is generally realized. A survey by Wolfendale (1980) revealed that 76 per cent of psychological services were involved in the in-service training of teachers, and management of behaviour problems was the most frequently offered topic. Another interesting finding was that courses offered by psychologists were more likely to be evaluated than courses offered by other agencies. However, psychologists have many duties, and the implementation of the 1981 Education Act is forcing many services to give priority to assessing individual children, so the current time allocation of 10–25 per cent is unlikely to increase in the near future.

This is most unfortunate, since educational psychology is the only scientific basis for teaching, and recent developments are of immediate practical use to teachers and of proven effectiveness. (This observation may come as a surprise to those teachers who still think educational psychology consists only of well-diluted Piaget.) There are a number of well-known writers who manage to blend intimate awareness of humdrum classroom events with a sound theoretical model and a basis of empirical research, most notably Kounin (1970), Gnagey (1975), and Robertson (1981). However, merely reading one of these works, albeit valuable, is not likely to result in changed classroom behaviour on the part of teachers, and is even less likely to result in behaviour changes in disruptive pupils. Well-structured in-service courses which go beyond mere information input are necessary to ensure that these stringent evaluative criteria are met (Topping and Brindle, 1979).

As might be expected, in-service courses to train teachers in behavioural methods have the best track record so far as evaluation is concerned — perhaps because they are the easiest to evaluate. A very large number of studies describing and documenting the success of such ventures are reviewed in Topping (1983), and a significant number are concerned with methods of changing disruptive behaviour in pupils up to the age of 19 years. Various training formats may be used. Information input in verbal and written form is a usual component, often backed up by group discussion. Modelling desired teacher behaviour by tutor role play or video can be followed by behavioural practice by the tutees, with feedback from self or group immediately or via video or audio recordings.

However, actual practice of the novel techniques in the classroom is highly desirable, to help ensure transfer of training. Course tutors might subsequently observe tutees in the classroom, or have teacher colleagues observe each other, or have tutees fill out behaviour checklists on themselves (self-recording), or have pupils record the teacher's behaviour. Some tutors have gone so far as to monitor classroom practice by closed circuit television and to provide prompts for the teacher in the form of visual or electronically transmitted signals suggesting when to implement specified action.

Some form of supervision of, and feedback about, attempted application of new techniques in the real situation is essential. Furthermore, some form of reinforcement for the teacher for using the techniques is also necessary, since improvement in the behaviour of the children may not be immediate and in any event may not be sufficiently reinforcing in itself to maintain the teacher's new behaviour. Praising teachers for praising their pupils has been shown to be more effective than merely telling teachers to do so, and the more immediate the positive feedback to the trainee can be, the more effect it will have.

All of this requires time and effort, manpower and money. But in-service training should be done properly, or it may as well not be done at all. Of course, there can be many practical difficulties. Those schools with the highest numbers of 'disruptive' pupils may also prove to be the schools whose teachers are least motivated to attend an in-service course on the topic (paradoxically enough), even though the course is mounted in their own school. With the problem of disruption having so many organizational ramifications for whole schools, it is only those courses which are totally concerned with how teacher behaviour in the classroom can *prevent* disruption which can usefully be based outside the schools in question. In any event, teaching is a highly institutionalized profession, and there may be difficulty in reshaping teacher behaviour after a very long and often over-learnt reinforcement history in non-compatible techniques. Furthermore, at a time when the morale of the teaching profession is being steadily eroded by the combination of increased societal expectations and accountability with decreased resources and staffing resulting from financial cutbacks, motivation to attend after-school courses may not be high. Teachers may be reluctant to accept responsibility for disruptive pupils, or reluctant to devote what they expect to be an increased amount of time to a small number of pupils, even where this already occurs using other or no strategies. Particularly in secondary schools, the inflexibility of ponderous organizations in meeting the needs of individual pupils can present many practical problems to teachers wishing to experiment with new techniques.

However, the techniques are at least now available, and are increasingly being packaged in structured format for the precise purpose of increasing the impact of in-service work. Monoghan's (1980) Learning Assessment Pack Unit 3 was a noteworthy early effort in this field. The final version of Grunsell's (1985) Inset pack titled 'Finding Answers to Disruption' will be most valuable. Most complete and thorough of all, perhaps, is the 'Preventive Approaches to Disruption' pack produced at Birmingham University (Chisholm *et al.*, 1983), although the emphasis is more on classroom management than strategy development at the level of the whole school organization.

Change at this latter level is perhaps unlikely as a sole result of an in-service venture, but an adept external consultant can develop the initiative of an in-service course into further arrangements for a more direct input into organizational development.

Consultancy and school organization

Schools seem curiously ill-organized to meet the needs of their pupils, especially the adolescents, and cynics may opine that this is because schools are primarily organized to meet the needs of teachers first, society second, parents third, and children last of all. Organizational development is a delicate and sophisticated task, for which relatively few consultative professionals are qualified, although the OD aspects of their work are increasingly interesting some educational psychologists (Topping, 1979). Nevertheless, it is rare for a psychologist to devote more than 20 per cent of her time to this kind of work.

It is perhaps unfortunate that the managers of educational institutions have negligible training in management. Yet there is a great deal of valuable literature in the area, and a growing body of knowledge on the successful management of organizational development input by external consultants into educational establishments—not all of which is low-level theorizing of little practical utility. As early as 1965, Bennis was offering his categorization of eight types of change programme for organizations. A paper by Keutzer *et al.* in 1971 described an attempt to create a 'new social system' among 35 strangers who were to comprise the entire staff of a new high school. Gallessich (1973) provided a useful framework for gathering and organizing data related to 'organizational phenomena' in a school, and discussed the implications for the consultant in determining priorities, assessing strengths and weaknesses, generating problem-solving strategies, and predicting consequents. Georgiades and Phillimore (1975) developed strategy guidelines to assist managers of change in the preparation of organizational climates which would facilitate and perpetuate innovation. Arends and Arends (1977) compiled a simple and speedily metabolized OD 'bag of tricks'—'ideas that can be tried out tomorrow'. Stratford and Cameron (1979) described a simple problem-solving strategy which is as applicable to organizational as to any other kind of problem. A useful review of the 'state of the art' of organizational development in schools was drawn up by Fullan *et al.* (1980) at the end of a productive decade—although 'the state of the science' seemed likely to become a more appropriate expression.

Of all the organizational subsystems of a school which impinge (or fail to impinge) upon disruptive pupils, the sanctions in routine use are perhaps the priority candidates for radical consultative intervention. Punishment is much more frequently employed in schools than reward, despite the massive amount of evidence that rewards have far more effect on behaviour. In so far as punishment can be effective at all, its use is frequently mismanaged in schools, and the conditions for effectiveness are not met. Teachers tend to have strong views about the usefulness of certain punishments which bear no relationship to the available evidence. What teachers intend to be punishing may not be so perceived by pupils, and what teachers intend as a reward may be perceived by pupils as punishing.

The simple and oft-used verbal reprimand is useless if too frequent, and can actually increase disruption. Van Houten and Doleys (1983) provide a useful review of the evidence on factors influencing the effectiveness of verbal reprimands. 'Detention' and 'lines' have little impact on pupil behaviour, although carefully and systematically operated 'response cost' schemes on behavioural lines can have some effect (Pazulinec *et al.*, 1983). There is massive research evidence that corporal punishment is at best ineffective and at worst damaging (British Psychological Society, 1980), but its use has declined only recently. There is no evidence that the practice of suspending a pupil results in any long-term improvement in the pupil's behaviour. The reluctance of schools critically to scrutinize their punishment systems, which are often based on folklore, myth, and emotional reaction, is paralleled only by their slowness to consider the development of reward systems. Again, this is particularly true of secondary schools.

Further information on these topics is available in Topping (1983) and the very useful book edited by Axelrod and Apsche (1983). Yet merely bringing this information to the attention of schools should not be expected to result in organizational change. The identification of key figures in the communication and power networks in the school is necessary, followed by careful and consistent efforts to persuade them, separately and in groups, of the positive outcomes to be gained from some system change. The aforementioned danger of compromise solutions proving self-sabotaging is particularly pertinent in this context. Ironically, however, compromise is inescapable, partly because the school in question must have enough of a problem with disruption to engender some motivation to innovate to solve the problem, but must not have so much of a problem with disruption that the whole organizational fabric of the school is in disarray and therefore cannot be influenced by the external consultant, except possibly randomly.

It is debatable whether consultative input on matters of curriculum development tends to be seen by teachers as more or less threatening than input on sanction systems. In any event, there is little doubt that over-academic curricula, under-resourcing of extra help for children with learning difficulties, and a heavy emphasis on giving pupils mechanical tasks with little physical involvement beyond note-taking, will all increase the probability of disruptive behaviour among the children, although the causal linkages may be complex and indirect. There are examples in the literature of specific curriculum development projects which focused on devising highly flexible individual work programmes for disruptive pupils and building in rewards for task completion, and these approaches were found to reduce disruption and absenteeism. However, many consultants would be concerned about the development of a 'special curriculum' for a small and fairly arbitrarily defined group of pupils, unless this was clearly an experimental stage intended to be preliminary to wider innovations involving more pupils. The dangers of establishing a 'special curriculum class' are fairly obvious.

A further area in which consultative input could be most valuable is in helping schools to develop a system of 'time-out', as an alternative to more blatantly punitive hierarchical reactions. The concept of time-out derives from the learning theory assumption that disruptive pupils must be getting something out of being disruptive which makes them go on doing it. Logically, therefore, when all else fails, a sensible intervention is to remove the pupil from the rewards in the social situation which are promoting the disruptive behaviour. So far there is little novel in this for the average teacher, but the crucial difference lies in the nature of the 'time-out' situation—which must not offer any alternative rewards, and should be totally non-stimulating.

If used properly and consistently, in accordance with the parameters for effectiveness laid out in Topping (1983) and Brantner and Doherty (1983), time-out can be a very powerful intervention with the most extreme kinds of disruptive behaviour, and without incurring unpleasant side-effects. However, teachers are by occupational habit more used to talking than listening, and it has been known for schools to grasp half the idea and proceed to perpetuate the most alarming and hyper-punitive procedures upon their 'real baddies'. In this area, it is most important for the consultant to stick with the development, ensuring that the end product conforms sufficiently to the behavioural analysis model to be viable and effective in the long run—and be ethically justifiable.

Coda

At this point the patient reader must be commended for the effort involved in sticking with a chapter that has had to cover so much ground in so small a space that it has ended up as more of a high-speed tour than anything else. The frustrated reader who still feels he doesn't know what consultants actually *do* must be directed elsewhere if the yearning to flesh out this skeleton is overwhelming. A blow-by-blow account of an unspecified period in the life of an educational psychologist is available in Topping (1982), although by no means all of the blows relate to disruptive pupils. A more immediately appealing source for teachers will be the book edited by Lindsay (1983), which is intended to provide both a theoretical overview and practical guidance for teachers, and is jointly written by teachers and educational psychologists.

Hopefully, readers will have formed some idea of the areas and issues to which consultants might help teachers, parents, and children to address themselves, with implications not only for dealing with immediate 'crises', but also for creating a milieu which renders disruptive behaviour unnecessary—a milieu which is good for everyone. For those teachers and parents who have never seen an educational psychologist, or any other breed of educational consultant, but who can clearly identify their need for consultation of a kind or kinds described herein, the moral is clear—seek and ye shall find. He who sits and waits to be helped, sits and waits for ever.

Notes

1 The author wishes it to be noted that the views expressed in this chapter are his alone and not necessarily those of Kirklees Metropolitan Council.
2 Pronouns referring to consultants are standardized in the female gender, for simplicity.

References

Arends, R. I., and Arends, J. H. (1977) *Systems Change Strategies in Educational Settings.* Human Sciences Press, New York.

Atkeson, B. M., and Forehand, R. (1976) Home-based reinforcement programmes designed to modify classroom behaviour: a review and methodological evaluation, *Psychological Bulletin,* **86** (6), 1298–1308.

Axelrod, S., and Apsche, J. (eds) (1983) *The Effects of Punishment on Human Behaviour.* Academic Press, New York.

Bennis, W. G. (1965) Theory and method in applying behavioural science to planned organisational change, *Journal of Applied Behavioural Science,* **1** (4), 337–360.

Brantner, J. P., and Doherty, M. A. (1983) A review of timeout: a conceptual and methodological analysis. In S. Axelrod and J. Apsche (eds), *The Effects of Punishment on Human Behaviour.* Academic Press, New York.

British Psychological Society (1980) *Report of a Working Party on Corporal Punishment in Schools.* British Psychological Society, Leicester.

Broden, M., Hall, R. V., and Mitts, B. (1971) The effect of self-recording on the classroom behaviour of two eighth-grade students, *Journal of Applied Behavioural Analysis,* **4**, 191–199.

Broughton, S. F., *et al.* (1981) Home-based contingency systems for school problems, *School Psychology Review* **10** (1), 26–36.

Cartledge, G., and Milburn, J. E. (1980) *Teaching Social Skills to Children.* Pergamon, Oxford.

Chisholm, B., Kearney, D., Knight, G., Little, H., Morris, S., and Tweddle, D. (1983) *Preventive Approaches to Disruption: A Resource of In-service Materials for Secondary School Teachers.* Faculty of Education, University of Birmingham, Birmingham.

Cooke, T. P., and Apolloni, T. (1976) Developing positive social-emotional behaviours: a study of training and generalisation effects, *Journal of Applied Behavioural Analysis,* **9**, 65–78.

D'Angelo, R. Y., and Walsh, J. F. (1967) An evaluation of various therapy approaches with lower socio-economic group children, *Journal of Psychology,* **67**, 59–64.

Ellis, R., and Whittington, D. (1981) *A Guide to Social Skill Training.* Croom Helm, Beckenham.

Forehand, R., *et al.* (1979) Parent behavioural training to modify child non-compliance: treatment generalization across time and from home to school. *Behaviour Modification,* **3**, (1), 3–25.

Freeman, A. G., and Topping, K. J. (1976) What do you expect of an educational psychologist? *Journal of the Association of Educational Psychologists,* **4,** (3), 4–9.

Fullan, M., *et al.* (1980) Organisation development in schools: the state of the art, *Review of Educational Research,* **50,** (1), 121–183.

Gallagher, P. A. (1972) Structuring academic tasks for emotionally disturbed boys, *Exceptional Children,* **38,** 9.

Gallessich, J. (1973) Organisational factors influencing consultation in schools, *Journal of School Psychology,* **11** (1), 57–65.

Georgiades, N. J., and Phillimore, L. (1975) The myth of the hero-innovator and alternative strategies for organisational change. In C. C. Kiernan and F. P. Woodford (eds), *Behaviour Modification with the Severely Retarded.* Associated Science Publishers, Amsterdam.

Glavin, J. P., and Quay, H. C. (1969) Behaviour disorders, *Review of Educational Research,* **39** (1), 83–102.

Gnagey, W. (1975) *The Psychology of Discipline in the Classroom.* Macmillan, New York.

Goldstein, A. P., Sprafin, R. P., Gershaw, N. J., and Klein, P. (1980) *Skillstreaming the Adolescent.* Research Press, Champaign, Ill.

Grunsell, R. (1984) Finding Answers to Disruption. Allen and Unwin, London.

Hall, M. C., and Nelson, D. J. (1981) Responsive parenting: one approach for teaching single parent parenting skills. *School Psychological Review,* **10** (1), 45–53.

Henry, S. E., and Killman, P. R. (1979) Student counselling groups in senior high school settings: an evaluation of outcome, *Journal of School Psychology,* **17** (1), 27–46.

Hopson, B., and Scally, M. (1981) *Life/Skills Teaching Programmes,* nos 1 and 2. Life Skills Associates, Leeds.

Horne, A. M., and Patterson, G. R. (1980) Working with parents of aggressive children. In R. R. Abidin (ed), *Parent Education and Intervention Handbook,* C. C. Thomas, Springfield, Ill.

Iscoe, I., Pierce-Jones, J., Friedman, T. S., and McGehearty, L. (1967) Some strategies in mental health consultation. In E. L. Cowen *et al.* (eds), *Emergent Approaches to Mental Health Problems.* Appleton-Century-Crofts, New York.

Johnson, C. A., and Katz, J. (1973) Using parents as change agents for their children: a review, *Journal of Child Psychology and Psychiatry,* **14,** 181–200.

Keutzer, C. S., Fosmire, F. R., Diller, R., and Smith, M. D. (1971) Laboratory training in a new social system: evaluation of a consulting relationship with a high school faculty, *Journal of Applied Behavioural Science,* **7** (4), 493–501.

Kolvin, I., Garside, F. R., Macmillan, A., Nicol, A. R., and Wolstenholme, F. (1981) *Help Starts Here: The Maladjusted Child in the Ordinary School.* Tavistock, London.

Kovitz, K. E. (1976) Comparing group and individual methods for training parents in child management techniques. In E. J. Mash *et al.* (eds), *Behaviour Modification Approaches to Parenting;* Brunner/Mazel, New York.

Kounin, J. S. (1970) *Discipline and Group Management in Classrooms.* Holt, Rinehart, and Winston, New York.

Lindsay, G. (ed.) (1983) *Problems of Adolescence in the Secondary School.* Croom Helm, Beckenham.

Lisle, J. D. (1968) The comparative effectiveness of various group procedures used with elementary pupils with personal-social adjustment problems, *Dissertation Abstracts Int.,* **28** (11), 448–A.

Lovitt, T. C. (1973) Self-management projects with children with behaviour disabilities, *Journal of Learning Disabilities,* **6,** 138–150.

McGee, C. S., Kauffman, J. M., and Nussen, J. L. (1977) Children as therapeutic change agents: reinforcement intervention paradigms, *Review of Educational Research*, **47** (3), 451–477.

McNamara, E. (1979a) Pupil self-management in the secondary school, *Journal of the Association of Educational Psychologists*, **5** (1), 26–29.

McNamara, E. (1979b) The use of self-recording in behaviour modification in a secondary school, *Behavioural Pyschotherapy*, **7** (3), 57–66.

McNamara, E., and Heard, C. (1976) Self-control through self-recording, *Special Education: Forward Trends*, **3** (2), 21–23.

Maloney, D. M., Harper, T. M., Braukman, C. J., Fixen, D. L., Phillips, E. L., and Wolf, M. M. (1976) Teaching conversation-related skills to pre-delinquent girls, *Journal of Applied Behavioural Analysis*, **9**, 371–375.

Minkin, N., Braukman, C. J., Minkin, B. L., Timbers, G. D., Timbers, B. J., Fixen, D. L., Phillips, E. L., and Wolf, M. M. (1976) The social validation and training of conversational skills, *Journal of Applied Behavioural Analysis*, **9**, 127–139.

Monoghan, P. J. (1980) *Learning Assessment Pack Unit 3*. Calderdale Psychological Service, Halifax.

Patterson, G. R. (1975) Multiple evaluations of a parent-training programme. In T. Thompson and W. S. Dockens (eds), *Applications of Behaviour Modification*. Academic Press, New York.

Patterson, G. R., and Fleischmann, M. J. (1979) Maintenance of treatment effects: some considerations concerning family systems and follow-up data. *Behaviour Therapy*, **10**, 168–185.

Pazulinec, R., Meyerrose, M., and Sajwaj, T. (1983) Punishment via response cost. In S. Axelrod and J. Apsche (eds), *The Effects of Punishment on Human Behaviour*. Academic Press, New York.

Pierce-Jones, J., Iscoe, I., and Cunningham, C. T. (1968) *Child Behaviour Consultation in Elementary Schools*. University of Texas Press, Austin, Texas.

Rinn, R. C., (1975) Training parents of behaviourally disordered children in groups: a three-year programme evaluation. *Behavioural Therapy*, **6**, 378–387.

Robertson, J. (1981) *Effective Classroom Control*. Hodder & Stoughton, London.

Rosenthal, T. L. (1976) Modelling therapies. In M. Hersen *et al.* (eds), *Progress in Behaviour Modification*, vol. 2. Academic Press, New York.

Russell, M. L., and Roberts, S. M. (1979) Behaviourally-based decision-making training for children, *Journal of School Psychology*, **17**, 3.

Russell, M. L., and Thoresen, C. E. (1976) Teaching decision-making skills to children. In J. D. Krumboltz and C. E. Thoresen (eds), *Counselling Methods* Holt, Rinehart, and Winston, New York.

Sanders, M. R., and Glynn, T. (1981) Training parents in behavioural self-management: an analysis of generalisation and maintenance, *Journal of Applied Behaviour Analysis*, **14**, 223–237.

Sarason, I. G., and Sarason, B. R. (1974) *Constructive Classroom Behaviour*. Behavioural Publications, New York.

Schneider, M., and Robin, A. (1976) The Turtle Technique: a method for the self-control of impulsive behaviour. In J. D. Krumboltz and C. E. Thoresen, (eds), *Counselling Methods*. Holt, Rinehart,& Winston, New York.

Schumaker, J. B., Hovell, M. F., and Sherman, J. A. (1977) *Managing Behaviour, Part 9: A Home-Based School Achievement System*. H. & H. Enterprises, Inc., Lawrence, Kansas.

Spence, S. (1980) *Social Skills Training with Children and Adolescents* NFER–Nelson, Slough.

Spence, S. H., and Marzillier, J. S. (1981) Social skills training with adolescent male offenders: II Short term, long term and generalised effects, *Behavioural Research and Therapy,* **19**, 349–368.

Spivack, G., and Shure, M. B. (1974) *Social Adjustment of Young Children: A Cognitive Approach to Solving Real Life Problems.* Jossey-Bass, San Francisco.

Spivack, G., Platt, J. J., and Shure, M. B. (1976) *The Problem-Solving Approach to Adjustment.* Jossey-Bass, San Francisco.

Stratford, R. J., and Cameron, R. J. (1979) Aiming at larger targets, *Occasional Papers of the Division of Educational and Child Psychology, British Psychological Society,* **3** (2), 47–62.

Stuart, R. B. (1971) Behavioural contracting with the families of delinquents. *Journal of Behaviour Therapy and Experimental Psychiatry,* **2**, 1–11.

Thacker, V. J. (1982) *Steps to Success: An Interpersonal Problem-solving Approach for Children.* NFER–Nelson, Slough.

Tharp, R. G., and Wetzel, R. J. (1969) *Behaviour Modification in the Natural Environment.* Academic Press, New York.

Thoresen, C. E., and Coates, T. J. (1976) Behavioural self-control: some clinical concerns. In M. Hersen *et al.* (eds), *Progress in Behaviour Modification,* vol. 2 Academic Press, New York.

Topping, K. J. (1977) The role and function of the educational psychologist, *Journal of the Association of Educational Psychologists,* **4** (5), 20–29.

Topping, K. J. (1978) Consumer confusion and professional conflict in educational psychology, *Bulletin of the British Psychological Society,* **31**, 265–267.

Topping, K. J. (1979) The psychology of organisations, *Journal of the Association of Educational Psychologists,* **5** (1), 2–4.

Topping, K. J. (1982) Psychology at work in education. In S. and D. Canter (eds), *Psychology in Practice: Perspectives on Professional Psychology.* Wiley, London.

Topping, K. J. (1983) *Educational Systems for Disruptive Adolescents.* Croom Helm, Beckenham.

Topping, K. J. (1985) *Parents as Educators: A Guide to Training Parents to Teach their Children.* Croom Helm, Beckenham.

Topping, K. J., and Brindle, P. (1979) The evaluation of in-service training, *British Journal of In-Service Training,* **5** (2), 49–51.

Topping, K. J., Monoghan, P. J., Brindle, P., and Freeman, A. G. (1981) Time-allocation, in-service training and evaluation, *Journal of the Association of Educational Psychologists,* **5** (7), 40–43.

Van Houten, R., and Doleys, D. M. (1983) Are social reprimands effective? In S. Axelrod and J. Apsche (eds), *The Effects of Punishment on Human Behaviour.* Academic Press, New York.

Walker, H. M. (1979) *The Acting-out Child: Coping with Classroom Disruption.* Allyn & Bacon, Boston, Mass.

Wolfendale, S. (1980) The educational psychologist's contribution to the in-service training of teachers: a survey of trends, *Journal of the Association of Educational Psychologists,* **3** (4), 45–53.

Management of Disruptive Pupil Behaviour in Schools
Edited by D. P. Tattum
©1986 John Wiley & Sons Ltd

3

Consistency management—school and classroom concerns and issues

Delwyn P. Tattum

Teachers as managers

In this chapter, the focus of which is effective school and classroom management, the importance of consistency will be discussed. Classroom consistency operates against the broader backcloth of school organization and management, and therefore, inasmuch as class teachers cannot claim total isolation (or immunity), we also need to examine the concept of school-wide consistency management, as teachers move about the building and exercise authority in a variety of settings. In the last few years we have witnessed a change in emphasis from class control to teacher management; this is more than mere semantics, as it does reflect a different way of approaching the problem of indiscipline. The approach switches our prime focus of attention from pupils' behaviours (outcomes) to teachers' planning, preparation, and practice (inputs), as a way of preventing indiscipline from occurring. Effective management pre-empts disciplinary problems, whilst control suggests that a problem already exists which requires action to resolve it.

In my development of this chapter I intend to combine consistency with coherence, as I regard their coalescence as implicit in effective teacher management. Coherence refers to thoughts and speech, that is, to the ways whereby plans and policies are formulated and articulated, whilst consistency refers to the behaviour whereby enunciated goals are set and procedures are put into operation. In fact, consistency and coherence of school goals, policies, and practices run through the growing literature on school and teacher effectiveness.

'The "atmosphere" of any particular school will be greatly influenced by the degree to which it functions as a coherent whole, with agreed ways of doing things which are consistent throughout the school and which have the general support of all staff'. (Rutter et al., 1979).

Disruptive behaviour and teacher consistency

When conducting research with disruptive pupils I regularly visited an off-site unit. Over a period of 2 years I observed and talked to more than 60 pupils of secondary school age and carried out extensive, semi-structured interviews with 29. The data were rich as the pupils described their experiences of schooling (and especially teachers) and explained why they behaved so violently (Tattum, 1982). They admitted that they had behaved very badly, but even the most aggressive claimed that they chose the classes in which they misbehaved. In the main they described their behaviour as a natural response to a situation or event which demanded a reaction. Unlike their more conformist peers they were unwilling to acquiesce to boredom, abuse, or injustices, and when asked whether there was any lesson they liked more than another, the majority regarded the teacher as the deciding factor rather than the subject. Not surprisingly, they said that they behaved worse with teachers who 'didn't teach you', 'were unfair', and 'didn't care'. In every school there is a teacher(s) who has more disciplinary problems than others, and we cannot ignore the possibility that a teacher's behaviour is a contributory factor to a pupil's indiscipline. In a study of an American high school, Duke (1978b) identified six categories of 'discipline problems': inconsistent rule enforcement, non-compliance with discipline policies, insensitivity to students, lack of discipline data, lack of classroom management skills, and inadequate administration of disciplinary policies.

An analysis of my own interview data produced five categories, and I present them in the vocabularies of motives by which the pupils explained and justified their behaviour (Tattum, 1982). They are:

(1) It was the teacher's fault.
(2) Being treated with disrespect.
(3) Inconsistency of rule application.
(4) We were only messing—having a laugh.
(5) It's the fault of the school system.

It is not possible in the space available fully to develop each vocabulary of motive, but the central position is given to inconsistent behaviour on the part of teachers, as this one was most frequently and most generally used. They were critical of inconsistencies between teachers and by the same teacher, and of preferential treatment being given to certain pupils. All claimed that they were picked on, and whilst they were not passive victims they did argue that inconsistency of rule application breeds a sense of grievance and precipitates confrontations. Rules operate where role fails, and disruptive pupils have invariably rejected the pupil role as defined by teachers, and so regulation by rule is the main control mechanism employed in their case. Schools are rule-governed organizations, and it is conceivable that every act a pupil performs is covered by some rule or other—if no specific rule exists then teachers' discretion permits them to create one to cover the case. An individual teacher's inconsistencies occur when he reacts differently towards different pupils for the same misbehaviours. Teachers should be seen to be fair, neither having favourites nor picking on individuals, but there is evidence that preferential treatment is given to certain pupils because of their social or academic status (Lufler, 1979; Hollingsworth *et al.*, 1984). Not all pupils are treated the same by teachers, for there is the human practice of rewarding those who conform most closely to the ideal pupil role as a teacher perceives it, and punishing those who deviate most prominantly from perceived expectations. Differential treatment based on reputation or organizational labelling is amply recorded (Hargreaves, 1967; Lacey, 1970). Inconsistencies among teachers are most evident as the teachers display variable commitment to the enforcement of school rules as they move about the building. Many teachers concentrate on maintaining good discipline in their own classrooms, and hold to the view that about-school discipline is the responsibility of the headteacher and other senior colleagues. Unfortunately, this differential response to good order results in different treatment for the same offence.

In discussions with teachers about school rules, many claimed that their school had very few rules, and that the guiding principle for all was that each person should show respect for the rights of others, or some alternative expression of the Christian ethic, 'Do unto others as you would they do unto you'. Duke (1978b) found quite the reverse, as many of the teachers he interviewed admitted to being inconsistent and justified their behaviour on the grounds that there were too many school rules for any individual to enforce effectively. In similar vein, only on a few occasions have teachers been able to recount how their school has engaged in a general staff discussion of their rule system in order to devise a school-wide policy. Yet rules are the fabric of school life; together with regulations, routine, and ritual, they are the main mechanisms used to achieve and maintain good order. They are implicit in all social relationships, and explicit instruments of authority and control. And as disruptive pupils (and no doubt their more conformist peers) claim, the inconsistency of rule application is a major source of dissatisfaction and disaffection. In an organization where such uncertainty is demonstrated amongst its senior members with responsibility for the maintenance of good order, we cannot be surprised that amongst those members who suffer the consequences of the inevitable inconsistencies an attitude of critical disdain exists.

A function of rules is to give structure to social interaction; by prescription and proscription they are, ideally, to reduce uncertainty, confusion, and ambiguity. Furthermore, they are intended to regularize justice and ensure fair treatment by teachers so that control is administered uniformly and not arbitrarily. They regulate the behaviour of both enforcer and enforced. Where this view of rules exists, senior persons seek to reduce the scope for action of lower ones through the imposition of additional rules, as freedom of action for pupils would be contrary to the internal mechanisms of predictability and calculability. But what of the consequences of granting discretion to those who apply the rules? We have observed that too many rules can create, as well as solve, problems. Inconsistent application is one problem; also, too many rules can become oppressive for the more conforming members who are also constrained by them.

But a closer examination of the relationship between rules and behaviour reveals that rules are not fixed and immutable, but are open to interpretation, negotiation, and modification. We cannot predict which rule a teacher will apply or whether a rule will be invoked at all—she may look the other way or select from a range of alternative responses. What is more, the violator may plead innocence, ignorance of the rule, provocation, or whatever, and so negotiate a modified response.

That schools are hidebound by rules has already been noted; their rules range from the legal and formal, through varying degrees of informality. At one point in their study of deviant behaviour in classrooms, Hargreaves *et al.* (1975) despairingly wrote: 'We were in danger of becoming depressed by the sheer quantity and complexity of what to us appeared to be the rules at work in classrooms. Rarely were these rules stated in any explicit form. How then, were we to make sense of the data in which we were steadily beginning to drown?' To try to give form to the rule structure they originally classified the school rules as: institutional, situational, and personal; the latter they subsequently elaborated around the themes of talk, movement, time, and teacher–pupil and pupil–pupil relationships.

In an attempt to produce a more comprehensive categorization of a complex and ambiguous rules system, Duke (1978a) devised the following list:

(1) Attendance-related rules
(2) Rules related to out-of-class behaviour
    (a) Criminal conduct
    (b) Non-criminal conduct
(3) Rules related to classroom behaviour
    (a) Classroom deportment
    (b) Conduct related to academic work

Duke later suggested 'that many of the student behaviour problems now perplexing education result from *inconsistencies* and *ineffective practices* connnected with school rules themselves. The implication is that some improvements in school discipline may be brought through organisational rather than behavioural change' (Duke, 1978a, my emphasis).

In chapter 13 in this volume, Professor Duke writes about one of the most recent trends in America to produce an organizational response to the indiscipline of pupils: School Discipline Plans, whereby many school districts have formulated codes to define pupil conduct with a list of consequences for disobedience.

In a further attempt to understand the complexity of school rules I have elaborated their extent and nature within a five-fold categorization (Tattum, 1982). The categories are not intended to be discrete, as they bring together the interaction between laws governing compulsory attendance and interpersonal negotiations between teacher and pupil.

(1) Legal/quasi-legal rules
(2) Organizational rules
(3) Contextual rules
(4) Personal rules
(5) Relational rules

School governance is a complex problem of which rules are only one aspect, but there is a growing body of knowledge which indicates that the ways in which schools organize themselves influence relationships and levels of disaffection.

Teachers' autonomy and discretion

A starting point in any discusion of disruptive pupil behaviour must be with the teacher as an authority figure, for in the final analysis it is the judgement of the teacher which determines what is or is not defined as unacceptable, and teachers have different standards, expectations, and tolerance levels. Teachers work predominantly in isolation and immunity from their colleagues, and whilst we may debate whether this stems from the formal organization of schools into the cellular model, or from the professional autonomy which teaching claims for itself, the outcome is that teachers enjoy considerable freedom in their management of pupils in their classrooms and beyond. Bidwell (1965) makes the point that the closed classroom promotes a structural looseness in general school organization, a looseness which is amplified by the flexibility required to cope with teaching large numbers of immature clients in a very fluid situation. Teachers have thus developed a management style in which 'immediacy' and 'autonomy' are regarded as practical necessities (Jackson, 1968). But it can be argued that the cherished professional appurtenances of autonomy and discretion contribute to the management inconsistencies that exist in schools. Having consideration for the educational climate current when this chapter was written, that is, pressure from the minister of education for greater teacher assessment and accountability, this analysis must not be construed as an argument for taking away teachers' autonomy. In fact, it is inconceivable that teachers could function effectively without the discretion that is an inevitable part of teachers' different styles and philosophies. But that does not mean that we should accept it uncritically, without examining ways whereby individual schools and individual teachers can bring a greater degree of consistency into their management of pupils.

> Even if discretion has subtle or hidden benefits, it may also have not-so-obvious costs.
> The most troubling thing about discretion, especially in the human services, is the possibility that it will lead to considerable unfairness. Discretion, uncontrolled, is capable of abusing clients (in this case, students). On the other hand, for some students discretion may result in many benefits. They may be able to cut classes and wander the halls without being noticed, to swear cruelly at other students, or to break rule after rule without remonstrance because so much discretion is involved in discipline. At some point, then, the discretionary system of school discipline becomes unfair. (Hollingsworth *et al.*, 1984)

The process of rule enforcement has a built-in discriminatory potential, as it progresses through detection, adjudication, and punishment. Consider the model shown in Figure 3.1, and how inconsistent treatment can occur at stages 2, 3, and 4.

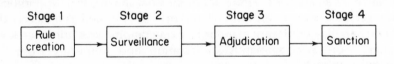

Stage 1	Stage 2	Stage 3	Stage 4
Rule creation	Surveillance	Adjudication	Sanction

FIGURE 3.1   Rule enforcement

The breadth of a teacher's responsibility extends beyond the classroom, but whilst the desirability of good class disciplinary standards is accepted by all, teachers view their about-school role with varying degrees of commitment. It is not just selective perception, but teachers vary in their orientation towards punishment, their desire to become actively involved, and their attitude towards the disciplinary responsibilities of senior management. Thus differential treatment occurs as some ignore problem behaviour, or, once involved, handle the misbehaviour themselves or pass the problem on to more senior colleagues. Hollingsworth *et al.* (1984) found that, whilst most teachers strongly favoured a tightening of the disciplinary regime, they held other teachers as not being strict enough and therefore responsible for disciplinary problems, but saw no need to change their own disciplinary methods. When we consider the consequences of being detected, the inconsistency of differential treatment continues along a discriminatory track. This can apply even towards behaviour which the staff would without dissent regard as serious; misbehaviour such as skipping lessons, bullying, defacing school property, and so on, may receive a reprimand from one teacher whilst another would promptly dispatch the pupil to the headteacher's office. The lack of pattern in detection and reaction also extends to punishment. The Government's Education (Corporal Punishment) Bill, 1985, is a charter for inconsistencies in schools, as it will promote discrimination between pupils on the basis of those who may be caned and those who may not be caned, according to a register of parental preferences. As a result of this legislation the unpredictability of the punishment system—as perceived by teachers and pupils alike—will confuse even further the discriminatory handling of punishments in schools.[1]

Finally, if one could be satisfied that teachers' discretion evened itself out between pupils I would not register so much concern, but evidence indicates that the system discriminates between pupils on the basis of cultural, social, and educational variables. Racial discrimination has been demonstrated as occurring in various ways in education, and in a review of research into the education of pupils of West Indian origin, Taylor (1981) summarizes teachers' attitudes to behaviour thus: 'To judge by teachers' reports in general and some of the evidence reviewed black pupils would appear to be much more deviant than whites.' On social class origins the ILEA study of support centres (Mortimore *et al.*, 1983) found an over-representation of pupils with parents in semi-skilled and unskilled occupations attending the centres. Hollingsworth *et al.* (1984) found that schools favoured middle-class pupils, but that the greatest positive discrimination favoured in-school achievers—so confirming early research findings.

> High-grade, high-achievement students are treated much more lightly when they do break school rules, controlling for frequency of rule-breaking. Students who are involved in extracurricular activities also enjoy some favourable discrimination. Discrimination in favour of achievers is, of course, very common in organisations. However, for a school with large numbers of other benefits available to achievers (class office, honour society), there seems no reason to exempt good students from punishments they deserve, if less academically achieving students incur them. (Hollingsworth *et al.*, 1984)

School-wide consistency

That school-wide disciplinary problems differ from classroom problems is evident to all, and many of the contributing factors have been touched on in the preceding section, points such as teachers' differing expectations, willingness to become involved, and uncertainty about the rule system. In a classroom, pupils see one authority figure with a given set of expectations and behaviours, but about the school there are teachers with different designations, secretaries, dining-room attendants and cooks, school nurse, caretaker, and senior pupils with prefectorial responsibilities. All have some degree of authority and different methods of enforcement. The sheer number and diversity of adults add to the problem of inconsistency.

In recent years we have seen a growing body of research literature on school effectiveness and teacher effectiveness, and although the studies have to some extent followed different paths they have complemented and reinforced each other. The 'good' schools research has concentrated on organizational characteristics which affect academic achievement and pupils' behaviour (Rutter *et al.*, 1979), whilst classroom researchers have looked at teachers' behaviours and management styles which equally bring about desirable outcomes from pupils. One of the correlates of effectiveness is strong leadership, and Edmunds makes the integrated point well in the following extract, although his main concern is with effective schools.

> One of the manifestations of instructional leadership is frequent principal-teacher discourse focused on diagnosing and solving instructional problems in the classroom. Principals who have intimate knowledge of the most effective techniques of classroom management and instruction are well prepared for discussions with teachers focused on the classroom. It is probably true to say that as schools acquire the characteristics of effective schools, they create a school climate more receptive to teacher use of the correlates of effective teaching. (Edmunds, 1982)

Research on effectiveness has highlighted a number of key variables which contribute to an ethos which brings success, but without entering too deeply into the issues it is evident that what happens is a *process* which involves the headteacher, staff, and pupils, and which, in consistency terms, flows through agreed policies, practices, expectations, norms, and rewards. In addition to strong leadership, characteristics of effective schools include well-defined goals and emphases, high staff expectations for pupil achievement, a sense of order, and a system for monitoring pupil progress and behaviour. Ethos has both content and process. Content refers to organizational structure, roles, norms and values, pupil grouping, teaching methods, and curriculum content. School process refers to the nature and style of social relationships and the flow of information within the school (Purkey and Smith, 1982). And although the focus in this section is on the school, the quality of the ethos at that level will enhance or diminish the quality of classroom activities. The school organization sets the context and defines the boundaries of teaching–learning and teacher–pupil interactions—and there are also reciprocal influences.

One of the important features of the school ethos approach is that it can take into account the structural looseness model discussed in the previous section. One of the problems of the bureaucratic model of schools is that its hierarchical structure fails to permeate the immediate classroom environment where teachers are largely independent of the headteacher's direct supervision. Furthermore, it is unlikely that greater consistency will be achieved by fiat from above. The discreteness of the structure and teachers' professional autonomy will be influenced more through gaining their commitment to policies via involvement in decision making. Rutter *et al.* (1979) found that 'outcomes tended to be better when both curriculum and approaches to discipline were agreed and supported by the staff acting together'. That is, that the school functioned as a coherent whole, with agreed ways of doing things which were consistent throughout the school, and that group planning provided opportunities for teachers to encourage and support each other. This approach assumes that changing schools necessitates changing staff attitudes and behaviour, as well as changing policies and structure. Consensus and commitment amongst colleagues is more relevant to professional development, thus the objective must be to gain staff cohesion in developing and enforcing policies about appropriate pupil behaviour, and in so doing to communicate to all that school is for learning and that behaviour which interferes with learning opportunities will not be tolerated.

Five recommendations are offered below which will contribute to the achievement of greater consistency among teachers in the application of rules and consequences. Whilst teachers have different teaching styles and management techniques, it would be unreasonable to expect major steps towards classroom consistency among teachers, but some measure of consistency about the school needs to be achieved as extreme differences of teacher reaction and response are untenable.

(1) Teachers and pupils should be closely involved in the creation and review of rules; a more open discussion will bring about a better understanding of their purpose and the problems they create for both parties. Wynne (1980), from his extensive investigation into American schools, observes that most lacked a disciplinary policy. He maintains that school rules are often vague or non-existent so that principals have the option to act *ad hoc* when challenged, and that unwritten rules create a vacuum in which neither staff nor pupils have clear standards on which to operate. He presented the question, 'Who makes the rules?', to which he claims he rarely received a straightforward or clear answer. In a further consideration of school rules, Duke (1982) engages the issues by discussing

their nature, number, and consequences—undoubtedly a useful guide for any individual school to follow in its review of disciplinary policies and practices. Finally, discussion can take place at various levels of formal assemblies. At some stage they might well include the other adult figures with authority mentioned at the beginning of this section.

(2) This recommendation follows naturally from the first; it is that rules must be communicated to teachers, pupils, parents, and other involved adults. Rules are of little use if they are not articulated to members of the organization, as order is based on the supposition that knowledge of the rules exists. The more persons involved in their creation and review the more widely they will be broadcast. School policy on discipline and consequences should be clearly stated in school prospectuses. In fact, parents tend as a group to favour stronger discipline than most teachers, and informing them is one step in obtaining their support and involvement. Whether individual schools should issue pupils with handbooks is worth considering, but conspicuous reiteration generates pressure for their observation and enforcement. Selective enforcement is unfair, and most pupils favour clear rules which are evenly and firmly applied. In absolute terms, consistency emerges as all teachers accept responsibility for all pupils, all of the time, and everywhere in the school. On consequences, Wynne (1980) found that 'almost all schools that have efficient discipline procedures also had efficient systems of recognising desirable conduct . . . Evidently, educators who can design and enforce discipline systems can also design systems to reward students'.

(3) By their own behaviour teachers communicate standards, which are translated and understood by pupils. Teachers must give respect if they want to receive it, they must expect success if they want pupils to achieve it, and they must present good models in their own behaviour if they want to influence pupil behaviour positively. A teacher's modelled behaviour can have a powerful effect on children and young people. Expressed positively it means that teachers take action to correct or check things as they move about the building, thus conveying the message that they care about the social and physical quality of life in the school. Negative examples are conveyed by teachers arriving late for lessons and leaving early, ill-prepared lessons, work unmarked or returned late, and the use of unofficial punishments. 'The inconsistency of "do as I say and not as I do' is also observed by pupils in matters of dress, smoking about the school, having a lunchtime drink, and even absenteeism. In fact, it appears to many pupils that teachers spend their time and energy in enforcing rules but are not subject to many rules themselves' (Tattum, 1982).

(4) Schools should keep accurate, up-to-date records of pupils' levels of attainment and behaviour. The practical advantage will occur when a pupil has to be severely disciplined, and staff are required to provide information

about problem areas in learning and relationships. More positively, it is when a school reviews its own control practices that it takes the step of relating them to educational objectives—an aspect of education which is receiving increased attention within the all-embracing accountability demands.

(5) Rules are an important part of the hidden curriculum as they give substance and expression to values; for whilst values are vague and general, rules are more specific and apply to identifiable situations. As creators and enforcers of school rules, teachers give meaning to their preferences for particular forms of behaviour that are deemed worthwhile and desirable; and the dominant value system in our schools is defined as that of the middle class. A more detailed examination of the rule system presented earlier would indicate that rules are concerned with more than neatness, decorum, and style: they are intent on bolstering and perpetuating a more deeply rooted system of values and beliefs (Tattum, 1982).

Jackson's (1968) analysis of classroom life recognized that survival is dependent on learning the hidden curriculum, and that conformity to its rule-governed expectations is an essential prerequisite to success in the formal curriculum. But what kind of learning takes place? Abundant literature confirms that the academic orientation of our schools disadvantages the majority of pupils as it constantly subjects them to experiences of failure and is an assault on their sense of worth and dignity. Most disruptive pupils are of average and below average ability and hence fall into this category. By their behaviour they are also pupils who regularly break rules and suffer the consequences—they are truly disaffected by their experiences of schooling. Unfortunately, the school facility which should be most supportive of disaffected pupils—the pastoral care system—is more involved in control than caring. Schools need to review the policies, structures, and practices of their pastoral care if they are to practise the 'rhetoric of caring' that they subscribe to in the prospectuses (Tattum, 1984). They need to devote more time to staff discussion about social and personal education, and about how they may work individually and collectively for the personal and social development of pupils. Schools devote considerable time, effort, and imagination to academic matters. They need equally to discuss, clarify, and develop openly their policies and practices in the social realm of education. This can be done within pastoral care, but Hargreaves (1984), in the ILEA report on *Improving Secondary Schools,* recommends an extension which will incorporate pastoral care but also include a range of initiatives in health education, consumer education, moral and political education, and others, and that these study areas should have a legitimate place on the timetable as part of the compulsory curriculum for all pupils. Ultimately, our concern has to do with more than order and discipline; it is necessary to create an ethos of worthwhile learning and to prepare young people to take their place in a challenging social and post-industrial milieu.

Classroom management and consistency

Classroom management has been described as 'Teacher behaviours that produce high levels of student involvement in classroom activities, minimal amounts of student behaviour that interfere with teachers' or other students' work, and efficient use of instructional time' (Emmer and Evertson, 1981). It includes the allocation of time and space, the distribution of materials, and careful record-keeping, as well as coping with pupil behaviour. The alternative to a consistent and coherent management style is an unsystematic 'bag of tricks', developed over time and through experience, but, unfortunately, it cannot be clearly articulated. There is considerable management knowledge in the profession, but it has not been freely observed and teachers have not been the most willing communicators of their accumulated skills. A most encouraging development in recent years has been the focus of research on direct observations of teachers teaching, so that we have a better understanding of teachers' behaviours and their effect on classroom management. A most influential series of studies on classroom discipline was undertaken by Kounin (1970). He investigated elementary school teachers' reaction to disruptive incidents. Through observations and subsequent analysis of videotapes and transcripts, he sought to distinguish between the techniques used by effective teachers to cope with indiscipline and those used by ineffective teachers. To his surprise the results indicated that both groups responded to control problems in much the same way; the significant difference lay not in their ability to cope with disruption once it occurred but in their ability to prevent it from happening in the first place. Successful teachers employed management techniques which were positively related to pupil involvement in their work and to a minimum of unwanted behaviour. They were better prepared and organized, coped effectively with competing and overlapping events, moved smoothly from one activity to another, maintained appropriate pace and momentum, and displayed class awareness as they constantly scanned the classroom to forestall potential problems. Using the same 'time-on-task' criterion to assess effective and ineffective teachers, Evertson and Emmer (1981) largely confirmed Kounin's findings. Following their Teacher Effectiveness Project, Brophy and Evertson (1976) distinguished between teachers who displayed 'proactive' behaviour, which was 'behaviour initiated by the teachers themselves, often prior to the beginning of the school year or the beginning of a particular day', and 'reactive behaviour that teachers show in situations when students do something that forces them to make some kind of immediate reactive response'.

Wragg (1984), in the extensive Teacher Education Project, also refers to 'first encounters', those initial teacher and class meetings, most especially those which take place at the start of a new school year. It can be claimed that the roots of a teacher's success or problems in class management can be observed in the first week of school. Established teachers regard these initial encounters largely in terms of management rituals, when they establish rules and routines, are precise and confident in their instructions, and generally lay down the patterns of behaviour for subsequent lessons. Importantly, good school managers follow similar procedures, making 'a massive communal effort at the start of the year with special assemblies, heads and senior teachers visiting all new classes, statements and re-statements about rules of conduct, dress, conventions, aspirations, expectations . . . a high degree of institutional control, an assertion of who was who and what was expected to transpire' (Wragg, 1984). In these early meetings the teacher's aim must be to command personal credibility as a behavioural and academic authority; to establish good work and behaviour habits. Research into pupils' expectations of teachers indicates that they prefer strict teachers who teach them, and when questioned away from peer influences most youngsters admit to wanting to work rather than filling in time—which they invariably describe as boring.

On returning to the theme that the key to effective classroom management is prevention of problems arising in the first place, the emphasis is on teachers' behaviour rather than control of pupils. It should also be noted that the findings which refer to the initial weeks are equally applicable to the rest of the school year. Following their extensive study of effective and ineffective teachers in elementary and junior high schools, Evertson and Emmer (1982b) identified three goals for management:

(1) to establish a climate for learning;
(2) to socialize children into the routine of classroom and school life;
(3) to organize the instruction and activities of a large group of children.

Children work better in a context that is secure and stable, they prefer to know what is required of them, to be occupied, and to be treated fairly. The twin concerns of consistency and coherence are important tools in the creation of a well-managed classroom that is task-oriented, and is predictable in that children know what is expected of them, and are clear about the consequences of not conforming to expectations.

A review of the literature on effective teachers presents a number of broad themes that can be most usefully concentrated on by both new and experienced teachers in their establishment and practice of consistent management.

(1) The first few lessons require detailed *planning and preparation*, which can be both short-term and long-term. Here the focus is on daily planning, which research indicates is conceptualized by teachers as a problem-solving process of how to structure the time and experiences of pupils in their classrooms (Calderhead, 1984). The pre-lesson thoughts of effective teachers

extend beyond subject matter, activities, and materials, and give due attention to pupil groups, basic rules and procedures, appropriate consequences, whole-class rather than group exercises, and assignments that promote success and involvement. Stanford *et al.* (1983) found that not only were new and ineffective teachers unaware of the amount of detailed planning necessary at the beginning of the year, but they did not know what to plan for. This is an area on which teacher educators need to concentrate, and schools would also forestall many behaviour problems if they ran staff development workshops focusing on the management of the beginning of the school year.

(2) Effective classroom managers introduce consistency into their lessons by carefully *teaching rules and procedures*. They take time to present, explain, and even discuss the rationales, some rehearse them with pupils (more so in primary schools), whilst others write them out and post them on a noticeboard. Pupils arrive from their previous classes with differing expectations of teachers. It is therefore the teacher's responsibility to identify and communicate appropriate rules and routines; and more so in schools where pupils attend the lessons of several different teachers during a day or week. Rules need to cover general classroom behaviour — entering and leaving the room, talking and shouting out, movement, the distribution and collection of materials, and so on — and work habits, that is, the manner in which learning activities are carried out — neatness, sharing, setting out work, and so on. In their Texas Project, Evertson and Emmer (1982a) found that less effective teachers had problems establishing a system to manage student–teacher and student–student contacts. Many teachers claim that they have only one or two rules, but these rules are vague 'catch-alls' which do not give pupils real limits and invite inconsistency on the part of the teacher. To have as few rules as possible is desirable, but they must be clear, specific, and positively stated.

(3) One of Kounin's off-beat words is 'withitness', that is, *frequent monitoring* of pupils' behaviour to prevent problems from arising. He found a strong association between 'withitness' and pupil involvement on task and lack of disruption — a correlation of 0.62 was scored when the whole class was engaged on an activity, which is a clear message for a teacher's planning of the beginning of the school year work. On an itemized analysis of observed responses by teachers, Evertson and Emmer (1982a) noted that effective teachers ignored disruptive behaviour less, and used their rules and procedures more frequently, thus consistently reinforcing the rule system and their own expectations. 'The less effective teachers were less vigilant or less inclined to intervene quickly, thus communicating inconsistent expectations . . .' In early encounters, consistency on the part of the teacher enables pupils to learn that their actions will result in consequences, in other words, they will, if detected, invoke a response from

teacher. I have used the word 'consequence' in preference to 'punishment' for two reasons. Firstly, because consequences do not have to be harsh or censorious, but rather need to communicate the teacher's alertness, and to convey a 'stop and think' warning; they do not necessitate a penalty. Teachers will also have a range of alternative responses according to the circumstances. Secondly, consequences can be rewards for good behaviour (and not just good work); and although critics of behaviour modification are reluctant to use positive consequences for various reasons, rewards do emphasize that which is desirable and discourage the attitude that the only way to gain attention is to misbehave.

(4) Alongside teachers' consistency of behaviour is *coherent communication* of instructions and information. Directions, objectives, and routines governing class activities and assignments need to be clearly stated in a step-by-step way so that pupils understand their tasks and know how to go about completing them. In this way effective teachers maintain a flow of work and can reasonably make pupils accountable for completing assignments. The establishment of a climate of learning was stressed earlier, and regular checking and early return of marked work conveys the expectation that class time is for work-related activities. In day-to-day classroom behaviour it means that a teacher circulates amongst the pupils, makes individual contact with as many of the class as possible, and so communicates involvement and awareness.

In conclusion

In a recent survey into classroom disruption in comprehensive schools, Dierenfield (1982) analysed the responses of 465 teachers from schools in 41 LEAs. The two factors on which teachers scored highest as influencing control of disruptive behaviour were establishing and maintaining behaviour standards early on (96.2 per cent very and moderately important) and consistent application of behaviour standards to all pupils (89.7 per cent very and moderately important). The indication from this sample is clear, namely, that good teachers apply appropriate management techniques, and that responding to pupils with consistency can minimize disruptive behaviour. I have no reason to think that this sample presents us with an unrepresentative viewpoint, and therefore, in this chapter, I have sought to offer practical suggestions to help teachers in their search for consistency in their classroom behaviour and as they move about the school. The recommendations are such that every school can set up its own discussion groups and workshops to develop a school-wide consistency management programme.

Note

1 Since writing this chapter the Government has withdrawn the Bill following its defeat in the House of Lords.

References

Bidwell, C. E. (1965) The school as a formal organisation. In March, J. G. (ed.), *Handbook of Organisations.* Rand McNally, Chicago.
Brophy, J., and Evertson, C. (1976) *Learning from Teaching: A Developmental Perspective.* Allyn & Bacon, Boston, Mass.
Calderhead, J. (1984) *Teachers' Classroom Decision-making.* Holt, Rinehart, & Winston, London.
Dierenfield, R. B. (1982) *Classroom Disruption in English Comprehensive Schools.* Macalester College, St Paul, Minnesota.
Duke, D. L. (1978a) Looking at the school as a rule-governed organisation, *Journal of Research and Development in Education,* 11 (4), 116–126.
Duke, D. L. (1978b) Adults can be discipline problems too! *Psychology in the Schools,* 15 (4), 522–528.
Duke, D. L. (1982) *Helping Teachers Manage Classrooms.* Association for Supervision and Curriculum Development, Alexandria, Virginia.
Edmunds, R. R. (1982) Programs of school improvement: an overview, *Educational Leadership,* December, 1982, 4–11.
Emmer, E. T., and Evertson, C. M. (1981) Synthesis of research on classroom management, *Educational Leadership,* January, 1981, 342–347.
Evertson, C. M., and Emmer, E. T. (1982a) Effective management at the beginning of the school year in junior high classes, *Journal of Educational Psychology,* 74 (4), 485–498.
Evertson, C. M., and Emmer, E. T. (1982b) Preventive classroom management. In Duke, D. L. (ed.), *Helping Teachers Manage Classrooms.*
Freiberg, H. J. (1983) Consistency: the key to classroom management, *Journal of Education for Teaching,* 9 (1), 1–15.
Hargreaves, D. H. (1967) *Social Relations in a Secondary School.* Routledge & Kegan Paul, London.
Hargreaves, D. H., Hester, S. K., and Mellor, F. J. (1975) *Deviance in Classrooms.* Routledge & Kegan Paul, London.
Hargreaves, D. H. (1984) *Improving Secondary Schools* (London: ILEA).
Hollingsworth, E. J., Lufler, H. S., Jr, and Clune, W. H., III (1984) *School Discipline. Order and Autonomy.* Praeger, New York.
Jackson, P. W. (1968) *Life in Classrooms.* Holt, Rinehart, & Winston, New York.
Kounin, J. (1970) *Discipline and Group Management in Classrooms.* Holt, Rinehart, & Winston, New York.
Lacey, C. (1970) *Hightown Grammar.* Manchester University Press, Manchester.
Lufler, H. S., Jr (1979) Debating with untested assumptions. The need to understand school discipline, *Education and Urban Society,* 11(4), 450–464.
Mortimore, P., Davies, J., West, A., and Varlaam, M. (1983) *Behaviour Problems in Schools: An Evaluation of Support Centres.* Croom Helm, London.
Purkey, S. C., and Smith, M. S. (1982) Too soon to cheer? Synthesis of research on effective schools, *Educational Leadership,* December, 1982, 64–69.
Rutter, M., Maughan, B., Mortimore, P., and Ouston, J. (1979) *Fifteen Thousand Hours.* Open Books, London.

Stanford, J. P., Emmer, E. T., and Clements, B. S. (1983) Improving classroom management, *Educational Leadership,* April, **1983**, 56–60.

Tattum, D. P. (1982) *Disruptive Pupils in Schools and Units.* Wiley, Chichester.

Tattum, D. P. (1984) Pastoral care and disruptive pupils: a rhetoric of caring, *Pastoral Care in Education,* **2** (1), 4–15.

Tattum, D. P. (1985) Control and welfare: toward a theory of constructive discipine in schools. In Ribbins, P., *Schooling and Welfare.* Falmer Press, London.

Taylor, M. J. (1981) *Caught Between. A Review of Research into the Education of Pupils of West Indian Origin.* NFER–Nelson, Windsor.

Wragg, E. C. (ed.) (1984) *Classroom Teaching Skills*, Croom Helm, London.

Wynne, E. A. (1980) *Looking at Schools. Good, Bad, and Indifferent.* Lexington Books, Lexington, Mass.

Management of Disruptive Pupil Behaviour in Schools
Edited by D. P. Tattum
©1986 John Wiley & Sons Ltd

_____**4**___

Classroom management in the United States: trends and critical issues[1]

Vernon F. Jones

Teachers in the United States continue to express considerable concern over student misbehavior. The National Education Association's 1983 *Nationwide Teacher Opinion Poll* reported that 45 per cent of all teachers responding indicated that student misbehavior interfered with teaching to either a 'great' (15 per cent) or 'moderate' (30 per cent) degree. Only 9 per cent of teachers reported no interference from student misbehavior. The extent of student misbehavior is also highlighted by the fact that nearly one student in ten is suspended from school during any given year, and school suspensions account for nearly 8 million lost school days each year (Hollingsworth *et al.*, 1984). A review of current data (Moles, 1983) suggests that although the amount of student misbehavior has not increased in the past few years, neither has it shown significant decreases.

Given the extent of student misbehavior, it is not surprising that several reports rate disruptive student behavior as a major factor contributing to teacher stress and job dissatisfaction. Feitler and Tokar (1982) reported that 58 per cent of their sample of teachers ranked 'individual students who continually misbehave' as the number one cause of job-related stress. In a study of 5000 Chicago teachers, Cichon and Koff (1980) reported that managing disruptive students ranked second to being involuntarily transferred as the major cause of stress.

Establishing an orderly classroom climate is an important teaching task as well as a pervasive concern of teachers. Walter Doyle (1985) stated that the role of classroom teacher involves the two major functions of establishing order and facilitating learning. Observational studies support Doyle's statement. Gump (1967) reported that approximately one-half of teachers' actions involved instruction. The remainder of teacher behavior involved such management functions as organizing and arranging students for instruction (23 per cent), dealing with misbehavior (14 per cent), and handling individual problems (12 per cent). A recent study (Wragg, 1984) of 36 British teachers observed during 213 lesson hours in mixed ability classes found that 54 per cent of teacher behavior involved management functions. Doyle (1985) presents an impressive research review indicating the interdependence of management and instruction functions. Simply stated, student learning is directly related to classroom order.

Parents echo teachers' concern regarding student behavior. Between 1969 and 1983, 14 of the 15 Gallup polls reported that Americans view discipline as the most important problem facing public schools. The 1983 poll (Gallup, 1983) indicated that 25 per cent of those sampled felt lack of discipline was the biggest problem facing local schools. Seven out of every ten respondents to the 1982 poll (Gallup, 1982) rated discipline problems in their local schools as either 'very serious' or 'fairly serious.' The 1982 poll also reported that 63 per cent of those surveyed viewed discipline problems in schools as a 'main reason why teachers are leaving their jobs.' Similarly, in the 1983 survey, those respondents who stated they would not want their children to become teachers rated discipline problems second only to low pay as their reason.

During the past two decades, the educational specialization labeled 'classroom management' has been developed in an effort to resolve continuing concerns regarding student misbehavior (Duke and Jones, 1984). Classroom management is defined to encompass teacher behaviors directed at maintaining orderly classrooms that facilitate student learning. Classroom management differs from school discipline in that the latter term focuses on student behavior outside the classroom and is less directly related to instruction and achievement. This chapter will examine 20 years of research and prescription in classroom management in the United States. This will be followed by a discussion of current classroom management issues.

In writing this chapter, I draw heavily on my practical experience. During the past 15 years I have served as a classroom teacher, special educator, junior high school vice principal, psychologist, researcher, staff trainer, consultant, and teacher educator. Information obtained while conducting studies of troubled schools and developing systems for reducing student behavior problems has proved valuable in supplementing current classroom management research.

Historical development of classroom management research and prescription

Research and prescription in classroom management have progressed dramatically during the past 20 years. An educator confronted with a student behavior problem in 1965 had few resources available and probably depended on advice from a colleague or information from an introductory educational psychology text for assistance. By 1985 an educator faced with a similar problem could turn to a myriad of resources including dozens of specialized books, hundreds of articles from professional journals, undergraduate and graduate courses on classroom management, numerous conferences, and a host of building or district specialists. In March 1984, a ten-member Panel on the Preparation of Beginning Teachers—chaired by Ernest L. Boyer, president of the Carnegie Foundation for the Advancement of Teaching—issued a report listing three major areas of expertise needed by beginning teachers (Boyer, 1984). These areas are: (1) a knowledge of how to manage a classroom, (2) subject matter knowledge, and (3) an understanding of the sociological backgrounds of their students. Similarly, in a recent publication from the Association for Supervision and Curriculum Development entitled *Effective Schools and Classrooms: A Research-based Perspective* (Squires *et al.*, 1984) the authors stated that effective teachers—teachers whose students demonstrated consistently high levels of achievement—possessed skills in '(1) planning, or getting ready for classroom activities; (2) management, which has to do with controlling students' behavior; and (3) instruction, which concerns providing for or guiding students' learning' (p. 10).

This dramatic growth in ideas and appreciation for the importance of skills in preventing and responding to disruptive student behavior has occurred through the development of several separate and relatively independent approaches to classroom management. These approaches have in turn reflected and responded to the social conditions and climate in the country. In order of their general development and popularization these approaches can be labeled (1) the counselling approach, (2) the behavioristic approach, and (3) the teacher effectiveness approach.

The counseling approach

During the 1960s and throughout much of the 1970s, the emphasis in dealing with student behavior was on discipline. What little training teachers received in dealing with student misbehavior focused on what to do after students misbehaved. Since the emphasis in psychology during the late 1960s and early 1970s was on personal growth and awareness, most methods focused on understanding students' problems, assisting students in better understanding themselves and working cooperatively with students to develop more productive behaviors. One of the earliest and most widely employed models was William Glasser's Reality Therapy (1965, 1969). Glasser's model derived from the belief that young people need caring professionals willing to assist them in taking responsibility for their behavior and for developing plans aimed at altering unproductive conduct. Rudolf Dreikurs and his associates (1971) developed a somewhat more clinical model based on the belief that acting-out children were making poor choices due to inappropriate notions of how to meet their basic need to be accepted. Dreikurs proposed a variety of methods for responding to children's misconduct, depending upon the perceived goal of the behavior. His model provided teachers and parents with strategies for identifying the causes of student misbehavior, responding to misbehavior with logical consequences, and running family and classroom meetings.

Emphasis on 'humanistic' psychology was most obvious in the models of self-concept theorists. Initially summarized by LaBenne and Greene (1969) and Purkey (1970), this work focused on the relationship between positive student self-concept, student learning, and productive behavior. This work was extended to include more practical aspects for teachers by Tom Gordon (1974), whose book *Teacher Effectiveness Training* provided teachers with techniques for responding to students' misbehavior with open communication and attempts at solving problems together.

Behavioristic methods

As social concern mounted regarding the disruptive behavior of youth, the focus of classroom discipline moved in the direction of teacher control. This increased concern with discipline was associated with the development and popularization of behavioristic methodology. Beginning in the mid 1970s, most courses aimed at helping teachers to cope with disruptive student behavior focused almost exclusively on behavior modification techniques. Teachers were taught to ignore inappropriate behavior while reinforcing appropriate behavior, to write contracts with recalcitrant students, and to use time-out procedures. This emphasis on control was most systematically presented to teachers in the form of Lee Canter's (1976) *Assertive Discipline*. Teachers learned to state clear general behavioral expectations, quietly and consistently punish disruptive students, and provide group reinforcement for on-task behavior.

Teacher effectiveness research

While counseling and control-oriented approaches vied for popularity, a new emphasis in classroom management was developing during the 1970s. This new direction placed an emphasis not on what teachers did in response to student misconduct, but rather on how teachers prevented or contributed to student misbehavior. This research, later labeled teacher effectiveness research or process-product research, is based upon correlating teacher behavior and student outcomes. This work has focused attention on three sets of teacher behaviors that influence student behavior and learning: (1) teacher skills in organizing and managing classroom activities, (2) teacher skills in presenting instructional material, and (3) teacher–student relationships.

Teacher organizational and management skills The study that initially highlighted the importance of teacher organizational and management skills was reported in Jacob Kounin's (1970) book, *Discipline and Group Management in Classrooms*. Kounin and his colleagues videotaped thousands of hours in classrooms which ran smoothly with a minimum of disruptive behaviors and in classrooms where students were frequently inattentive and disruptive. The videotapes were then systematically analyzed to determine what teachers in these two very different types of classrooms did differently when students misbehaved. The results showed no systematic differences. Effective classroom managers were not notably different from poor classroom managers in how they responded to student misbehavior. However, further analysis demonstrated clear and significant differences between how effective and ineffective classroom managers behaved prior to student misbehavior. Effective classroom managers employed a variety of teaching methods that prevented disruptive student behavior.

The Texas Teacher Effectiveness study was a second landmark in dealing with organizing behavior. In this study, reported in *Learning from Teaching* by Jere Brophy and Carolyn Evertson (1976), the researchers observed 59 teachers over 2 years. Teachers were selected to provide two groups whose students differed consistently in terms of performance on standardized achievement tests. Classroom observations focused on a variety of teacher behaviors previously suggested as being related to effective teaching. The results of the study supported Kounin's findings that effective teachers engaged in a variety of organizational and interactional behaviors that prevented disruption and facilitated learning by creating smoothly run classrooms.

These findings were expanded by Emmer, Evertson, and Anderson (1982) in the Classroom Organization and Effective Teaching Project carried out at the Research and Development Center for Teacher Education at the University of Texas at Austin. In the first of a series of studies, these researchers observed 28 third-grade classrooms during the first several weeks of school. The research findings showed that the smooth functioning found in effective teachers' classrooms throughout the school year was largely the result of effective planning and organization during the first few weeks of school. Effective classroom managers provided students with clear instruction in desirable classroom behavior and carefully monitored student performance—reteaching behaviors that students had not mastered.

Effective teachers also made consequences for misbehavior clear and applied these consistently. This study was followed by research in junior high school classrooms (Evertson and Emmer, 1982a) that verified the importance early planning and instruction in appropriate behavior plays in secondary school settings.

Recent studies building upon those cited above have demonstrated that when teachers are provided with information about skills associated with effective teaching and receive feedback on how their behavior in the classroom matches criteria for effective teaching, they can become much more effective teachers (Good and Grouws, 1979; Evertson *et al.*, 1982; Fitzpatrick, 1982; McDaniel, 1983; Mohlman, 1982; Sanford, 1983; and Stallings, 1983).

Instructional skills How teachers present material to students is a second area of investigation concerning teacher behavior that prevents disruptive student behavior and enhances learning. The earliest and most long-standing work in this area has been conducted by Madeline Hunter (1981). Her ITIP (Instructional Theory Into Practice) program has for nearly two decades attempted to translate findings in educational psychology into practical strategies that improve instruction. While her work has emphasized some of the skills highlighted by researchers interested in classroom organization and teacher–student relationships, her major contribution has been in assisting teachers in understanding the necessity of developing clear instructional goals, stating these to students, providing effective direct instruction, and monitoring student progress. Recently this work has been expanded and researched by Jane Stallings (1983).

Studies have also been conducted to examine the relative merits of competitive, cooperative, and individualized instruction. This work, carried out by R. and D. Johnson from the University of Minnesota, has demonstrated that cooperative learning activities are associated with a wide range of desirable learning outcomes. Students who work cooperatively on learning tasks tend to relate more positively to their peers, view learning as more positive, and learn more information (Johnson and Johnson, 1975, 1983; Johnson *et al.*, 1984). Additional work in cooperative team learning has been carried out by Slavin (1983), who has developed the Teams-Games-Tournaments approach, and by Sharan (1980).

Another area of study has examined the variability in how students learn (Doyle, 1983) and how teachers can adjust instruction to respond to students' individual learning styles. Work carried out by Rita Dunn (Dunn, 1983; Dunn and Dunn, 1978), Joseph Renzulli (1983), Anthony Gregorc (1982), and others has shown that when teachers allow students to study using approaches to learning that are most productive for each student, students learn much more effectively and behave more appropriately.

Teacher–student relationships   The third major research area within the teacher effectiveness paradigm has focused on the effect teacher–student interactions have on student achievement and behavior. This field of study can be divided into two basic areas: (1) studies exploring the impact of the frequency and quality of teacher–student interactions on student achievement, and (2) studies emphasizing the personal, affective dimension of teacher–student relationships and its effect on student attitudes and, to a lesser degree, achievement.

Robert Rosenthal and Leonore Jacobson's (1968) book, *Pygmalion in the Classroom*, generated tremendous interest in the impact teacher–student relationships have on student achievement. These authors reported that teachers' expectations for student performance became self-fulfilling prophecies. In other words, students seemed to perform as teachers expected them to. The important research issue then became discovering how teachers communicated high or low expectations to students. This question was initially studied by Jere Brophy and Tom Good (1971, 1974) at the University of Texas. These researchers, who have been leaders in the field of classroom management for 15 years, found that teachers responded very differently to high- and low-achieving students. They also discovered that the type and quantity of teacher interaction with students were associated with marked differences in student performance (Brophy, 1983a, 1983b; Brophy and Good, 1974). This research has been replicated and expanded to include an examination of attribution theory and factors related to teachers' sense of control (Brophy, 1983a, 1983b; Cooper and Good, 1983).

The second area of study has involved the affective quality of teacher–student relationships and its effect on student attitudes and self-concept. This research was first widely reported in the late 1960s and early 1970s in books such as LaBenne and Greene's (1969) *Educational Implications of Self-Concept Theory* and William Purkey's (1970) *Self Concept and School Achievement*. While there was less emphasis on interpersonal relationships in the classroom during the mid 1970s, research and practical ideas in this area have received increased attention during the early 1980s (Purkey, 1978, 1984).

Current trends in classroom management

Who is responsible for student behavior?

There is currently considerable debate over the role teachers should play in creating and maintaining a safe and productive learning environment. In his book, *Teaching—The Imperiled Profession*, Daniel Duke (1984) states that three roles receive support. The first argues for limited teacher involvement in handling student misconduct. Teachers are viewed as responsible only for teaching, with discipline problems referred to administrators or handled by an increasing array of resource people. A second option involves simplifying the teacher's role regarding classroom management. Teachers are encouraged to systematize their disciplinary role in order to minimize time spent on behavior problems. Teachers using this approach generally establish and consistently enforce clear, specific classroom rules. The third option would have teachers expand their skills in handling classroom discipline. This view suggests that teachers need to become familiar with the increasingly broad range of research and related skills in the area of classroom management (Brophy, 1980; Evertson and Emmer, 1982b; Jones, 1980, 1982) and incorporate these into a new type of classroom leadership.

Viewing the student and school administration as responsible   Recent studies dealing with excellence in American public schools have tended to support the first role—limited teacher responsibility for student behavior. The National Commission on Excellence in Education report, *A Nation at Risk: The Imperative for Educational Reform*, (Yinger, 1983b) includes the following recommendation: 'The burden on teachers for maintaining discipline should be reduced through the development of firm and fair codes of student conduct that are enforced consistently, and by considering alternative classrooms, programs and schools to meet the needs of continually disruptive students' (pp. 29–30).

A similar statement appears in the Task Force on Education for Economic Growth of the Education Commission of the States report, *Action for Excellence* (Yinger, 1983a). Indeed, schools have been moving in this direction for several years. It has been estimated that three out of every four schools have some form of printed disciplinary code (Safer, 1982). In some districts, teacher contracts now mandate that each school have a published procedure for handling student discipline (Jones, 1984). The 1983 National Education Association's *Nationwide Teacher Opinion Poll* states that 71 per cent of teachers responding report that their school districts have a written policy on student truancy. (See Duke, chapter 13.)

Providing teachers with simple, usually control-oriented classroom management methods   Based on research supporting the value of high rates of on-task behavior (Borg, 1980; Sirotnik, 1982) and the value of consistency (Rutter *et al.*, 1979), educational consultants have developed management techniques that train teachers to use punishment and reinforcement to insure high rates of student attending behavior. Lee Canter's (1976) Assertive Discipline has been the most widely implemented of these control-oriented programs. More complex programs such as the Program for Academic Survival Skills (Greenwood *et al.*, 1974) have also received wide acclaim.

The problem with the first two roles available to teachers is that they are based on the assumption that the instruction and classroom climate are always at least adequate. Responsibility for student behavior is placed outside the classroom, i.e. with the student or administrator. In essence, these roles imply a 'Sit down, shut up, or get out' stance. The teacher is viewed as having limited responsibility for student misbehavior. This stance is contrary to most educational research conducted since Jacob Kounin's (1970) classic study on classroom management. For well over a decade we have known that teachers make a difference. Numerous studies (Brophy and Good, 1974; Emmer *et al.*, 1982; Evertson *et al.*, 1982; Good and Grouws, 1979; Fitzpatrick, 1982; Rutter *et al.*, 1979; Stallings, 1983) report that teachers trained in specific classroom management and instructional skills elicit better student behavior and greater learning gains than control groups.

In addition to ignoring much of the best educational research of the past decade, emphasizing 'get tough' measures and ignoring classroom factors that cause misbehavior is sure to eliminate many potentially capable students from our schools. One out of every twelve students in the US is absent from school every day, and 25 per cent of white students, 44 per cent of Blacks, and 46 per cent of Hispanic students drop out of school (Plisko, 1983). To give up on these students by failing to examine school and classroom factors that affect their ability to learn and their desire to attend school is analogous to physicians only treating patients whom they can cure with penicillin. Indeed, given all the rhetoric about striving for excellence in American education, it seems strange that most excellence studies recommend firmer discipline and higher standards without recommending massive efforts to improve the quality of school life for students.

Viewing the teacher as responsible The third role suggests that teachers are responsible for developing excellence in instructional and management skills. This role focuses on teachers' responsibility for preventing mis-behavior by effectively organizing the classroom, implementing teaching strategies that increase on-task student behavior, and involving all students in appropriate academic tasks. The majority of recent research related to classroom management has dealt with this preventive role. Indeed, the gradual change in terminology from 'classroom discipline' to 'classroom management' reflects the change in focus from an after-the-fact counseling or corrective role to a preventive role emphasizing instructional and organizational excellence. Based on increasingly solid research, programs have been developed for training teachers in these skills (Emmer *et al.*, 1982; Evertson *et al.*, 1982; Fitzpatrick, 1982; Good and Grouws, 1979; Hunter, 1981; Jones and Jones, 1981, 1985).

The importance of considering rather than ignoring classroom factors can be seen by examining studies of students' attitudes to school. When Jane Norman and Myron Harris (1981) surveyed 160 000 teenagers for their book, *The Private Life of the American Teenager*, they discovered that only 42 per cent of the students described school as 'necessary,' 21 per cent found it 'interesting', and 27 per cent said school was 'boring.' Additionally, 60 per cent of the students said they studied primarily to pass tests rather than to learn. Similarly, a national poll conducted by the University of Michigan's Institute for Social Research reported that the number of students who thought what they learned in school was 'very important' or 'quite important' declined from 70 per cent to 50 per cent in the decade 1970–1980. Another study conducted by the National Center for Educational Statistics reported that more than half of all high school seniors sampled found their part-time jobs more enjoyable than school. When John Goodlad (1984) asked students to identify the best thing about school, 34.9 per cent said 'friends,' 13.4 per cent said 'sports,' 7 per cent said 'nothing.' Given these findings, it is not surprising that over 55 per cent of teenagers state they cheat in school (Norman and Harris, 1981). When one considers that these responses came not from a group of dropouts or disruptive students but from a cross-section of American youth, it seems imperative that we focus on teachers' and the schools' responsibility for enhancing learning and reducing disruptive student behavior.

The extent of student apathy suggested by the studies presented above was validated when the Carnegie Council on Higher Education surveyed school principals for its 1979 study 'Giving youth a better chance.' Forty-one per cent of the principals surveyed rated student apathy as 'very serious' or 'serious.' In fact, principals rated apathy ahead of absenteeism as a leading school problem. Since other chapters examine the relationship between school factors and student behavior, the remainder of this chapter will explore issues related to improving teachers' skills.

Problems with current approaches to improving teacher skills

While several programs have proven effective in providing teachers with skills that are associated with increased student on-task behavior and gains on standardized achievement tests, the attempt to increase teacher skills as a means of improving classroom management faces serious problems — some of which are described in sources generally considered supportive of this approach.

Practical Problems

First, teachers are dramatically lacking in their knowledge and use of effective instructional and management skills. Brophy and Rohrkemper

(1981) observed and interviewed 44 teachers from inner-city schools in a large metropolitan school district and 54 teachers in a smaller city. Most of the teachers had 10 or more years experience and half of the teachers were nominated by their principles as outstanding in working with problem students. The researchers found that few of the teachers had any pre-service or in-service training in classroom management. The study also reported that few of the teachers (including those rated most effective) had a clear, consistent philosophy or understanding of how to manage their classrooms. Instead, they tended to rely on an unsystematic 'bag of tricks' approach developed through experience.

The author's extensive work in in-service teacher training strongly supports Brophy and Rohrkemper's findings. Indeed, it is not surprising that teachers are poorly trained in classroom management techniques. The majority of research and prescription in both effective teaching and classroom management has been reported in the past 10 years. Therefore, many teachers received their pre-service teacher training before the majority of knowledge was available. Furthermore, a combination of factors has prevented this material from being incorporated into teachers' repertoire of classroom behaviors. Firstly, there is always a timelag between research findings and their incorporation into applied prescriptions. Secondly, limited staff development funds have required schools to focus on isolated aspects of effective instruction and classroom management. Thirdly, teachers are heavily burdened with large classes and multiple curricular and bureaucratic demands. Fourthly, the teaching profession has been unable to attract academically gifted individuals (Robertson, Keith and Page, 1983; Schlechty and Vance, 1981; Vance and Schlechty, 1982; Weaver, 1979). Fifthly, schools' economic conditions have intensified the problem. Duke (Duke, 1984; Duke and Cohen, 1983; Duke, Cohen and Herman, 1981; Duke and Meckel, 1980) has poignantly highlighted the problems created by current economic conditions in education. Declining enrollments, inflation, and taxpayers' conservatism have led to an era of retrenchment. Budget cuts lead to a 'downward spiral' characterized by reduction in funds, increased class sizes, reduced teacher morale, reduced student achievement, and increasing parent, student, and teacher dissent (Duke and Cohen, 1983). Within this context, survival rather than professional growth tends to be the prevailing issue.

Limited teacher skill and the lack of resources to ameliorate this situation are major practical reasons why educators have been frustrated in attempts to change student behavior by improving teacher skills and have instead tended to focus on control-oriented measures that minimize the teacher's role in handling classroom management problems. However, there is also scholarly evidence suggesting that the problem may lie partially in the inappropriate or incomplete nature of teaching methods currently emphasized when training teachers to prevent or respond to disruptive student behavior.

Scholarly Concerns

The classroom management and instructional methods being presented to teachers are—due partly to imposed limits of time and funding available for staff development—often superficial, and in some cases highly question-able (Good, 1983; Jones, 1983). For example, many classroom teachers do not know how to monitor their interactions with different types of students — e.g. to see whether they interact differently with high- versus low-achieving students. Suggestions presented during in-service training sessions often include such simple recommendations as calling on all children equally—a prescription that is not supported by the research. Instead, the expectation literature should be used to help teachers become aware of their classroom behavior and its effect on students, and then to make thoughtful decisions about how to interact with various students.

The overemphasis on time-on-task and direct instruction as key factors related to learning also highlights the danger in superficial interpretation of research findings. While recent studies support the value of high time-on-task rates (Borg, 1980; Sirotnik, 1982), other studies challenge this contention. Karweit (1983) concluded from her review of eight studies of engagement rates that the relationship between time and learning is 'weak and inconsistent.' Good (1983) also questions blind acceptance of the relationship between time-on-task and learning. Good (1983) noted that among the many reasons why time measures do not better predict learning is that (1) students may be assigned learning tasks that are inappropriate or irrelevant, (2) students may be poorly prepared for seatwork assignments, and (3) students may be assigned tasks that fill time but do not logically extend their understanding of the content. Doyle's (1983) creative analysis of academic work suggests that teachers often fail to match effectively the instructional activity with the desired academic goal. Soar and Soar (1980) found that the degree of student attention to a task was positively related to low cognitive level tasks but negatively related to high cognitive level learning.

The popularization of Assertive Discipline provides a concrete example of educators' acceptance of a simplistic model. Rather than being asked to examine why students misbehave and how the curriculum and instruction might be altered so as to reduce disruptive behavior, teachers are taught a simple method for eliciting appropriate behavior. Because the method can be mastered in several in-service hours, school districts around the country have spent hundreds of thousands of dollars to train their teachers in this simplistic, control-oriented approach. However, no research exists to support the academic or personal benefits to students from using this approach. Furthermore, the negative, control-oriented aspects of Assertive Discipline frequently dominate while the positive aspects are discarded. Finally, the method clearly focuses on the student as the sole cause of misbehavior, and the approach is often used to support ineffective teaching.

Even some of the best in-service training materials can be abused if presented in isolation. Recently I worked with a middle school whose staff had been well trained in Madeline Hunter's ITIP methods. However, the organization of the school day, the curriculum, and the instructional methods reflected those of most high schools. Students had no consistent contact with an adult or peer group, learning material was generally quite abstract, and instruction was predominantly teacher-centered. Furthermore, the school employed Assertive Discipline rather than an approach that helped students develop important personal and problem-solving skills. The school district had mistakenly assumed that training teachers in one aspect of instructional excellence assured effective teaching and good classroom management. Instead, the methods taught to teachers inadvertently reinforced many teaching methods that were not in the best interests of middle school children (Dorman, 1981; Lipsitz, 1980, 1984; Toepfer, 1980).

These examples highlight a key problem associated with classroom management research and prescription in the United States. As mentioned throughout this chapter, isolated methods are too often presented as comprehensive solutions. Table 4.1 lists the six general categories into which classroom management prescriptions have been presented and the major researchers and writers in each area. As discussed in the final section of his chapter, teachers need to become familiar with each of these approaches to classroom management and then make decisions about which aspects to adopt in their classroom.

In search of an answer

The research and prescriptions of the past 10 years have both aided and complicated teachers' attempts to answer the persistent question, 'How can I motivate students and minimize student misbehavior?' While classroom management research has moved far beyond a mere focus on counseling or punishing recalcitrant students to provide teachers with a myriad of methods for preventing misbehavior, some currently popular management methods and much that has been written about schooling suggests that teachers should play a limited role in dealing with disruptive student behavior.

Although there is no simple answer to the complex issue of student behavior, several thoughtful, in-depth studies and educational models offer both philosophical guidelines and some specific prescriptions. In his

Table 4.1 Continuum of classroom management strategies

Interpersonal relationships	Classroom organization and management	Instruction	Problem solving	Behavioristic	School-wide discipline
Jack Canfield and Harold Wells	Jere Brophy	Walter Doyle	Rudolf Dreikurs	Wesley Becker	Lee Canter
Tom Gordon	Ed Emmer	Rita Dunn	William Glasser	Lee Canter	Daniel Duke
William Purkey	Carolyn Evertson	Tom Good	Tom Gordon	Frank Hewett	William Glasser
Richard and Pat Schmuck	Tom Good	Madeline Hunter	Frank Maple	Daniel O'Leary	William Wayson
	Madeline Hunter	David and Roger Johnson	William Morse	Hill Walker	
	Jacob Kounin	Bruce Joyce	Robert Spaulding		
	Jane Stallings	Robert Slavin			
		Bob Soar			
		Jane Stallings			

well-conceptualized and intensive study of 38 schools, John Goodlau (1984) carefully examined teacher and student behaviors. Goodlad's work highlighted the central importance of instructional excellence and painted a picture of student behavior as significantly affected by the quality of instruction. Goodlad (1984, pp. 123–124) summarized his findings by noting:

> First, the dominate pattern of classroom organization is a group to which the teacher most frequently relates as a whole. . . . Second, each student essentially works and achieves alone within a group setting. . . . Third, the teacher is the central figure in determining the activities, as well as the tone of the classroom. . . . Fourth, the domination of the teacher is obvious in the conduct of the classroom. . . . Fifth, there is a paucity of praise and correction of students' performance, as well as of teacher guidance in how to do better next time. . . . Sixth, students generally engage in a rather narrow range of classroom activities—listening to teachers, writing answers to questions, and taking tests and quizzes. . . . Seventh, the patterns summarized above describe early elementary classes less well than they do classes in higher grades. . . . Eighth, large percentages of students we surveyed appeared to be passively content with classroom life. . . . Ninth, even in the early elementary years there was strong evidence of students not having time to finish their lessons or not understanding what the teachers wanted them to do.

Goodlad's study suggests that student misbehavior is caused not so much by lack of teacher control or adequate disciplinary codes as by a failure to engage students actively and meaningfully in the learning process.

In her sensitive and insightful book, *The Good High School*, Sara Lawrence Lightfoot (1985) examined six successful secondary schools. Among her many useful insights, she points to teachers' central role in educational excellence. 'It is their closeness to students and their direct engagement in the educational process that makes teachers the primary adult actors in schools and the critical shapers of institutional goodness' (p. 334). Lightfood states that teachers desire increased educational involvement and responsibility and notes that this is instrumental in creating a positive, engaging learning environment. Similar findings have been reported by Joan Lipsitz (1984) in her book, *Successful Schools for Young Adolescents* and by Ted Sizer (1984) in his sensitive and thoughtful book, *Horace's Compromise*.

The earlier work of Rutter *et al.* (1979), reported in the book *Fifteen Thousand Hours*, supports the findings of these more recent studies. Rutter and his associates reported major differences in effectiveness between schools serving similar student populations. Several key factors differentiating the more from the less effective schools involved factors dealing with teacher behavior. Rutter *et al.* wrote:

> Factors as varied as the degree of academic emphasis, teacher actions in lessons, the availability of incentives and rewards, good conditions for pupils, and the extent to which children were able to take responsibility were all significantly associated with outcome differences between schools. All of these factors were open to modification by the staff, rather than fixed by external constraints. (p. 178)

These researchers also pointed to factors such as ample teacher praise, harmonious staff relationships, teacher availability to students, and a variety of specific classroom management skills as instrumental in influencing student behavior and achievement. The influence teachers have on the school atmosphere was highlighted by the statement: 'Standards of behavior in school are also set by the behavior of the staff. . . . This means that pupils are likely to be influenced—either for good or ill—by the models of behavior provided by teachers both in the classroom and elsewhere' (pp. 188, 189).

Educators are not without a practical model that incorporates much of what researchers such as Goodlad, Lightfoot, Lipsitz, Rutter, and Sizer have reported. For over a decade, educators concerned about quality education for young adolescents have attempted to create school environments in which positive personal interactions, meaningful curricula, and appropriate instructional methods are central to improving student behavior and enhancing learning. This focus on meeting the unique educational needs of young adolescents (often termed the middle school movement to emphasize the desirability of treating young adolescents as unique rather than as *junior* high school students) is based on several premises: (1) the importance of understanding students' personal and cognitive development, (2) establishing educational goals in the light of students' developmental characteristics, (3) implementing instructional and school organizational patterns that are responsive to student characteristics and selected learning goals, and (4) focusing on institutional rather than student factors when goals are not met. These premises place teachers in the critical, responsible role suggested by writers who have closely investigated school settings.

From theory and research to prescription

There is ample evidence to support the proposition that teachers should be the first and primary line of defense in dealing with disruptive student behavior. Although seldom intentionally, teachers are a primary (although

Table 4.2   Teacher skills needed to develop responsible classroom mangement

Correction		School-wide discipline programs Implementing behavioristic techniques Employing problem-solving approaches
Prevention	Organization and instruction	Incorporating teaching methods that motivate students by adopting multiple learning styles and instructional goals Implementing teaching that maximizes on-task behavior Developing effective classroom rules and procedures
	Interpersonal relationships	Working with parents Creating positive peer relationships Establishing positive teacher–student relationships
Theoretical foundation		Understanding students' personal and academic needs

certainly not the sole) factor responsible for students' disruptive school behavior. This position places a heavy emphasis on dramatically improving teachers' classroom management skills. Table 4.2 provides an outline of the skills classroom teachers need in order to prevent and respond effectively to disruptive student behavior.

Table 4.2 suggests that teachers need to develop a wide yet clearly definable set of classroom management skills. Since few teachers possess these skills (Brophy and Rohrkemper, 1981; Joyce and Clift, 1984), this view implies that teachers must be given an opportunity to become familiar with a wide range of educational research and prescription. As our knowledge of the teaching and learning process becomes more thorough, it is increasingly clear that simple prescriptions will not suffice. Teachers need large amounts of time to familiarize themselves with new educational research as well as curricular changes and innovations. Similarly, time must be provided for developing new approaches and analyzing and discussing the results. An approach to classroom management that places major emphasis on teacher skill and decision making argues convincingly for the importance of providing teachers with daily schedules that allow them to spend considerably more time preparing creative lessons and talking with individual students. Perhaps as several major studies on excellence in education suggest, schools should operate 220 days a year. However, each teacher should teach only 180 of these days. The remaining time should be set aside for professional growth and planning. As numerous reports have suggested, we must also alter teachers' working conditions and salaries so as to attract and retain professionals who can understand and thoughtfully implement an increasingly complex level of educational research, curricula and technology. Only in this way will teachers become able to carry out adequately and responsibly their role as the key factor influencing student behavior and achievement.

Note

1 Portions of this chapter are adapted with permission from *Comprehensive Classroom Management* by Vernon F. Jones and Louise S. Jones, copyright 1985, Allyn & Bacon, Inc.

References

Borg, W. (1980) Time and school learning. In C. Denham and A. Lieberman (eds), *Time to Learn*. National Institute of Education, Washington, DC.

Boyer, E. (1984) *High School: A Report on Secondary Education in America*. Harper & Row, New York.

Brophy, J. (1983a) Supplemental group management techniques. In D. Duke (ed.), *Helping Teachers Manage Classrooms*. Association for Supervision and Curriculum Development, Alexandria, Va.

Brophy, J. (1983b) Research on the self-fulfilling prophecy and teacher expectations, *Journal of Educational Psychology*, **75**, 631-661.

Brophy, J., and Evertson, C. (1976) *Learning from Teaching: A Developmental Perspective*. Allyn & Bacon, Boston, Mass.

Brophy, J., and Good, T. (1971) Teacher's communication of differential expectations for children's classroom performance: some behavior data, *Journal of Educational Psychology*, **61**, 365-374.

Brophy, J., and Good, T. (1974) *Teacher-Student Relationships: Causes and Consequences*. Holt, Rinehart, & Winston, New York.

Brophy, J., and Rohrkemper, M. (1981) The influence of problem ownership on teachers' perceptions of the strategies for coping with problem students, *Journal of Educational Psychology*, **73**, 295-311.

Canter, L. (1976) *Assertive Discipline*. Lee Canter Associates, Inc., Los Angeles.

Cichon, D., and Koff, R. (1980) Stress and teaching, *NASSP Bulletin*, **64**, 91-104.

Cooper, H., and Good, T. (1983) *Pygmalion Grows Up*. Longman, New York.

Dorman, G. (1981) *Middle Grades Assessment Program*. Center for Early Adolescence, Chapel Hill, NC.

Doyle, W. (1983) Academic work, *Review of Educational Research*, **53**, 159-199.

Doyle, W. (1985) Classroom organization and management. In M. C. Wittrock (ed.), *Handbook of Research on Teaching*, 3rd edn. Macmillan, New York.

Dreikurs, R., Grunwald, B., and Pepper, F. (1971) *Maintaining Sanity in the Classroom: Illustrated Teaching Techniques*. Harper & Row, New York.

Duke, D. (1984) *Teaching—The Imperiled Profession*. State University of New York Press, Albany.

Duke, D., and Cohen, J. (1983) Do public schools have a future? A case study of retrenchment and its implications, *Urban Review*, **15**, 495-506.

Duke, D., Cohen, J., and Herman, R. (1981). Running faster to stay in place: New York schools face retrenchment. *Phi Delta Kappan*, **63**, 13–17.

Duke, D., and Jones, V. (1984) Two decades of discipline—assessing the development of an educational specialization, *Journal of Research and Development in Education*, **17**, 25–35.

Duke, D., and Meckel, A. (1980) Disciplinary roles in American schools, *British Journal of Teacher Education*, **6**, 37–50.

Dunn, R. (1983) Learning style and its relation to exceptionality at both ends of the spectrum, *Exceptional Children*, **49**, 496–506.

Dunn, R., and Dunn, K. (1978) *Teaching Students through Their Individual Learning Styles: A Practical Approach*. Reston Publishing Co., Division of Prentice-Hall, Inc., Reston, Va.

Emmer, E., Evertson, C., and Anderson, L. (1980) Effective management at the beginning of the school year, *Elementary School Journal*, **80**, 219–231.

Emmer, E., Evertson, C., Sandford, J., Clements, B., and Worsham, M. (1982) *Organizing and Managing the Junior High Classroom*. Research and Development Center for Teacher Education. Austin, Tex.

Evertson, C., and Emmer, E. (1982a) Effective management at the beginning of the school year in junior high school classes. *Journal of Educational Psychology*, **74**, 485–498.

Evertson, C., and Emmer, E. (1982b) Preventive classroom management. In D. Duke (ed.), *Helping Teachers Manage Classrooms*. Association for Supervision and Curriculum Development, Alexandria, Va.

Evertson, C., Emmer, E., Sanford, J., and Clements, B. (1982) *Improving Classroom Management: An Experimental Study in Elementary Classrooms*. Research and Development Center for Teacher Education, University of Texas, Austin.

Feitler, F., and Tokar, E. (1982) Getting a handle on teacher stress: how bad is the problem; *Educational Leadership*, **39**, 456–458.

Fitzpatrick, K. (1982) The effect of a secondary classroom management training program on teacher and student behaviour. Paper presented at the annual meeting of the American Educational Research Association, New York.

Gallup, G. (1982) Gallup poll of the public's attitudes toward the public schools, *Phi Delta Kappan*, **64**, 37–50.

Gallup, G. (1983) The 15th annual Gallup poll of the public's attitudes toward the public schools, *Phi Delta Kappan*, **65**, 33–47.

Glasser, W. (1965) *Reality Therapy*. Harper & Row, New York.

Glasser, W. (1969) *Schools Without Failure*. Harper & Row, New York.

Good, T. (1983) Classroom research: a decade of progress. Paper presented at the American Educational Research Association, Montreal, April.

Good, T., and Grouws, D. (1979) The Missouri mathematics effectiveness project. *Journal of Educational Psychology*, **71**, 355–362.

Goodlad, J. (1984) *A Place Called School*. McGraw-Hill, New York.

Gordon, T. (1974) *Teacher Effectiveness Training*. Wyden, New York.

Greenwood, C., Hops, H., Delquadri, J., and Walker, H. (1974) *PASS: Program for Academic Survival Skills*. Center at Oregon for Research in the Behavioral Education of the Handicapped, Eugene, Oreg.

Gregorc, A. (1982) *An Adult's Guide to Styles*. Gabriel Systems, Inc., Maynad, Ma.

Gump, P. (1967) *The Classroom Behavior Setting: Its Nature and Relation to Student Behavior*. Office of Education, Bureau of Research, Washington, DC. (ERIC document no. EDO 15515.)

Hollingsworth, E., Lufler, H., and Clune, W. (1984) *School Discipline: Order and Autonomy*. Praeger, New York.

Hunter, M. (1981) *Increasing your Teaching Effectiveness*. Learning Institute, Palo Alto, Calif.

Johnson, D., and Johnson, R. (1975), *Learning Together and Alone: Cooperation, Competition and Individualization*. Prentice-Hall, Englewood Cliffs, NJ.

Johnson, D., Johnson, R., Holnbee, E., Roy, P. (1984) *Circles of Learning: Cooperation in the Classroom*. Association for Supervision and Curriculum Development, Alexandria, Va.

Johnson, R., and Johnson, D. (1983) Effects of cooperative, competitive, and individualistic learning experiences on social development, *Exceptional Children*, **49**, 323-329.

Jones, V. (1982) Training teachers to be effective classroom managers. In D. Duke (ed.), *Helping Teachers Manage Classrooms*. Association for Supervision and Curriculum Development, Alexandria, Va.

Jones, V. (1980) *Adolescents with Behavior Problems: Strategies for Teaching, Counselling, and Parent Involvement*. Allyn & Bacon, Boston, Mass.

Jones, V. (1983) Current trends in classroom management: implications for gifted students, *Roeper Review*, **6**, 26-30.

Jones, V. (1984) An administrator's guide to developing and evaluating a building discipline program, *NASSP Bulletin*, **68**, 60-73.

Jones, V., and Jones, L. (1981) *Responsible Classroom Discipline: Creating Positive Learning Environments and Solving Problems*. Allyn & Bacon, Boston, Mass.

Jones, V., and Jones, L. (1985) *Comprehensive Classroom Management: Increasing Learning by Preventing and Solving Discipline Problems*. Allyn & Bacon, Boston, Mass.

Joyce, B., and Clift, R. (1984) The Phoenix agenda: essential reform in teacher education, *Educational Researcher*, **13**, 5-18.

Karweit, N. (1983) Time-on-task: a research review. Report # 332, Center for Social Organization of Schools. The Johns Hopkins University, Baltimore, Md.

Kounin, J. (1970) *Discipline and Group Management in Classrooms*. Holt, Rinehart, & Winston, New York.

LaBenne, W., and Greene, B. (1969) *Educational Implications of Self-concept Theory*. Goodyear, Pacific Palisades, Calif.

Lightfoot, S. L. (1983) *The Good High School: Portraits of Character and Culture*. Basic Books, New York.

Lipsitz, J. (1980) The age group. In M. Johnson (ed.), *Toward Adolescence: The Middle School Years Seventy-Ninth Yearbook of the National Society for the Study of Education*. University of Chicago Press, Chicago.

Lipsitz, J. (1984) *Successful Schools for Young Adolescents*. Transaction Books, New Brunswick, NJ.

McDaniel, T. (1983) On changing teachers' attitudes toward classroom management. *Phi Delta Kappan*, January, **1983**, 374-375.

Mohlman, G. (1982) Assessing the impact of three inservice teacher training models. Paper presented at the annual meeting of the American Educational Research Association, New York, April.

Moles, O. (1983) Trends in student discipline problems. Paper presented at the meeting of the American Educational Research Association, Montreal, Canada, April.

National Education Association (1983) *Nationwide Teacher Opinion Poll*. National Education Association, Washington.

Norman, J., and Harris, M. (1981) *The Private Life of the American Teenager*. Rawson, Wade Publishers, Inc., New York.

Plisko, V. (ed.) (1983) *The Condition of Education*, 1983 edn. US Government Printing Office, Washington, DC.

Pollard, A. (1980) Teacher interests and changing situations of survival threat in primary school classrooms. In P. Woods (ed.), *Teacher Strategies: Explorations in the Sociology of the School*. Croom Helm, London.

Purkey, W. (1970) *Self Concept and School Achievement*. Prentice-Hall, Englewood Cliffs, NJ.

Purkey, W. (1978) *Inviting School Success: A Self-concept Approach to Teaching and Learning*. Wadsworth, Belmont, Calif.

Purkey, W., and Novak, J. (1984) *Inviting School Success: A Self-concept Approach to Teaching and Learning*, 2nd edn. Wadsworth, Belmont, Calif.

Renzulli, J. (1983) The assessment and application of learning style preferences: a practical approach for classroom teachers. Paper presented at the annual meeting of the American Education Research Association, Montreal, Canada, April.

Robertson, S., Keith, T., and Page, E. (1983) Now who aspires to teach? *Educational Researcher*, **12**, 13–21.

Rosenthal, R., and Jacobson, L. (1968) *Pygmalion in the Classroom: Teacher Expectation and Pupils Intellectual Development*. Holt, Rinehart, Winston, New York.

Rutter, M., Maughan, B., Mortimore, P., Ouston, J., and Smith, A. (1979) *Fifteen Thousand Hours*. Harvard University Press, Cambridge, Mass.

Safer, D. (1982) *School Programs for Disruptive Adolescents*. University Park Press, Baltimore, Ma.

Sanford, J., Emmer, E., and Clements, B. (1983) Improving classroom management, *Educational Leadership*, **41**, 56–60.

Schlechty, P., and Vance, V. (1981) Do academically able teachers leave education? The North Carolina case, *Phi Delta Kappan*, **63**, 106–112.

Sharan, S. (1980) Cooperative learning in small groups: recent methods and effects on achievement, attitudes, and ethnic relations, *Review of Educational Research*, **50**, 241–271.

Sirotnik, K. (1982) The contextual correlates of the relative expenditures of classroom time on instruction and behavior: an explanatory study of secondary schools and classes, *American Educational Research Journal*, **19**, 275–292.

Sizer, T. (1984) *Horace's Compromise: The Dilemma of the American High School*. Houghton Mifflin, Boston, Mass.

Slavin, R. (1983) *Cooperative Learning*. Longman, New York.

Soar, R., and Soar, R. (1980) Setting variables, classroom interaction and multiple pupil outcomes, *JSAS Catalog of Selected Documents in Psychology*, **10**, 2110.

Squires, D., Huitt, W., and Segars, J. (1984) *Effective Schools and Classrooms: A Research-based Perspective*. Association for supervision and Curriculum Development, Alexandria, Va.

Stallings, J. (1983) An accountability model for teacher education. Paper presented at the annual meeting of the American Association of Colleges for Teacher Education, Detroit.

Toepfer, C. Brain (1980) Growth periodization data: some suggestions for re-thinking middle school education, *High School Journal*, **63**, 222–227.

Vance, V., and Schlechty, P. (1982) The distribution of academic ability in the teaching force: policy implications, *Phi Delta Kappan*, **62**, 22–27.

Weaver, T. (1979) In search of quality: the need for talent in teaching. *Phi Delta Kappan*, **61**, 29–32.

Woods, P. (1976) Having a laugh: an antidote to schooling. In M. Hammersley and P. Woods (ed.), *The Process of Schooling: A Sociological Reader*. Routledge & Kegan Paul, London.

Wragg, E. (ed.) (1984) *Classroom Teaching Skills*. Nichols Publishing Co., New York.

Yinger, R. (1983a) *Action for Excellence: A Comprehensive Plan to Improve our Nations Schools*. Report by the Task Force on Education for Economic Growth, Education Commission of the States, Washington, DC.

Yinger, R. (1983b) *A Nation at Risk: The Imperative for Educational Reform*. Report by the National Commission on Excellence in Education, Washington, DC.

Yinger, R. (1980) A study of teacher planning. *Elementary School Journal*, **80**, 107–127.

Management of Disruptive Pupil Behaviour in Schools
Edited by D. P. Tattum
©1986 John Wiley & Sons Ltd

_____*5*___

The management of aggressive behaviour in young children

Alice F. Laing and Maurice Chazan

Introduction

It is difficult to know precisely what behaviour is being referred to when the term 'aggressive' is applied to young children. The word nearly always has a negative connotation, and its use implies that the child's behaviour is undesirable. However, much aggressive behaviour is entirely natural in the early years. As young children grow in self-awareness and independence, they will at times attempt to assert their authority against their parents in a physical way, e.g. by biting, hitting, or kicking. In the course of their social development, as they begin to play with other children rather than just near them, they will frequently resort to fighting and squabbling over space and toys, until they learn more socially acceptable ways of achieving their ends. As Erikson (1963) points out, during the phase of childhood when a sense of autonomy is being acquired (roughly between 18 months and 4 years), children often experience frustration because they cannot do certain things, either because they are not allowed to or because what they wish to achieve is beyond their level of maturity; and frustration tends to lead to aggression (Dollard et al., 1939; Sears, Maccoby and Levin, 1957). Since it is important that children gradually develop independence skills, a certain amount of aggressive behaviour can be regarded not only as natural but as desirable. Manning et al. (1978) suggest that not all types of hostility in under-5s are associated with poor adjustment. In their view, young children showing 'specific hostility' (occurring in a situation which annoys or frustrates the aggressor, who is thus able to get his/her own way) tend to be socially well-adjusted, such behaviour helping an assertive child to manipulate the environment. In contrast, 'games hostility' (very intimidating activities which occur in a rough and tumble or fantasy game, such as hurling to the ground or gripping round the throat) and 'harassment' (unprovoked aggression directed at an individual, often the same one repeatedly) are to some extent maladaptive styles of behaviour.

This chapter will not attempt to deal comprehensively with the development or function of aggressive behaviour in the early years (for relevant discussions, see Maccoby, 1980, chapter 4; also Manning and Sluckin, 1984) but rather will focus on those forms of over-reactive behaviour which cause concern to adults, particularly nursery and infant school teachers and other staff involved with groups of young children. It will be concerned mainly with children in the age range 3 to 7+ years, and aggressive behaviour will be taken to include conduct which tends to be described as 'hostile', 'antisocial', 'disruptive', or 'difficult to control'. The chapter will cover identification (screening schedules and prevalence), general principles underlying appropriate assessment, and management strategies.

Identification

Teachers seldom have any difficulty in picking out children who are aggressive. Usually they identify themselves. Take, for example, the case of Martin. At the age of 5+, he was a member of a rather large reception class (29 in number), his teacher, Mrs Smith, having some assistance from a teaching aide. Martin was a very active child in the classroom, constantly flitting from one activity to another, although he seldom used the various materials as they were intended. If he was checked in any way, he would shout out rudely and would often have a temper tantrum if he could not get what he wanted. He disliked any physical contact and would shy away from it, stiffening and even crying. The other children did not like him (or were afraid of him). They shunned his company and so his play was more alongside the others than with them. He could be spiteful towards timid children. For example, he was found hitting a quiet, new boy with his coat, claiming that the boy was stretching the coat. On the other hand, if he enjoyed an activity, he would behave well.

Clearly, such a child is difficult to handle and Mrs Smith regarded him as 'naughty' and 'a nuisance'. Indeed, she could find little to say in his favour and saw his school experience as a series of crises which she was only too willing to catalogue. He existed in the classroom against a background of threats and exhortations, frequently involved in confrontations with adults and children alike.

Even though teachers can fairly easily identify aggressive children, the use of simple screening schedules or checklists may be found helpful. Such schedules enable teachers to look more precisely at the behaviour which they are finding difficult and to compare it with that shown by the other children in the class. Objections have been raised to the use of systematic identification procedures, particularly in the case of young children. It is argued that such 'labelling' has negative effects, that screening instruments are often unreliable and have limited predictive value, and that such instruments encourage the adoption of a medical model which may be inappropriate (Leach, 1981). Nevertheless, used sensitively and positively, with the emphasis on giving children the help which they need rather than on predicting the course of their future development, screening schedules can assist teachers in sharpening their classroom observation and in clarifying their thoughts about individual children.

Screening schedules

In recent years, a variety of schedules have been developed for the systematic screening of behaviour difficulties at school or in the home. A selection of instruments suitable for use by teachers of young children will be discussed briefly here (for information on schedules designed for parents, see Richman *et al.*, 1982 and Jenkins *et al.*, 1980 and 1984). The most widely used school-based schedules are perhaps Rutter's Child Behaviour Scale B (Rutter, 1967; Rutter *et al.*, 1970) and Stott and Marston's (1971) *Bristol Social Adjustment Guide: Child in School.* The Rutter Scale B (for teachers) consists of 26 statements of possible behaviour problems, the teacher having to check whether the statement 'certainly applies', 'applies somewhat', or 'doesn't apply' to the individual concerned. This scale has been used mainly with older children but there is a shortened form for infant school children (aged 5–7+), and Behar and Stringfield (1974) have produced a modification of the original questionnaire for 3–6-year-olds (see also Osborn *et al.*, 1984). The Rutter Scales have been carefully validated and are easy to administer, but their format (all negative items) may lead teachers to adopt a negative set towards particular children (Fitton, 1972).

The revised version of the Bristol Social Adjustment Guide: Child in School, which is meant for children aged 5–16 years, adopts a rather different format, providing a comprehensive variety of phrases (both positive and negative) describing a child's behaviour. Although the teacher has to do no more than underline those phrases which most nearly describe the individual's behaviour, the guide may be somewhat time consuming if a whole class is to be screened. Teachers may prefer to complete, initially, the six adjustment pointers (checked on a four-point scale) used by Stott (1981) in a study of a sample of 5–6-year-olds, and then to employ the full guide in the case of those children who seem to present a problem. The scores on the Bristol Social Adjustment Guide form the basis for picking out children with varying degrees of 'over-reactive' or 'under-reactive' behaviour in terms of categories ranging from 'stability and near stability' to 'severe maladjustment' (see Stott, 1975). Norms are provided for 'hostility', regarded as one of the five core syndromes scored by the guide, and for 'peer-maladaptiveness' (domineering or aggressive attitudes to age-peers), which is one of the associated groupings. For children aged 3–5 years, the Effectiveness Motivation Scale (Stott and Sharp, 1976), which includes items relating to disruptive and quarrelsome behaviour, may also be found useful.

Other relevant screening scales or checklists for young children include the Swansea Behaviour Checklist (see Chazan *et al.*, 1983) and the Infant Rating Scale (Lindsay, 1981), the latter being available at two levels (Level 1 for 5–5½-year-olds and Level 2 for 7–7½-year-olds). The Infant Rating Scale has been standardized on a substantial sample of children and contains subscales on Behaviour and Social Integration which help to identify aggressive and disruptive children. In the USA, Kohn and Rosman (1972, 1973) have developed two teacher rating instruments, the Problem Checklist and the Social Competence Scale, which aim to measure two major dimensions of social–emotional functioning in preschool children, namely (1) Interest-Participation versus Apathy-Withdrawal and (2) Cooperation-Compliance versus Anger-Defiance.

Whatever instruments are used, it is important that screening should be regarded not as a means of labelling children in a stereotyped way, but as the first stage in assessing those in difficulties and in providing them with appropriate help and support.

Prevalence of aggressive behaviour

Estimates of the prevalence of behaviour difficulties in children aged 3–7+ have been surprisingly high. It is difficult to compare the findings of different studies, since these will vary according to the measures used, the size and composition of the sample, and the raters involved. For example, little correlation exists between ratings of behaviour at home and adjustment in school (Coleman *et al.*, 1977). Although sex differences are not found in all areas of behaviour, boys tend to present more behaviour problems than girls, especially with respect to overactivity, restlessness, and antisocial behaviour (Richman *et al.*, 1982). However, a number of estimates of the prevalence in the age range in question of behaviour problems which cause at least some concern to parents or teachers have been in the region of 11–14 per cent (Davie *et al.*, 1972; Chazan and Jackson, 1974; Hughes *et al.*, 1979; Chazan *et al.*, 1980). Where 3-year-olds have formed all or a substantial proportion of the sample (Coleman *et al.*, 1977; Richman *et al.*, 1982), or where estimates are based on ratings by both teachers and parents (McGee *et al.*, 1984), prevalence figures have been even higher.

It is even more difficult to provide meaningful estimates of the prevalence of *aggressive* behaviour in young children than it is to give an overall indication of the number of children presenting behaviour difficulties, as the findings of several studies show. Chazan *et al.* (1980), in a survey of 7320 4-year-olds in two LEAs in England and Wales, found that 3.4 per cent of their sample (0.9 per cent severe, 2.5 per cent mild) showed aggressive behaviour, with destructiveness reported in 2.3 per cent (0.3 per cent severe, 2.0 per cent mild) — these categories overlap somewhat as far as individual children are concerned. In a further study of 375 children (193 boys, 182 girls), with ages ranging from 36 to 63 months, 52 (13 per cent of the total sample) displayed aggressive behaviour, in 25 cases along with other patterns of behaviour such as overactivity, withdrawal, or dependency (Laing, 1984). Osborn *et al.* (1984), using their own scales of 'antisocial' and 'neurotic' behaviour derived from Rutter's Child Behaviour Scale, found 4.1 per cent of 13 135 5-year-olds reported as 'destructive', 4.2 per cent as 'frequently fighting with others', 12.1 per cent as having temper tantrums at least once a week, and 1.5 per cent as bullying (if mild forms of such behaviours are included, the figures are very much higher). Chazan and Jackson (1971, 1974), using an older version of Stott's six pointers (Stott, 1966), reported that teachers of 5-year-olds considered nearly 6 per cent of the children in their charge to be 'very aggressive', the figure being only slightly lower in the case of 7-year-olds. Stott (1981), using the revised form of his six questions, found 5.19 per cent of children aged 5–6 years to be hyperactive, 2.09 per cent to be impulsive, and 0.85 per cent to be hostile. A much higher prevalence of antisocial behaviour is reported by McGee *et al.* (1984) in a study of 7-year-olds in New Zealand: on the basis of the Rutter Child Behaviour Scale B, 22.6 per cent of 492 boys and 14.2 per cent of 459 girls were rated as 'antisocial' either at home or at school. These high figures may be due to the inappropriateness of the scale's cut-off points (determined for rather older children) in the case of 7-year-olds.

The above estimates, although varying widely, suggest that most nursery staff and infant school teachers will have at least one moderately or severely aggressive child needing special attention in their class or group.

Persistence of aggressive behaviour

There is evidence that aggression in normal children tends to decline fairly rapidly after about 5 or 6 years. Children who remain highly aggressive at the stage when other children's aggression is lessening are likely to be immature or disturbed (Maccoby, 1980). Some of the early problems arising from aggressive or destructive tendencies which cause concern to adults are therefore transitory, but by no means all. Macfarlane *et al.* (1954) suggested that children with many problems at the preschool stage are more likely than others to present later difficulties. Westman, Rice and Bermann (1967), in a study of nursery school children in the USA, found that difficulties in peer relations, temper tantrums, and overactivity were among the symptoms most predictive of poor adjustment later on. In a follow-up study of children first seen at 3 years, Richman *et al.* (1982) report that as many as 62 per cent of children presenting behaviour problems at that age remained at 8 years with some degree of disturbance, and that the outcome of early problem behaviour was more likely to be antisocial in type than neurotic. Boys showing antisocial tendencies at 8 years were much more likely to have been rated 'difficult to control', 'overactive, restless', or 'having poor relations with siblings' at 3 years of age than boys with no disorder at 8 years. On the basis of longer-term studies carried out in the USA and elsewhere (see Robins, 1966 and 1972), Rutter (1975) concludes that the prognosis for children with serious and widespread 'conduct' or 'antisocial' disorders is poor, particularly when behaviour of this kind is shown in early childhood. The outlook for these children is much worse than that for children with 'emotional' or 'neurotic' disorders.

Questions relating to the persistence of problem behaviour are always difficult to answer, particularly because circumstances may change over time and because any intervention undertaken has to be taken into account. Intensive follow-up studies are needed, even over a fairly short span of time, if our understanding of the development of aggressive behaviour in children is to be increased.

Assessment

Role of teacher

The assessment of behaviour difficulties involves obtaining maximum information about the nature of the problem and the development of the child concerned, in the context of the family and the school. The Warnock Report (DES, 1978) recommended that there should be five stages of assessment for children with special educational needs, ranging from internal assessment by school staff to assessment by a multiprofessional team. Although some children with behaviour difficulties will require an assessment involving an educational psychologist, psychiatrist, social worker, or other professional, teachers as well as parents always have a crucial part to play in assessing problem behaviour. They can contribute their own knowledge of the child's functioning in classroom and play-ground, knowledge which is unique to them; but they need to understand that the causation of behaviour difficulties is very complex, and that aggressive behaviour in young children is usually related to an interaction between temperamental, developmental, family, and school factors. Some of the general principles which should be considered by teachers in making a contribution to assessment will be outlined here (for a more detailed discussion of the role of the teacher in the assessment of behaviour difficulties in young children, see Chazan *et al.*, 1983).

General principles in assessment

(1) It is only too easy to label children 'aggressive' and then to see only their aggressive behaviour. As Mrs Smith admitted about Martin, their nuisance rating is high. The first step in dealing with them is probably to become more precise and more objective about the aggressive incidents which occur. By noting carefully when the incidents take place (i.e. exact time of day), what triggers them off, who is the focus of the aggression (e.g. one particular child/any children; adult/child; boy/girl; younger/older child), where the incidents occur and what is the result of each incident, a pattern often begins to emerge (Leach and Raybould, 1977). When teachers look carefully at aggressive behaviour over a period of time, they sometimes realize not only that they can begin to predict trouble but also that there are occasions on which aggressive behaviour does not occur.

(2) To get aggression into perspective, it is also useful to note any positive aspects in the children's behaviour. To view children from a negative angle only, exacerbates the situation and leaves no way out of the confrontations. Even Martin was not without his strengths. He was not unintelligent; he had good motor skills, useful hand–eye coordination, and an interest in books, with well-developed receptive and expressive language skills; and he liked active play. These positive attributes indicate areas where Martin could have been given the attention he so clearly was seeking and which might have led to a change in how he interacted with others.

(3) It is useful to find out whether the aggression is displayed only in school or whether it is part of the children's behaviour outside of school as well. As previously mentioned, problem behaviour is often specific to a particular situation. Discussion with parents can be very enlightening, especially as studies have frequently found considerable disagreement between parents and teachers as to which children have problems (e.g. Touliatos and Lindholm, 1981). Furthermore, close liaison with parents is important because the family situation usually has a considerable bearing on the development of aggressive behaviour in the child. Within the family setting, children can learn aggression in a variety of ways, including through the parents' own models of behaviour and child-rearing practices (Maccoby, 1980). Richman *et al.* (1982) found evidence that disharmonious family relationships were often important in the development of both antisocial and neurotic behaviour. In particular, they established that mothers who were depressed and anxious when their children were 3 years old tended to have disturbed children at 8 years to a greater extent than other mothers.

Help for the family will, therefore, often be needed in addition to any other strategies adopted to help the child, and if this help is to be appropriate, information should be obtained on the family situation.

(4) The close observation of the pattern of aggressive behaviour in children, which was advocated as the first step in coming to terms with the problem, should also include a consideration of the classroom environment and the organization of the day-by-day teaching in it. The kind of daily programme of activities arranged by particular teachers and the methods of control used by them seem to influence the amount of aggression occurring in any classroom group of young children (Patterson, Littman and Bricker, 1967). Martin's classroom was rather gloomy and cramped, posing organizational difficulties for Mrs Smith. Perhaps because of this, she had adopted a highly organized routine in which children were moved from activity to activity on a prearranged rota, rather than because of their needs or interests. In addition, all the children were expected to participate in certain activities (like watching television programmes, art work) whether they were interested or not. Such a tight organizational pattern made things difficult for Martin (and indeed for others in the class), disrupting him once he had settled down and also increasing his opportunities for aggression, especially when he was bunched together with the whole class. Hughes *et al.* (1979), in their study of children's difficulties on starting infant school, have shown that poor concentration was judged by the teachers concerned to be the main problem displayed and that this remained a major worry for teachers 18 months later. 'Restlessness' has been similarly identified as adversely affecting disadvantaged children's responses to the infant school programme (Chazan and Jackson, 1971 and 1974). On occasion, the classroom routine followed by Mrs Smith was distracting Martin rather than encouraging persistence.

(5) Since an association has been established between reading difficulties and antisocial behaviour even in infant school children (McMichael, 1979), it is important to take into account the child's educational progress as part of the assessment procedures, with a view to taking any necessary remedial action. Little agreement exists as to whether reading difficulties produce behavioural problems or whether initial poor adjustment is a major factor in the causation of poor progress in reading. It is probable that in some cases immaturity or disturbance on entry to school leads to difficulties in learning to read; in others, conduct disorders stem from these difficulties; while in yet a third group both reading problems and behavioural difficulties may be related to some common cause, such as social disadvantage (Sturge, 1982). Where aggressive behaviour is associated with lack of educational progress, the nature of the link should be explored as fully as possible.

Management strategies

Helping aggressive children through the normal programme

In individual work situations, such as basic skills work, aggressive behaviour may be at its minimum, provided that sufficient apparatus is readily available, the activities have been well chosen for each child's particular needs, and the seating arrangements are sensible. Opportunities for aggression may be greater in sessions given over to free play or creative activities. Yet it is precisely in these areas that deliberate attempts could be made to help children to release pent-up feelings or to begin to learn to control them.

Advice on how teachers can structure play so as to enhance the children's experience without dominating it can be found in a report by Manning and Sharp (1977). The two aspects to which teachers should pay particular attention are language stimulation and the emergence of imaginative play. The presence of an adult in a play episode is particularly rewarding (Smith and Connolly, 1980; Sylva *et al.*, 1980). For a small group to be talking intently and meaningfully about a play activity is valuable for any member of it and certainly for an aggressive child, one of whose problems may be that he has not acquired sufficient language skills to negotiate his demands. Martin, it will be remembered, did not fall into such a category. He had good linguistic development but did not choose to use it. In his case, opportunities to see how language could be used productively with other children and adults might have been helpful. He was an only child until just after he came to school and both of his parents had had full-time jobs, his father being a prison officer and his mother a comprehensive school teacher. Although he may well have been brought up in a home where language was important, it would be interesting to know whether he regarded language as a medium for control (as his teacher frequently used it in his case) or as a means through which he could make his point of view known. To find that an adult would be willing to listen to him and act on his suggestions or that he could, through verbal communication, carry the group along in an activity to a successful conclusion could have led him to realize that there were alternatives to his use of force or using language for verbal abuse.

Children less fortunate in their preschool language experiences than Martin may need planned language activities (see Chazan and Laing, 1982; Harris, 1984) to give them enough language ability to be able to appreciate the effect of verbal communication. There is also a very good case for discussing with parents aspects of the development of receptive and expressive language skills relevant to their children. For a variety of reasons, dialogue may not occur very often at home, yet it is in the home that there are much greater possibilities of its occurrence than in school, where there is usually little chance of a prolonged one-to-one interchange (Tizard *et al.*, 1982; Tizard and Hughes, 1984).

The reasons why imaginative play has been singled out as being particularly important are that it often leads to better use of language as children define roles or situations; that it enables children to think about other people's points of view; that it gives opportunities for trying out or practising new skills; and that it may, on occasion, help children to come to terms with their worries or anxieties. Yet another feature is that imaginative play usually requires some interaction with others in order to explain what is going on or to enlist some cooperation so that the game may continue. Aggressive children may well avoid imaginative play, or other children may not want to play with them as their games are too rough and noisy or the scenario too brief and undeveloped, always finishing in wild chasing or running or pushing. Brief small-group activities to help aggressive children develop awareness of others or try out other roles than Batman can be set up (see Chazan *et al.*, 1983). These activities are useful not just for aggressive children but for others too. No special programme is required. Teachers can simply select or adapt existing activities which appear suitable.

There are many opportunities for successful peer interaction as well as for cognitive development in creative activities. Participation in music, singing, movement, and drama can lead to cooperative efforts in which all can take pride and the discipline inherent in the subjects themselves can lead to better self-control. They can also lead, of course, to greater disruption, and the part in them to be played by aggressive children should be carefully considered so that demands too far beyond the children's levels of tolerance are not made. A fine balance is required between not allowing sufficient time for the children to come to terms with the experience and prolonging the activity until the children are bored with it.

Art and crafts have the bonus of offering individual expression of feelings if the experience has been so organized. The control of media such as paint, paper, or clay to create and re-create symbols can help children to work towards releasing worries and fears or solving conflicts. It is not enough, however, to provide the materials and leave aggressive children to get on with it in the belief that they will then work things out for themselves. They need to be supervised unobtrusively and, where appropriate, helped to develop their work by using colours and tools as skilfully as possible.

Helping aggressive children through special programmes

The suggestions made so far for the classroom management of aggression may not be adequate for fairly severe problems. In these cases, it will probably be essential to work along with the parents as any particular programmes developed in the classroom will stand a much better chance of success if they are backed up by a similar approach at home. Two such programmes will be briefly discussed now, further details of them being available in Chazan *et al.* (1983).

A problem-solving approach It has been suggested (Spivack and Shure, 1974) that children can be helped towards bringing their social behaviour under their own verbal control if they are encouraged to discuss alternative ways of behaving and the consequences of such behaviour. Aggressive children are often impulsive and are inclined to lash out unthinkingly. If they could be helped to appreciate the effect of their actions on others, through a realization of their own feelings in similar circumstances, and then to consider the peer (or adult) confrontation as a problem with several possible solutions, the instant 'scream-up' might be avoided. Actual incidents become the basis for discussion among children, the adult's role being a strictly neutral one as the intention is not to impose any particular solution for a behavioural problem, but rather to get children to follow through for themselves the possible consequences of whatever solutions they have proposed. The emphasis is not on telling the children *what* they should be thinking, but teaching them *how* to think. Children who act aggressively because their language has not developed sufficiently for them to employ verbal negotiation would find a problem-solving approach fairly unproductive, but such an approach might have helped Martin, if built onto the opportunities to use his good language skills more effectively.

It is important, therefore, for teachers who might be considering the use of this approach, to take into account the children's levels of communicative skill and to choose the correct time for the discussion between the pupils concerned, once the immediate crisis has passed. The way in which the teacher proposes to guide the discussion has also to be thought about and patience is required to wait until the children work towards more acceptable solutions without pressurizing them to adopt the behaviour the teacher would find acceptable. If adults hold rather negative attitudes towards certain children, it is particularly difficult to achieve the role of facilitator which is required. Hopefully, however, the close examination of children's aggressive behaviour and the concentration on the 'positives' they have to offer, as advocated earlier in this chapter, will have led staff to review their own attitudes and change them if necessary. Spivack and Shure (1974) also suggest that, if children do respond to this approach and begin to bring their behaviour under more thoughtful (and verbal) control, this bodes well for their future social development.

A behaviour modification approach   It is not possible in the confines of this chapter to give a detailed account of the procedures involved in behaviour modification. Teachers can find this in a number of books (e.g. Herbert, 1981), and a fuller description of the approach linked to case studies of its use with 3- and 4-year-olds is in the handbook already mentioned (Chazan *et al.*, 1983). The unacceptable behaviour has to be systematically assessed; the desired behaviour has to be precisely described; effective rewards to encourage the children to display, or move towards displaying, this acceptable behaviour have to be selected; and a consistent and concerted approach by all adults concerned has to be agreed upon with regard to the programme being implemented. It is no use one person giving a child attention and praise for a certain action if another gives attention to the very behaviour which the first person is trying to ignore and therefore get rid of. Obviously, if a similar programme were to be carried out in the home, results would probably be seen much more rapidly, as the parent may unwittingly be cutting across the programme if the method and the objectives have not been fully discussed.

The fundamental idea behind behaviour modification is simple—children (and, indeed, all of us) respond better to praise than to reproof. If any action is immediately followed by clear social approval, it tends to be repeated, especially if a highly satisfying response is always elicited by this action from others important to the individual concerned. The techniques based on this idea do, however, call for considerable thought and discussion and for careful planning, especially in a classroom with other children present. It is, nevertheless, worthwhile investigating its possibilities. An understanding of the techniques may enable teachers to see a way round difficult behaviour and the close study of children's behaviour which they call for is frequently very illuminating. Teachers have been known to change their minds completely about a child's behaviour when they have actually counted the number of times it occurs and thought about how it could be modified.

Objections are sometimes raised to this approach, mainly on the grounds that manipulation of another person's behaviour is not ethically justifiable. While there is certainly some force in this argument, it has, nevertheless, to be said that we are all busily trying to 'shape' behaviour in the direction we want it to go from the moment the baby is born. Behaviour modification techniques owe their power to systematic positive suggestion and, as such, are much to be preferred to unsystematic or negative strategies. If the behaviour acquired through these methods is satisfying to the children concerned, approved by their teachers, and enables them to get on more effectively in school (and/or at home), it would seem reasonable for teachers to make use of them, either by themselves or in combination with any of the other approaches discussed in this chapter.

Infant teachers more than any others should be willing to consider strategies for helping aggressive children. If the latter have not been helped towards controlling their aggression in the infant school, such behaviour may become established and long lasting (Richman *et al.*, 1982). Time is not always the great healer. While children are young enough to be helped towards substituting acceptable for unacceptable behaviour, it would indeed be sad if no help were given, either because of exigencies of time or space, or because of pressures on staff, or because staff were unwilling to consider the problem objectively, to view aggressive children positively, and to work out suitable programmes.

Much of this discussion on classroom procedures has been based on a child in a reception class. The first move from home, whether to school or preschool (Blatchford *et al.*, 1982; Cleave *et al.*, 1982), is an important one, as patterns of behaviour with regard to school may be established at that point, whether for good or ill. All teachers of young children, therefore, should consider strategies for coping with difficult behaviour. Indeed, it has been shown (Kolvin *et al.*, 1981) that teachers in the primary school can play an important role in helping children with adjustment problems. To see this as part of teaching young children is a responsibility additional to the normal maintenance of classroom control but it is a responsibility with considerable hidden benefits for the teacher. If aggression is merely prevented by adult threat or strictures, it may well reappear in another guise. If, on the other hand, children can be led to adopt other behaviour, this will make for happier relationships with everyone concerned—peers, teachers, and parents.

References

Behar, L., and Stringfield, S. (1974) A behaviour rating scale for the pre-school child, *Dev. Psychol.*, **10**, 601–610.

Blatchford, P., Battle, S., and Mays, J. (1982) *The First Transition*. NFER–Nelson, Windsor.

Chazan, M., and Jackson, S. (1971) Behaviour problems in the infant school, *J. Child Psychol. Psychiat.*, **12**, 191–210.

Chazan, M., and Jackson, S. (1974) Behaviour problems in the infant school: changes over two years, *J. Child Psychol. Psychiat.*, **15**, 33–46.

Chazan, M., and Laing, A. F. (1982) *Children with Special Needs: The Early Years*. Open University Press, Milton Keynes.

Chazan, M., Laing, A. F., Jones, J., Harper, G., and Bolton, J. (1983) *Helping Young Children with Behaviour Difficulties*. Croom Helm, London.

Chazan, M., Laing, A. F., Shackleton Bailey, M., and Jones, G. (1980) *Some of Our Children: The Early Education of Children with Special Needs*. Open Books, London.

Cleave, S., Jowett, S., and Bate, M. (1982) *And So to School*. NFER–Nelson, Windsor.

Coleman, J., Wolkind, S., and Ashley, L. (1977) Symptoms of behaviour disturbance and adjustment to school, *J. Child Psychol. Psychiat.*, **18**, 201–210.

Davie, R., Butler, N., and Goldstein, H. (1972) *From Birth to Seven.* Longman, London.

Department of Education and Science (1978) *Special Educational Needs.* (The Warnock Report.) HMSO, London.

Dollard, J., Doob, L. W., Miller, N. E., Mowrer, O. H., and Sears, R. R. (1939) *Frustration and Aggression.* Yale University Press, New Haven, Conn.

Erikson, E. H. (1963) *Childhood and Society,* 2nd edn. W. W. Norton, New York.

Fitton, J. B. (1972) 'Use of the Rutter Behaviour Scales', *J. Assoc. Educ. Psychologists,* **3**, 45–47.

Harris, J. (1984) Early language intervention programmes: an update, *Newsletter of Assoc. Child Psychol. Psychiat.,* **6** (2), 2–20.

Herbert, M. (1981) *Behavioural Treatment of Problem Children: A Practice Manual.* Academic Press, London.

Hughes, M., Pinkerton, G., and Plewis, I. (1979) Children's difficulties on starting infant school, *J. Child Psychol. Psychiat.,* **20**, 187–197.

Jenkins, S., Bax, M., and Hart, H. (1980) Behaviour problems in pre-school children, *J. Child Psychol. Psychiat.,* **21**, 5–17.

Jenkins, S., Owen, C., Bax, M., and Hart, H. (1984) Continuities of common behaviour problems in preschool children, *J. Child Psychol. Psychiat.,* **25**, 75–90.

Kohn, M., and Rosman, B. L. (1972) A social competence scale and symptom check-list for the pre-school child: factor dimensions, their cross-instrumental generality and longitudinal persistence, *Dev. Psychol.,* **6**, 430–444.

Kohn, M., and Rosman, B. L. (1973) A two factor model of emotional disturbance in the young child: validity and screening efficiency, *J. Child Psychol. Psychiat.,* **14**, 31–56.

Kolvin, I., Garside, R. F., Nicol, A. R., Macmillan, A., Wolstenholme, F., and Leitch, I. M. (1981) *Help Starts Here—The Maladjusted Child in the Ordinary School.* Tavistock, London.

Laing, A. F. (1984) The extent and nature of behaviour difficulties in young children, *Links,* **10**, 21–25.

Leach, D. J. (1981) Early screening for school learning difficulties: efficacy, problems and alternatives, *Occ. Papers of Div. of Educ. and Child Psychol.,* **5** (2), 46–57. British Psychological Society, Leicester.

Leach, D. J., and Raybould, E. C. (1977) *Learning and Behaviour Difficulties in School.* Open Books, London.

Lindsay, G. A. (1981) *The Infant Rating Scale: Manual.* Hodder & Stoughton, London.

Maccoby, E. E. (1980) *Social Development: Psychological Growth and the Parent-Child Relationship.* Harcourt Brace Jovanovich, New York.

MacFarlane, J. W., Allen, L., and Honzik, M. P. (1954) *A Developmental Study of the Behaviour Problems of Normal Children between 21 Months and 14 Years.* University of California Press.

McGee, R., Silva, P. A., and Williams, S. (1984) Behaviour problems in a population of seven-year-old children: prevalence, stability and types of disorder—a research report, *J. Child Psychol., Psychiat.,* **25**, 251–260.

McMichael, P. (1979) The hen or the egg? Which comes first—antisocial emotional disorders or reading disability? *Brit. J. Educ. Psychol.,* **49**, 226–238.

Manning, K., and Sharp, A. (1977) *Structuring Play in the Early Years at School.* Ward Lock Educational, London.

Manning, M., Heron, J., and Marshall, T. (1978) Styles of hostility and social interactions at nursery, at school, and at home: an extended study of children. In *Aggression and Anti-Social Behaviour in Childhood and Adolescence* (ed. L. A. Hersov and M. Berger). Pergamon Press, Oxford.

Manning, M., and Sluckin, A. M. (1984) The function of aggression in the pre-school and primary school years. In *Disruptive Behaviour in Schools* (ed. N. Frude and H. Gault). John Wiley, New York.

Osborn, A. F., Butler, N. R., and Morris, A. C. (1984) *The Social Life of Britain's Five-Year-Olds.* Routledge & Kegan Paul, London.

Patterson, G. R., Littman, R. A., and Bricker, W. (1967) Assertive behaviour in young children: a step toward a theory of aggression, *Monographs of the Society for Research in Child Development.* **35** (5).

Richman, N., Stevenson, J., and Graham, P. J. (1982) *Pre-School to School: A Behavioural Study.* Academic Press, London.

Robins, L. N. (1966) *Deviant Children Grown Up.* Williams & Wilkins, Baltimore, Md.

Robins, L. N. (1972) Follow-up studies of behaviour disorders in children. In *Psychopathological Disorders of Childhood* (ed. H. C. Quay and J. S. Werry). John Wiley, New York.

Rutter, M. (1967) A children's behaviour questionnaire for completion by teachers, *J. Child Psychol. Psychiat.*, **8**, 1–11.

Rutter, M. (1975) *Helping Troubled Children.* Penguin Education, Harmondsworth, Middx.

Rutter, M., Tizard, J., and Whitmore, K. (eds) (1970) *Education, Health and Behaviour.* Longman, London.

Sears, R. R., Maccoby, E. E., and Levin, H. (1957) *Patterns of Child Rearing.* Row Peterson, Evanston, Ill.

Smith, P. K., and Connolly, K. J. (1980) *The Ecology of Pre-school Behaviour.* Cambridge University Press, Cambridge.

Spivack, G., and Shure, M. B. (1974) *Social Adjustment of Young Children.* Jossey-Bass, San Francisco.

Stott, D. H. (1966) *Bristol Social Adjustment Guides: Manual,* 3rd edn. University of London Press, London.

Stott, D. H. (1975) *Bristol Social Adjustment Guides: Manual,* 5th edn. University of London Press, London.

Stott, D. H. (1981) Behaviour disturbance and failure to learn: a study of cause and effect, *Educ. Research,* **23**, 163–172.

Stott, D. H., and Marston, N. C. (1971) *Bristol Social-Adjustment Guides: The Child in School,* 2nd edn. Hodder & Stoughton Educational, London.

Stott, D. H., and Sharp, J. D. (1976) *Effectiveness Motivation Scale (Manual).* NFER Pub. Co., Windsor.

Sturge, C. (1982) Reading retardation and antisocial behaviour, *J. Child Psychol. Psychiat.*, **23**, 21–31.

Sylva, K., Roy, C., and Painter, M. (1980) *Childwatching at Playgroup and Nursery School.* Grant McIntyre Ltd, London.

Tizard, B., and Hughes, M. (1984) *Young Children Learning: Talking and Thinking at Home and at School.* Fontana Books, London.

Tizard, B., Hughes, M., Pinkerton, G., and Carmichael, H. (1982) Adults' cognitive demands at home and in nursery school, *J. Child Psychol. Psychiat.*, **23**, 105–117.

Touliatos, J., and Lindholm, B. W. (1981) Congruence of parents' and teachers' ratings of children's behaviour problems, *J. Abnorm. Child Psychol.*, **9**, 347–354.

Westman, J. C., Rice, D. L., and Bermann, E. (1967) Nursery school behaviour and later school adjustment, *Amer. J. Orthopsychiat.*, **37**, 725–731.

Management of Disruptive Pupil Behaviour in Schools
Edited by D. P. Tattum
©1986 Andrew Pollard. Published by John Wiley & Sons Ltd

_____6___

An ethnographic analysis of classroom conflict

Andrew Pollard

Introduction

Conflict between teachers and young children cannot always be avoided. This is likely to be true for at least as long as our primary school system is based on the taken-for-granted assumption that one adult can satisfactorily educate about 25 children simultaneously by providing structured activities in a classroom. Whatever educationists may think about the inherent difficulties posed by this situation, the fact still remains that something like it is a reality for the vast majority of teachers and children in schools within the state systems of Western countries. In many parts of the world, teacher–pupil ratios and other conditions are much worse.

As in the case of the other approaches represented in this book, there is very little that ethnographic studies can actually *do* about this basic reality. Perhaps, though, they can begin to offer a way of rebutting those who say that such ratios do not matter. Such arguments are usually based on comparisons between measured level of pupil achievement obtained with different class sizes. Simple quantifiable outputs are often used such as maths or literacy scores which imply the use of a very narrow set of educational criteria. The main issues which are omitted are, of course, qualitative, and concern the experience of the teacher and the child of the social processes which are the typical consequence of large classes. Ethnography can be useful here because, as a form of sociological inquiry, it has evolved a set of relatively systematic procedures designed to provide description and analysis of the subjective perspectives which people tend to develop as they act. Ethnography thus provides a way of addressing the vital qualitative elements of classroom life and of taking account of the perspectives which make it meaningful to the participants. In a sense, such perspectives are always unique to each individual, but it is also the case that, because of the similarity of the basic structural factors which influence classroom life, identifiable *patterns* in the perspectives of teachers and children do tend to emerge. The accumulation of case studies makes comparison possible and in this way a deeper understanding of the meaning which classroom processes have for school participants can be constructed.

The result of such an analysis is sometimes that even aspects of classroom life which may be very familiar are rendered partially strange. Lest this peculiar achievement be misunderstood, I must immediately suggest that this strangeness is a vital ingredient for the type of incisive reflection which in my view is needed in teaching. Another way to put it is to say that while common sense derived from experience is a fine way to reach quick, workable decisions at one level, there are other situations where it can be a barrier to reflective thinking — thinking which may have more power and value in the long run. I would thus suggest that what we need as teachers are the ability and skill to adopt a type of practical theorizing. Such practical theorizing has been usefully defined by Reid (1978, p. 43) as 'an intricate and skilled intellectual and social process whereby, individually or collectively, we identify the questions to which we must respond, establish grounds for deciding on answers, and then choose among the available solutions'.

This volume has its focus on disruptive behaviour in schools, and I have, in a sense, simply taken the issue of disruption in primary school classrooms as my focus. However, in my view, this issue is only a symptom of underlying problems in what are socially structured and partially constrained teacher-pupil relationships. An ethnographic analysis of classroom interaction and relationships can offer one way of getting behind the surface phenomenon of disruptive behaviour to help identify what Reid calls the underlying 'questions to which we must respond'.

The analysis which is presented here is derived from work in primary schools with class-based systems, work which is grounded largely on interview and observational data and which is reported in a more complete and detailed form elsewhere (Pollard, 1985). In this chapter I attempt to tease out some of the implications of such ethnographic analyses for teachers wishing to reflect on the issue of disruption in normal classroom situations. In particular I draw attention to the ways in which the teaching strategies and policies which teachers adopt in their classrooms are often reflected in the coping strategies which children adopt — and disruption, of course, can be seen as one child strategy which has had a particularly long history.

'Disruption' and teaching policies

The concept of disruption is premised on the idea that there is a sense of order in most classrooms which can be disrupted. Whilst this may generally be the case, the existence of order is not something which can be assumed.

As has been pointed out on many occasions, there is an inherent conflict in the teacher–pupil relationship. For instance, as long ago as 1932 Waller described teachers as 'the enemy of the spontaneous life of groups of children'. More recently, Shipman (1975) suggested that 'the very existence of school is a limit on freedom' and argued that 'clashes of interest will occur even in the most progressive schools'.

To understand the nature of these potential clashes of interest is a vital step towards understanding 'disruption' or other forms of conflict in classrooms. In my own studies of primary schools I identified personal interests and concerns which the teachers (Pollard, 1980) and children (Pollard, 1984) appeared to be most concerned about in the immediacy of their classroom experiences. These 'interests-at-hand' are summarized in Table 6.1.

Table 6.1 Classroom interests-at-hand of teachers and children

Teachers	Children
SELF	SELF
—self-image	—self-image
—workload	—control of stress
—health and stress	—enjoyment
—enjoyment	—dignity
—autonomy	
ORDER	PEER GROUP MEMBERSHIP
INSTRUCTION	LEARNING

The most important point which is implied in this table is that both parties maintain a primary concern with their 'self'. Of course, this interest becomes apparent in a number of ways and various facets of the concern are thus indicated. In the case of teachers some common factors which are suggested are: a desire to control the workload involved in teaching, expectation of deriving intrinsic pleasure and enjoyment from classroom life where possible, an attempt to control the level of stress and tension involved in the job, and, more generally and significantly, ambitions to maintain whatever particular self-image, with regard to teaching, that has been adopted by each teacher. This latter may relate to factors such as educational philosophies, characteristic forms of teaching, levels of commitment, etc. In addition, I found that many primary school teachers tend to want to work within a defined area of autonomy and, where this is established, they will act to maintain and protect it. Teachers' interests-at-hand of order and instruction are in a slightly different category and can be seen as providing a means of maintaining the various facets of self. As a middle school teacher once explained to me, 'It's simple really, there's a lot of 'em [children in each class] and if you don't keep them under control they'll run all over. The easiest way to do that is to keep 'em interested and keep 'em working.'

The interests-at-hand of young children seem to take a form similar to that of teachers, although there is considerable variation for children in different structural positions within each class in the way in which each concern is manifested. There are various facets of the primary interest of 'self'. For instance, children wish to control the levels of stress which they experience in their classrooms. Stress can be seen both positively and negatively. For instance, some children may see the element of stress which is related to risk taking and mischief as a necessary part of these experiences. On the other hand, most primary school children seek to avoid stress when it is being introduced or imposed by a teacher. Enjoyment is a second major concern for young children, and in the immediacy of their classroom experiences it is a prominent criterion by which such experiences are judged and in response to which new courses of action are contemplated. The maintenance of dignity is a further facet of self. This concern is often under threat from academic criteria in the evaluative contexts which schools provide, but it is also very important to children when teachers seek to control them behaviourally. The way this is done is crucial, with children often responding adversely if they feel themselves to have been humiliated or treated unfairly. The final facet of the interest-at-hand of self which I have identified here is that of self-image. This relates to children's sense of their own identity and to their attempts to sustain and develop it. Of course, this sense of identity is being formed continuously, but each child's biography, home background, and friendships will give some significant substance to their sense of identity at any particular point in time and this is something which each child will seek to maintain in the classroom. Children's interest-at-hand of peer group membership and learning are, as with order and instruction for teachers, in a slightly different category because they essentially provide a means of satisfying the various facets of self. Peer group membership is particularly significant for children who may be doing less well at school and learning is often of greater importance for more successful children. The priorities placed on these enabling interests thus represent alternative ways of satisfying the immediate concerns which are associated with each child's sense of 'self'.

We should not be alarmed by a discussion of the significance of the sense of 'self' held by teachers and children for it is not intended to imply any type of 'selfishness' as such. Indeed, the concept of self is used here in the symbolic interactionist sense (Mead, 1934) to represent an essential quality of being a person with an identity in society. Interests-at-hand take the form which they do because classrooms are always potentially threatening for the self-image of both teachers and children. This is built into their very structures and purposes. In simple terms, the teacher faces relatively large numbers of children and is expected to educate them, whilst each child faces the evaluative power of the teacher and is expected to learn.

The classroom threat to the self-image of both parties is thus inherently high and is reciprocally applied. It is no wonder, then, that teachers and children put considerable efforts into developing ways of coping with the situation. These represent a means of attaining their primary goal.

How, then, is order achieved? Logically, if we accept that there is a basic conflict of interests, there are only two possibilities: either order is imposed by the teacher using her power or there is negotiation between the teacher and her class so that a set of social understandings which define order is constructed. Fortunately the ethos of most primary schools has always placed great emphasis on establishing good relationships with children and consciously coercive teachers are rare. However, it is not unusual for teachers who lack negotiative skills and who feel their interests to be threatened in particular situations to fall back on coercion. Tension, anxiety, and frustration often accompany this response.

Whilst the strategy may work in the short term it has unfortunate side-effects, and essentially these are caused because the coercive strategy can only be made to succeed at the expense of the children's interests. When a teacher 'becomes angry', 'goes mad', 'gets eggy', they are likely to act in ways which will be seen by children as being 'unfair'. Children then report being 'picked on', 'shown up', 'done over', and humiliated. Children, throughout the primary age range, are quick to discern when the expectations made of them and the sense of order in the classroom begin to be based more on the use of teacher power rather than on a sense of justice.

Justice is perhaps rather a high-flown word to use here but I think that is essentially what is under consideration. I suggest this because a shared sense of the moral order of the classroom, with social conventions, expectations, tacit rules, and thus a sense of justice, is the normal outcome of a successfully conducted round of negotiations. Such negotiations are particularly significant at the start of a school year and they last until understandings about the parameters of behaviour for teacher and children are established and accepted (Ball, 1980). The expectations must take account of the particular interests and concerns of all the participants. The agreement that is reached amounts, in a sense, to a mutual exchange of dignity and in the sociological literature has been termed a 'working consensus' (Hargreaves, 1972) or a 'truce' (Reynolds, 1976). Whatever it is called, an accommodation between the teacher and the children is essential if the inherent conflict of classroom life is to remain latent and if order is to be sustained. This is so because if the fundamental concerns of either party are not satisfied then it becomes in their interests to disrupt the *status quo*. If this happens, the latent conflict will become manifest in the creativity of children's deviance and of teacher responses or, conversely, in unilateral teacher actions and child responses.

An implicit point here which is worth making clear is that strategies of teachers and children tend to mesh because of the interactive nature of classroom life. Thus the particular actions of a teacher will yield reactions from the children which they deem to be appropriate, given their subjective perceptions of the situation and their interests in it. The same applies in reverse, with the teacher reacting to child behaviour in ways which she perceives to be appropriate. This dynamically evolving interactive process almost always stabilizes in a class as each party comes to know the other and becomes able to predict, interpret, and respond adequately to the other's actions.

This stabilization of relationships as strategies mesh can be very productive. For instance, consider the model of a positive cycle shown in Figure 6.1—a model seen from the children's perspective. In this model it is first suggested that teacher initiatives lead to children enjoying a sense of their own dignity. Secondly, it is postulated that children are stimulated by the curriculum or learning activities provided for them by the teacher. These are judged to be interesting and appear likely to satisfy the children's concern for learning. Thirdly, the situation is regarded as being fair. There are two aspects of fairness here, relating to the way the children are ordered and controlled and to the nature of the tasks which they are presented with. Regarding the first, let us assume that the children and teacher are operating within established organizational and social frameworks, and that they have thus negotiated and understand the parameters of permissible action. Order thus has a secure base. The other aspect of fairness concerns the appropriateness of the match between the task which the children are faced with and their ability and motivation to do it. If the task is well matched then the children are likely to accept its challenges and attempt to grapple with it with vigour.

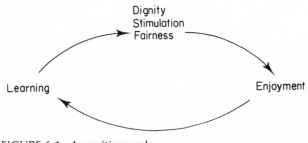

FIGURE 6.1   A positive cycle

The result of the existence of this sense of dignity, stimulation and fairness is postulated in the model as being children's enjoyment and then their learning. This is brought about essentially because the children's interests-at-hand are satisfied by the teacher's provision and action from the start. The further and crucial result of this child enjoyment and learning is that *teacher* interests-at-hand are thereby satisfied. Order is maintained, instruction is effective, and teacher self-esteem can flourish, with the likely result that the teacher will feel able to inject further energy and care with which again to project the dignity, stimulation, and fairness to fuel another cycle. The cyclical process can then spiral into learning experiences of higher and higher quality. Sometimes teaching goes just like this.

On the other hand, we must also recognize the existence of negative cycles which instead of spiralling upwards can lead to a decline into suspicion, hostility, and unpleasantness. Again, this can be represented by a model seen from the children's perspective.

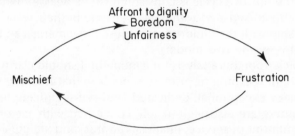

FIGURE 6.2 A negative cycle

In this model, shown in Figure 6.2, it is suggested that teacher initiatives threaten the children's main interest-at-hand on three counts. Firstly, they represent an affront to the children's dignity as people. Teacher actions may be seen as being dismissive, high-handed, or even aggressive. Secondly, the learning activities provided for the children are seen as being boring. In other words, they are badly matched to the ability and concerns of the children. They are too hard, too easy, or too lacking in any connection with the children's interests to provide any significant motivational attraction. Thirdly, the teacher is seen to be acting unfairly. In other words, the teacher is not abiding by negotiated understandings about her behaviour or that of the children. The teacher is acting unilaterally.

The children will, in a situation of this sort, feel and express a great deal of frustration. Their interests-at-hand, far from being satisfied, are being ignored or threatened, whilst at the same time they are relatively powerless to defend themselves. And yet they do have a degree of defensive power which comes from their numbers, friendships, and peer group membership and this collective solidarity is likely to be used to neutralize the damage done by the teacher—with a shrug of the shoulders or a wink to 'mates'—or to respond in kind with forms of resistance such as 'mischief', 'mucking about', and 'having a laugh' at the teacher's expense. Work evasion, rather than learning, is a probable outcome.

Ironically, the further result of this, which completes the cycle, is likely to be *damage* to the teacher's interests-at-hand. Order in the classroom will be constantly challenged if it is essentially oppressive; attempts to instruct will not be matched by quality in learning if children have not been offered an appropriate motivation to learn rather than being made fearful. If children are coerced then the deviant responses which tend to result will constantly threaten the teacher's self-esteem and autonomy. Such resistance is likely to reduce further the teacher's enjoyment but to increase the stress and the potential workload which are faced.

Fortunately, there are not many classrooms where this situation endures but regrettably, if we are to believe HMI and other reports, there are not many where the positive cycle is consistently at its peak either. However, teachers are able to sense movements over time in their teaching and in their relationship with the children, and these movements can be seen as variations between the two models.

Stepping back from this analysis for a moment, I should clarify my belief that the reality of teaching in primary schools is that it is a *very* difficult job. Whilst many exceptional, dedicated, and self-sacrificing teachers do exist many others are also legitimately concerned with factors such as workload, conditions of service, financial rewards, and life outside school. At the present time more and more pressures and expectations are being applied to the education service but resources are being cut and constraints reinforced. It is no wonder that morale in the profession is sometimes low.

This, I would argue, is one reason why negative cycles sometimes evolve. When people become tired and disenchanted with their job, the energy, care, and conscientiousness which is required to maintain the positive cycle is less likely to be forthcoming. Ironically, the interactive nature of classroom life, analysed in this case by the negative cycle, suggests that such disenchantment and withdrawal is likely to make the job even harder and less rewarding.

If we polarize the issue for analytical purposes one can postulate two possible ways of approaching it as a teacher. One is rather despondent: accepting the difficulties and seeking comfort from other members of the profession who feel the same way. The difficulties which are faced in class can thus become transmuted into reflections of the 'difficult catchment area', 'awkward parents', 'centralist government', 'miserly local authority', 'intransigent children', 'autocratic head teacher', etc. A rationalization is provided which defends convenient, habitual, and minimalist responses to classroom events whatever the apparent effects which those teaching methods may have. The die is cast and the blame lies elsewhere. At the other pole, it is possible to stand back from the immediacy of surviving in the interactive mesh with the children to reflect on what is happening with the intention of taking positive action. Such an approach is founded on a teacher taking direct responsibility for what happens in the classroom. Of course, this is not in reality an entirely fair allocation of responsibility and I will return to that point; however, if we can allow the partial illusion we will see that the effect of endorsing such a sense of responsibility is very significant.

As symbolic interactionists have argued since W. I. Thomas (1928), the way in which people define situations is a crucial factor influencing the ways in which they act. Thus, if teachers perceive themselves as being responsible for their classrooms, for the people who work in them, and for events which take place in them, then they have, in a sense, seized a degree of power over each situation and taken up a commitment to exert active control over it. This may sometimes require an optimistic disposition, but I would argue that even on instrumental grounds it makes good sense if one is looking for satisfaction from one's work.

In my view, such an initiative is often essential if an unproductive mesh of teacher–child coping strategies is to be broken and recast in a more constructive form, for really it is only the teacher who can be expected to have the analytical capacity to identify sources of difficulty, to consider possible solutions, and to then implement them. This brings us to perhaps the most important argument to be presented in this chapter. It is that teachers should develop long-term *social policies* as a basis for daily practice and decision making in their classrooms.

A social policy is one possible outcome of the type of practical theorizing which was suggested by Reid (1978) and discussed earlier, and it can be particularly applied to relationships in the classroom and to the question of discipline. It is based on careful analysis of one's actual teaching and on the making of judgements about teaching strategies for the long term. It can thus be contrasted with the mechanistic, technical, and tip-based solutions to incidents and difficulties which may arise. Such short-term responses may well be skilled but they will always constitute a relatively superficial treatment of surface phenomena unless the underlying issues influencing teacher–child relationships are exposed. Coping in such a way on a day-to-day basis is not only exhausting but it offers little hope. It is like treating the symptoms of an illness but failing to investigate its cause.

As many of those advocating classroom-based action research have found (e.g. Nixon, 1981; Rowlands, 1984), a consideration of 'underlying issues' can be very challenging. Perhaps one reason, then, why such rigorous types of analysis are not commonly undertaken by teachers is that we ourselves are inevitably a significant factor in the quality of what goes on in the classroom. Teaching is a very personal activity and teachers have a great influence on their classes whatever other factors also obtain. The challenge of self-reflection is thus potentially very great indeed. I well remember, a few years ago, when experiencing some ups and downs with my class of vertically grouped infants, concluding once again that the only real solution to my problems was to try to control aspects of my personality so that my tendency to lapse into counterproductive responses in class could be transformed into something more constructive. I am sure (and I know others who would certainly agree!) that I never entirely succeeded in solving the problem, but the identification of the issue and the commitment to do something about it was, in my view, crucial, and certainly led to improvements based on the identification of my own weaknesses.

Classrooms are very complicated places. There are always a lot of things going on involving many people. Such events normally occur simultaneously and there are numerous dimensions and issues to be considered. Fast, decisive, and appropriate initiatives and responses are required from the teacher. One of the things which teachers thus have to do is reduce that complexity. A policy enables that simplification to be made in a positive, constructive, and consistent way because it is based not on instant pressured response but on considered analysis and reflection. It also makes it possible for the teacher to take the initiative more confidently and more coherently—the children know where they are going. As a result, children are offered a relatively stable and consistent pattern of actions from the teacher and are likely to be more able to identify and to adjust to them. This can produce the beginning of a more positive mesh of teacher–child strategies with the enormous benefit that the creativity and energy of the children are used in ways which are supportive of educational concerns and of teacher interests rather than against them.

So what policy issues might be considered by a classroom teacher in a primary school with regard to disruption? Since the immediate source of disruption in a classroom comes from children, the obvious area on which to focus is the children themselves. However, I have already argued that children will be disruptive if their interests-at-hand in the classroom are not satisfied to a reasonable degree, and it is therefore necessary to turn the focus on ourselves as teachers too. To do this we can consider children's interests-at-hand in turn (see Table 6.1) and note the implications which their concerns have for teachers.

In my view, children's sense of self is the most important single factor. The self-image which any individual holds of himself or herself is an essential element affecting the way in which they are able to present themselves in social situations and to act. This sense of self develops through interaction with others and particularly through the influence of significant others such as teachers. But teachers have a complex job to do and they work within a society which routinely classifies and values people in different ways. The result is that such classification is also common in classrooms in both overt and tacit ways. Hierarchies based on ability, social class, sex, race, or age inevitably create a sense of superiority in some and a sense of inferiority in others, and have results which can only be divisive. Those whose dignity is affronted must defend themselves by developing alternative valuation systems and this may well mean that, by rejecting the dominant set of values, they act in ways which are regarded as being disruptive. A crucial policy question which we face when teaching thus concerns the way in which we protect and foster the self-image of *all* the children in the class. A likely direction for finding a solution lies in the systematic search for and celebration of success.

Enjoyment is another major concern of children in class and this can be linked with the work tasks which they are offered. There are three common criteria for children here. As they often put it, is work 'easy' or 'hard', is it 'interesting' or 'boring', is it 'useful' or 'pointless'? Sometimes the work set for children is seen by them as being 'hard', 'boring', *and* 'pointless'. Some children will respond with evasion and disruption. They will seek to 'have a laugh', 'muck about', or 'get out of it'. Such actions are a creative way of reclaiming time for themselves which was to have been 'wasted'. The policy implication has to be that we must continuously strive to match learning tasks and activities to the motivation of children. This does not mean, however, that the curriculum should be dictated solely by children's concerns. The key point is motivational and it follows that whatever is presented to children must have the quality and appropriateness to attract and sustain their interest. This is not easy to achieve, but it remains a key issue which requires an active and positive response—accepting its importance is not enough. What is needed is constant appraisal of the quality and task structure of the curriculum which is offered to the children. This requires considerable knowledge of various curriculum areas as well as the flair to present them attractively. It is thus an area in which each teacher's policy decision to review their practice regularly, and to refine and extend their knowledge of particular curricular areas, can make a very significant contribution to the avoidance of disruption. That in itself, though, is an insignificant baseline position compared with the other gains which are to be achieved if the children's interest in learning can be harnessed. There is plenty of evidence that children both want and need to learn as they develop. The only points of difference between children and adults in this respect concern *what* and *how* they should learn. However, curiosity and 'pleasing teacher' need not necessarily lead in different directions if the curriculum is stimulating and attractive and is pitched at an appropriate level of challenge.

A third area for classroom policy making is that of interpersonal skills, particularly in relation to the children's concern to control levels of stress and to maintain dignity. The way a teacher handles deviant incidents and flashpoints in the classroom are of particular significance here. In such a situation any child is very vulnerable. He or she is likely to know that the understandings of the working consensus have been broken and that censure is legitimate—but what form will that censure take?

Unfortunately, it is often the case that the child in such a situation is personally blamed, told off, or castigated. This is reasonable in a sense since each child, as an individual, is in control of his/her own actions. Such a response also serves as a tangible means to give vent to frustration on the teacher's part. However, I would argue that it is unlikely, in the long run, to help matters much since the child is almost forced onto the defensive by rejecting the teacher and what s/he stands for. When personal dignity is attacked it will be recouped in an alternative way and even in a primary school classroom this is likely to be by harnessing the creative mischief-making powers of other children who have been similarly confronted.

An approach to censuring a deviant act—or managing a flashpoint which, on the basis of ethnographic evidence, seems to be much more productive—is that of focusing on the act itself rather than on the child or children who carried it out. Being firmly told that 'hitting people in the playground is not kind and must stop' and being asked to think about 'better ways to play' is quite different from being informed that 'you are a very nasty and thoughtless little child' and told to 'stay in till after playtime'. The latter is closed, final, aggressive, and offers little hope. The former is clear, firm, and instructive, but it is not personally damaging or vindictive and it leaves the way open for a fuller acceptance. Hargreaves, Hestor and Mellor (1975) coined the terms deviance-insulative and deviance-provocative for these contrasting approaches. It is quite simple to understand the point but far harder to think, when classroom pressures mount, in the cool and constructive way which is suggested. That is why a policy decision is necessary. Without it one is a hostage to one's own frustration and annoyance if and when it emerges.

The final area of policy making which I would identify as being relevant to the issue of disruption is that which relates to children's peer group membership, culture, and friendship patterns. It was the Opies who made the significant points some time ago (1959) that child culture is the children's *own* and that adults know relatively little about it. We are gradually learning more about it (Sluckin, 1981; Davies, 1982; Pollard, 1985) but we still have, in my view, only a rudimentary understanding at the present time. Two points which are clear, however, are firstly that children's culture and children's friendship groups generate norms, values, rules, understandings, and a sense of social structure which is extremely complex and sophisticated, and secondly that these provide a means by which children make sense of and cope with the adult world when it impinges on them. There are thus a lot of things about children and the ways in which they think that we simply do not understand, and the social side of this is as important as the cognitive. Disruption in class may be regarded as being totally senseless and obtuse behaviour by a teacher, but for children it is often thought of as being entirely rational, appropriate, and justified. It will almost certainly be socially structured by children's understandings about how effective strategies for disruption should be carried out.

There are, in other words, two major and discrete social worlds and sets of perspectives which come together in a classroom. In my view, the wise teacher will do everything possible to understand the children's culture and social structure. If this is done the way is open to work *with* it and to harness the energy and enthusiasm of the children to educational goals.

Conclusion

The argument which I have presented in this chapter is a deliberate attempt to suggest ways of improving classroom practice in primary schools through a critical and socially aware self-reflection. This is all very fine, but one may well ask, 'Is it fair or practical?' This brings us back to the point where we began about the pupil–teacher ratio and resourcing. When class sizes are high and resources are limited, teachers are forced to deal with 'crowds' of children and to juggle with resource constraints. Is it then fair or reasonable to expect them to concern themselves with such things as classroom social policy when they face so many basic practical difficulties in their work? I would make three points about this.

In the first place I would agree that such arguments are intrusive and that teachers are being asked to maintain and improve the quality of educational provision in increasingly difficult circumstances. As I pointed out earlier, whilst the inherent conflict in the relationship between the teacher and the taught can never be eliminated altogether, it is considerably exacerbated by the inadequate resourcing for education which is accepted as normal at present. Teachers, pupils, and many parents know this intuitively. I would argue further that the quality of educational experiences could be enormously improved if increased resources could be put to use in ways which are interpersonally constructive—at the moment disruption seems to be a very reasonable response to some of the situations with which our children are faced. Nevertheless, the necessary arguments cannot be won in finance committees and the treasury because the benefits of educational spending are seen as being intangible and the rationale for expenditure is seen as being unproven.

On the other hand, I would also argue that the adoption of social policies, such as those which have been discussed in this chapter, can *ease* teacher problems in the long run and lead to a great sense of personal and professional fulfilment. The sense of perspective which policies can provide offers support when coping with real-life pressures.

This brings me to my third point, and it is based on the recognition that as teachers we lack a shared and coherent conceptual framework and vocabulary with which to analyse our practice. Without such a basic professional resource we are collectively weakened when we need to make a case such as the one that refuses to accept disruption as being simply a problem of child pathology or of cultural deficit. I would suggest that we need to work on this problem and that the use of the conceptual frameworks provided by ethnographers (more extensively described by Woods (1983), for instance) can contribute to the development of this means of professional discourse. For teachers to reflect rigorously on classroom social policies could thus be useful in helping them to cope, and could also contribute to the future development of the profession—quite apart from the anticipated benefits to the children themselves.

Disruption is a provocative topic—it may be more significant in highlighting fundamental issues which we should consider than it is as a classroom 'problem' as such. After all, whose problem is it?

References

Ball, S. (1980) Initial encounters in the classroom and the process of establishment. In Woods, P. (ed.), *Pupil Strategies.* Croom Helm, London.

Davies, B. (1982) *Life in the Classroom and Playground.* Routledge & Kegan Paul, London.

Hargreaves, D. H. (1972) *Interpersonal Relationships and Education.* Routledge & Kegan Paul, London.

Hargreaves, D. H., Hestor, S. K., and Mellor, F. J. (1975) *Deviance in Classrooms.* Routledge & Kegan Paul, London.

Jackson, P. (1968) *Life in Classrooms.* Holt, Rinehart, & Winston, New York.

Mead, G. H. (1934) *Mind, Self and Society.* University of Chicago Press, Chicago.

Nixon, J. (ed.) (1981) A Teacher's Guide to Action Research. Grant McIntyre, London.

Opie, I., and Opie, P. (1959) *The Lore and Language of School Children.* Clarendon Press, Oxford.

Pollard, A. (1980) Teacher interests and changing situations of survival threat in primary classrooms. In woods, P. (ed.), *Teacher Strategies.* Croom Helm, London.

Pollard, A. (1984) Goodies, jokers and gangs. In Hammersley, M., and Woods, P. (ed.) *Life in School.* Open University Press, Milton Keynes.

Pollard, A. (1985) *The Social World of the Primary School.* Holt, Rinehart, & Winston, London.

Reid, W. A. (1978) *Thinking about the Curriculum.* Routledge & Kegan Paul, London.

Reynolds, D. (1976) The delinquent school. In Hammersley, M., and Woods, P. (ed.), *The Process of Schooling.* Routledge & Kegan Paul, London.

Rowlands, S. (1984) *The Enquiring Classroom.* Palmer, London.

Shipman, M. (1975) *The Sociology of the School.* Longman, London.

Sluckin, A. (1981) *Growing Up in the Playground.* Routledge & Kegan Paul, London.
Thomas, W. I. (1928) *The Child in America.* Knopf, New York.
Waller, W. (1932) *The Sociology of Teaching.* Russel & Russel, New York.
Woods, P. (1983) *Sociology and the School,* Routledge & Kegan Paul, London.

Management of Disruptive Pupil Behaviour in Schools
Edited by D. P. Tattum
©1986 John Wiley & Sons Ltd

_____*7*___

Promoting positive behaviour in the classroom

David A. Lane

Introduction

The Islington Educational Guidance Centre was established to provide short-term intervention for children aged 3–16 years who were referred for severe conduct disorders. As originally conceived, it was concerned with older children who had a history of previously unsuccessful intervention, either for antisocial behaviour in school or for delinquency in the community. Most pupils were likely to have a history of learning difficulties. Pupils, by the time they reached the centre, had usually developed severe hostility to adults and were highly impulsive and took a 'couldn't care less' attitude to authority. They were often labelled as 'impossible' to deal with by those professionals involved with them. A separate programme for non-attenders was subsequently added to the centre's services.

The formal point of referral was intended to be the individual child; however, in practice the individual never represented the primary focus of the work. Previous research (Lane, 1973a, b, 1974a, b) had established the importance of looking at the individual in the context of the school system. The centre's policy was therefore based on assumptions derived from the research, the services provided arising out of those assumptions. The central assumption was that it was not enough simply to look at characteristics within the individual for explanations of behaviour labelled antisocial, but rather it was necessary to look at the response of the child to the environment and its response in return. Thus, that interaction became the main focus for attention. Certain principles are applied within the framework of that assumption.

(1) No intervention can be predetermined in advance of an analysis of the situation and the construction of a formulation which explains why the

behaviour occurs in a given context. Any intervention has to be based on the formulation.

(2) As far as possible, interventions should take place in the context in which difficulties were reported.

(3) The principle is maintained that any action taken should be aimed at the minimum level of intervention necessary to achieve agreed objectives in the setting.

(4) The range of response offered should be flexible, to ensure rapid movement between levels of intervention, as necessary.

The referrals received by the centre might originate from a number of sources—teachers, psychologists, educational welfare officers, child guidance, etc.—and take a variety of forms. A teacher might ask for help with a child who is disruptive in class, a head of department might seek help with a whole class which was proving difficult, a headteacher might be looking for advice to set up a programme to deal with problems in the playground at breaktime, a child guidance guidance clinic might want to establish a joint family/school intervention, a psychologist might be seeking a behavioural assessment of a group of children to support other data obtained, or a group of teachers/probation officers, etc., might be seeking a training input. To meet these needs, the centre provides the following services:

(1) Advice, analysis, and intervention directly within the school or other setting, in close partnership with those directly involved.

(2) The centre may also carry out a joint teaching programme in the school, with the family, or part-time at the centre, in association with other concerned individuals or agencies.

(3) Following intervention at (1) or (2) above, follow-up support would be provided for as long as was needed to ensure that gains were maintained and new objectives which arose were met.

(4) Training and ongoing supervision of practitioners in a variety of settings would be available as necessary.

(5) A counselling service for pupils and practitioners would be provided when no alternative sources were available.

The success of the programmes developed at the centre depends upon the combined efforts of the schools, the children, the families, other agencies, and the centre in pooling resources and skills to meet complex problems and the use of validated techniques of analysis and intervention. The importance of that partnership has been established at the experimental, theoretical, and practical level.

The individual and the system

In establishing the Islington Educational Guidance Centre 10 years ago, and in developing school-based work prior to that, the concern was with the influence of both individual and system factors. In those earlier days it was the emphasis on the schools' contribution which generated the heat; most people were happy to accept explanations which focused on the individual or the family.

Currently, most of the attention in the literature is focused on the school and the centre's concern with individual components causes some dispute. The view is taken that promoting positive behaviour in the classroom does involve a variety of factors. It cannot be achieved simply by a more relevant curriculum or better classroom management. The research will therefore be briefly considered. It was originally argued that it was important to focus, not on the single difficulty which might be most visible, but on the stress faced by all pupils, the point being that individual difficulties find their expression, are shaped, or are an output of the school structure. The main cause of failure to learn 'appropriate' behaviour was therefore seen as a lack of exposure to appropriate learning experiences. Teachers concerned with learning difficulties and behaviour problems should, it was felt, consider the overall structure of the school, not simply the child's deficits. However, to achieve that, teachers needed adequate personal and pro-fessional support in order to deal with these interactive patterns (Lane, 1970, 1973a, b, 1974a, b).

One example of the type of pattern of interaction referred to above arose in earlier research (Lane, 1976b, c). This research was concerned with children who had failed to make progress in remedial groups specializing in learning problems. A variety of models of intervention were tried and it was found that the average gains by the groups in different models varied significantly. However, the individual gains varied within one group more than within another. So the success of the pupil depended upon the group to which s/he was assigned, but even within this pattern differences appeared according to personality type. For some children a supportive counselling framework for remedial education suited them, for others a structured model with a clear relationship between behaviour and consequence proved more valuable. The implication was that the pupils' remedial education should be matched to their personal style of learning. However, if situational constraints or a management imposed philosophy determined when, where, and how the remedial input was to be provided, the gains for the pupils were fewer and the stress on the class teacher higher. Unfortunately, too often teachers were observed teaching in a style which suited neither them nor their pupils because of the priorities of the management structure within the school. It is important to recognize such management priorities in resource allocation. More often than not the difficulties faced are multiple (Graziano, 1971; Wall, 1979; Brown and Madge, 1982), and the critical role of management in schools is well documented (Reynolds and Sullivan, 1979, Galloway *et al.*, 1982).

Recent reports (HMI, 1978; Topping, 1983) indicate similar findings, in that staff in special units set up to support children are left with inadequate support for themselves. Management groups might similarly establish pastoral systems which incorporate 'sanctuaries' within the school to support the child, but fail to write terms of reference to add supports which are realistic for the staff running them. They may express considerable public pride in their pastoral care when outside observers see little of value (see, for example, Hargreaves, 1984).

A major study was therefore undertaken to consider features which could affect remission from difficulties in the long term. The results (Lane, 1974b, 1976b, 1978a, 1983) confirmed the idea that outcome depended upon features of (1) the individual, (2) the family, and (3) the school.

(1) *The individual*   The behaviour exhibited by the child early in the school career was predictive of later difficulties, and the initial type of behaviour provided a guide to the final pattern. The findings confirmed the work of other researchers (Rutter, 1975) indicating that conduct disorders in particular are predictive of later difficulty. However, the personality characteristics of the individual were also implicated, since features such as levels of extraversion, emotional stability, and toughmindedness (Allsopp and Feldman, 1974) were found to relate to outcome (Lane and Hymans, 1982).

(2) *The family*   The level of deprivation faced by the child was correlated with a high level of initial difficulty in school; however, it was the continuation of such deprivation, or increasing stress, which related to long-term negative outcome. The impact of social class, family background, and parental experience existed in complex interaction with individual and school features.

(3) *The school*   The long-term outcome for the child was strongly correlated with the action of the school. Positive attempts by the school to support the child and positive structural changes in the school were related to changes in the child being maintained over extended periods.

In essence, the findings indicated that certain children and certain behaviours were more resistant to change than others, and a difficult family situation was an important but not an inevitable feature of problem behaviour in school; however, what happened to the child subsequently was the primary issue of concern. Schools could and did play a major role in generating and maintaining change, or in ensuring the continuation of failure. They had a choice.

What might be done?

If schools matter, what might be done? A wide range of suggestions are available to teachers, and over the last decade large sums of money have been allocated to provisions for disruptive pupils, ranging from off-site centres and alternative schools to curriculum change and the manipulation of routine sanctions. Yet, as Dawson (1980) has indicated, many such provisions remain unevaluated according to any criteria whatsoever. The major review by Topping (1983) of 21 alternative systems concludes, among other things, that many of the less sophisticated options are more valuable.

The problem, therefore, is not a lack of ideas, but an absence of evaluated workable solutions. Nevertheless, such solutions are increasingly emerging and a few such are discussed below, aimed at the levels of analysis previously identified — the individual, the family, and the school.

The individual

The major contribution to developing programmes related to individual and classroom behaviour problems is found in 50 years of the behavioural literature. Contributions such as those of Olson (1935), O'Leary and O'Leary (1972), Leach and Raybould (1977), and the recent Batpack materials (Wheldall and Merrett, 1984) have provided a clear methodology for defining a problem behaviour and developing a programme of intervention. However, while the behavioural literature has attended to the fact that certain behaviours are more difficult than others to change, it has largely ignored the evidence that certain individuals are more difficult to influence. Thus, the literature on individual differences (McWilliams, 1975; Eysenck and Eysenck, 1975b) indicating that outcome does vary by personality type remains ignored. The major attempt described by Coulby (1980) to provide input for problem behaviours does in part meet this criticism, and offers key reading in this area. The earlier Teacher–Child Interaction Project (Berger and Wigley, 1980) also had much to commend it in clarity of purpose and methodology. Wakefield (1979) has — unusually — looked at individualizing learning through personality, and while much of the literature has concentrated on lower age groups there are a few notable exceptions (Presland, 1980; Galloway, 1979).

The family

The family of the child presenting problems has been the subject of much speculation, but few evaluated interventions. Several interesting projects are described by Apter (1982) although, as Topping (1983) points out, some caution is needed in the interpretation of results. Extensive schemes to work with the family have been developed within the Portage Project,[1] and while this model was developed with the under 5s, the precision teaching involved (Lindsey, 1967) provides a general model for family work. Precision teaching concepts (Williams *et al.*, undated), while in the main developed for remediating learning problems in school, may be usefully extended to dealing with behavioural, emotional, and developmental problems within the home or a residential setting. (See, for example, the residentially based Bereweeke System and the home-based Superparents series.) Several other interesting schemes for family work (such as Steps to Independence)[2] provide approaches to teaching by parents which could be effectively applied in schools. The potential overlap between home- and school-based teaching systems is itself an interesting area, and much can be learnt about effective teaching in schools through a consideration of effective home-based education. The work initiated by Few (1978) at the Islington Educational Guidance Centre provided an interesting framework in which the same models of analysis and intervention could be applied in the home and the school, thereby establishing a flow of ideas between the settings, with parent and teacher in creative partnership. Few's later work in the context of the Lea Green School in Waltham Forest, under Cliff Giles's pioneering leadership, greatly extended the home–school link. The work of the Pakeman Unit (Reay *et al.*, 1984) to provide a bridge between home and school further demonstrates the use of home–school partnerships and the value of combining the skills of teachers and social workers. The home–school partnerships take on an even more critical role in respect of attendance problems. Green (1980) has graphically illustrated how children become labelled as 'truants' through an administrative but highly subjective process. Her work in 1973 with truants in the Open Class Project also illustrated the importance of the home–school partnership (Turner, 1974; McInnes, 1974).

The school

That the school is important is clear from the work of Galloway and his associates (1982). This work should be prime reading as it demonstrates that differences in policy influence outcome in schools. The recent report by the Inner London Education Authority (Hargreaves, 1984) lists 104 recommendations for action to improve achievement and behaviour in schools and certainly repays careful reading, in spite of drawing on a highly selective literature. The problems highlighted by Hargreaves raise the complex issue of choice in programmes for change, given that so many difficulties arise. Unfortunately, Hargreaves does not help on this point as the report provides a prescriptive rather than an analytic approach to intervention. Burden (1978) does provide a framework for a schools system analysis, based upon the concept of the project team, and this model has much to commend it. There are also an increasing number of school-based initiatives available (Button, 1981; Grunsell, in press; ILEA, 1984; Oldroyd *et al.*, 1984; but also see White and Brockington, 1978). Topping's (1983) review does give some grounds for optimism in that he lists a number of studies which demonstrate that change is possible and can be maintained in schools. My own long-term research (Lane, 1983) lends support to Topping's position.

Change is possible, but how is it to be achieved?

It appears that change is possible and positive classroom behaviour can be promoted. Many ideas for intervention are available in the literature and numerous books containing the 'tricks of the trade' or craft or art of teaching exist, developed by experienced practitioners. A major problem occurs, however, in applying these 'good practices' in the ordinary classroom. The key difficulties lie in:

(1) deciding which of the numerous good ideas to try,
(2) achieving a match between problem and method, and
(3) Working out why the good idea failed in any given example from one's own practice.

It has been argued (Galloway, 1979; Berger, 1979) that the reason for failure may lie in the mindless application of a technology of behaviour change—a prescription to be swallowed rather than an analysis to be understood. Similar criticisms may be levelled at the concept of an 'innovation exchange', the idea that good ideas can be transferred from one school to another. There are several problems with such an exchange since every school is unique in terms of its pupils, staff, layout, structure, and resources. Realistic change can only be brought about by an active process of analysis of their own problems on the part of schools; solutions must then be worked for, with input and advice as necessary. The imported solution approach inhibits that process and deskills those teachers involved.

Concern about a technique-based approach to intervention has gained increasing urgency as misunderstood concepts of 'behaviour modification' have found their way into schools. Lane (1977) strongly argued that a technique for change must be derived from a careful analysis. Wheldall (1984) has similarly stressed the dangers of an intervention without a preliminary 'applied behavioural analysis'. Unfortunately, the choice to act first and analyse afterwards, if at all, appears to be preferred in the management style of some practitioners. In running workshops in various parts of the country (and abroad) it has become apparent to the author that two poles of a dimension for problem solution exist.

The 'end product' or crisis style of management tends to focus on finding a solution to the immediate crisis; once that crisis is solved that is the end of the matter. In the 'process' or analytic style of management the emphasis is on explanations rather than immediate solutions. However, even process-oriented managers tend to use informal or *ad hoc* methods of analysis, and rarely does anyone suggest that in their school they might formally and periodically review a series of behavioural incidents to see what lessons might be learnt. Even more rarely does anyone suggest that they might use an experimentally derived management analysis.

Yet, if the argument about the mindless application of techniques is valid, a more analytically oriented approach to the promotion of positive behaviour in schools is necessary. Many schools across the country have taken to the concept of an analytic style of management. So, what might such an analysis look like? One of the most useful concepts seems to be that of a project team set up in and by a school to analyse a specific aspect of their operation. The system model developed by Burden (1978) provides an excellent example of such an approach. The peripatetic advisory team working on an analytic basis in schools described by Coulby (1980) provides an effective framework to involve schools in the development of such an approach. My own present scheme is described in detail elsewhere (Lane, 1974c, 1978b). However, it is not the use of any particular scheme which matters but rather the establishment of a commitment to a process-oriented approach to management.

The preference for immediate or long-term solutions is, of course, a choice behaviour. An end product approach is equivalent to selecting a small reward available immediately, in preference to a larger reward much delayed by the process of analysis; furthermore, the value of the reward is uncertain. Analysis entails a commitment to that uncertainty. A commitment to analyse does not represent a choice to act upon a particular end decision, such as 'promoting positive classroom behaviour'. The analysis may result in a school deciding to exclude more difficult pupils. That is the hard lesson which those who seek to advise must learn. These uncertainties explain the powerful appeal of the end product approach; it is immediately reinforcing.

The analysis of the situation

The definition phase

When faced with a 'problem' situation, what might the practitioner do? The answer is, any one of a number of things, all of which might work. The suggestions which follow here represent an abbreviated account of one possible approach, if the choice to analyse is made.

Where does one start? One starts with a description by someone of a situation they consider to be a problem, i.e. 'The worst class I have ever taught—somebody must do something about it.' Contained within that statement are two elements, the behaviour which is causing concern and the objective of the referring agent. Both the behaviour and the objective need to be clarified.

A start can be made with the behaviour. What is it that the class, or members of it, actually do? Those behaviours have to be operationally defined so that a naïve observer could sit in the class and reliably record the occurrence of any given instance of the behaviour.

The question then becomes, 'Why is that behaviour a problem?' For example, does it interfere with a specific piece of learning, or does it disturb others, and to whom is it a problem? If one can determine that the behaviour is a problem and to whom, it might prove possible to clarify objectives.

To define objectives, it is necessary to determine the actors involved in any situation, and those who are not involved but who might have a legitimate interest in the situation. All of those involved may have objectives they are trying to achieve and the clarification of those possibly diverse objectives must be undertaken.

If this preliminary discussion reveals the existence of a problem definition and a set of objectives which can be usefully analysed, a process of assessment can follow.

The assessment phase

The purpose of assessment is to gather necessary information and test hypotheses in order to arrive at a formulation of the problem. The emphasis is on necessary, reliable, and refutable information, not every conceivable bit of information which might be available. For example, if at the initial stage it appears that a problem exists in one class between one teacher and one pupil, a whole school analysis would be unwise. If, subsequently, the situation was seen to reflect a general problem for staff in the school— in, for example, not knowing the approved procedures for dealing with 'incidents'—then a more widely drawn analysis might be necessary.

There are a number of ways in which a situation might be assessed, the choice being determined by the nature of the problem, its setting, and the objectives of those involved. Subject to that initial choice when encouraging a teacher to undertake an analysis, two levels—predisposing (e.g. trait) and controlling (e.g. state)—are usually considered as a starting point, given the research data on their respective importance. These two concepts, for the purpose of this discussion, are defined as follows.

Predisposing elements Predisposing elements do not explain why a response occurs at any given moment. They represent preferential response tendencies which increase or decrease the likelihood that a given behaviour will occur. They do not control its occurrence, but improve the prediction. For example, if a child was taught by a parent that you should hit someone who insults you, it might make it more likely than when insulted s/he would hit out. It would improve the prediction for that behaviour. If it did not improve the prediction it would not be counted, in spite of any speculative appeal it might hold. Whether or not the child did hit out at a given moment would depend on the precipitating factors at the time and the maintaining consequences which would follow the behaviour. Thus, s/he might hit out only when insulted in the presence of a teacher who failed to offer protection from racial abuse. These precipitating and maintaining factors are called 'state' elements in this model.

Predisposing elements exist for both the individual and the organization. They are usually viewed as being derived from two sources:

(1) Constitutional elements, which for the individual include specific impairment (deafness, etc.) and physiological factors (autonomic reactivity). For the organization they include formal definitions of role, rules, physical resources, political structures, etc.
(2) Experiential elements, which for the individual include prior learning (e.g. history, models), and for the organization, informal variations of the formal procedures and adaptations of those procedures evolved by experience.

Thus, in considering predisposing elements in a given case of a class presenting difficulties, one might look at the abilities of the pupils, the history of the relationship between the teacher and pupils, the resources available to teach given materials, etc.

Controlling elements Controlling elements explain why, at any given moment, one rather than any other behaviour occurred. For example, why a child hit out on one occasion, but not on another. There are a number of elements of influence, the four usually critical state features are considered.
(1) *Setting events* The settings in which the behaviour occurs and any in which it does not occur are identified. Differences between those settings can then be investigated.
(2) *Precipitating factors* The event(s) which immediately preceded the behaviour, the 'antecedent' is the potentially precipitating factor, and the actual precipitating factor is that which triggers the behaviour in question. It may be one specific event (stimulus) or a combination of them, e.g. insult plus non-protecting teacher.

(3) *The behaviour* The precise nature of the resulting behaviour must be determined. It might include cognitive (thinking that he shouldn't insult me), autonomic (feeling tense), motoric (throwing a punch), or other modalities; or, of course, one might be the stimulus for the other.

(4) *The consequence* This concerns the events which immediately follow the behaviour in question and serve to reinforce it (increase the likelihood it will be repeated) or punish it (decrease the likelihood it will be repeated). For example, if, following a punch, racial abuse ceased the likelihood would be increased that the response of punching would be used again in the same circumstances.

The three components, antecedent (A), behaviour (B), and consequence (C), compare what is known as a functional analysis.

The formulation phase

Once all the information is obtained, the process of formulation can begin. The aim is to provide an explanation which demonstrates why given behaviours occur. On the basis of the formulation, predictions are possible about the likely impact of any changes introduced into the situation. Our colleague, Julius Malkin, was once asked to whom he was accountable, and he replied that we were all accountable to our formulation. That neatly underlines the status of a formulation. It is not simply a descriptive account of a child's score on a test, or a list of needs in a profile, or a diagnostic label; it is the predictive explanation of why the behaviour occurs, out of which the intervention is designed. If the intervention fails, you look for shortcomings in your formulation; thus the formulation itself is a hypothesis which can be experimentally tested.

The formulation is not usually just one person's explanation; it has been established through a cooperative process of information gathering and hypothesis testing. It has then been further discussed and refined, and any suggestions for intervention talked through so that eventually one arrives at an agreement. The agreement consists of the formulation, intervention options, a definition of each participant's role, the objectives to be met, and the end product.

The intervention phase

In the intervention phase, the particular actions which are to be undertaken are specified and a contract between the parties is entered. The contract is run and monitored to see that it works as predicted. The ongoing process of evaluation is critical and enables the formulation to be tested and, if necessary, altered.

The reader may have noticed that very little has been said about intervention. This is deliberate. Often, teachers new to analysis worry that, having arrived at a formulation, they will not be able to think of techniques for change. In practice, that is rarely a problem. Once you have your formulation, the rest will usually follow from the skills available and experiences already received.

The follow-up phase

This is the key phase to ensure that gains are maintained, that new objectives are met, and that reflection on the whole process takes place for future benefit. A formal process of review must follow every intervention and, periodically, groups of interventions. Otherwise, poor techniques will not be eliminated and necessary changes in the school structures will not be clarified. Poor practices continue for far too long in most settings because they are not periodically challenged.

Promoting positive behaviour

One brief example will be considered (based on material provided by a former colleague, Linda Corlett), chosen simply to illustrate the variety of features that have to be taken into account.

In undertaking an analysis of any given example certain features are frequently identified as playing a key role. The reader may care to consider which, if any, of these are present in the example provided.

(1) Praise and ignoring behaviour—what is praised and when, what is ignored, and what receives attention (O'Leary and O'Leary, 1972)?

(2) Rules—How is compliance sought? Is it considered legitimate by those from whom it is sought (Brown 1984; Lane, 1973a)? Are there clear rules governing the occurrence of learning and behaviour (O'Leary and O'Leary, 1972)?

(3) Aims—do the participants understand and share the purpose of the learning (Lane, 1972)?

(4) Individual needs—how are pupils/teachers labelled and what implications follow upon attachment of a label? In particular, are children labelled in terms of their 'special needs'? Are these 'needs' then met within the classroom/school or considered a matter for expert external help? Does the child/teacher know how to ask for/offer help (Scheff, 1966; Ullman and Krasner, 1975; Galloway *et al.*, 1982)?

(5) System organization—does the system realistically plan to meet objectives in a way that recognizes diverse needs, and the value of divergence (Galloway *et al.*, 1982, Topping, 1983)?

(6) Escalation—are problems dealt with at source or passed up the hierarchy? Is support available to staff at source (Brown, 1984; Galloway *et al.*, 1982)?

The point must be emphasized that the example provided only partially reports the situation. A full analysis is not supplied nor is any formulation.

Example

The headteacher of a primary school referred five boys from one class, who had been the centre of considerable disturbance for 2 years. They were said to be impulsive and easily distracted and they interfered with the work of other children, failed to respond to correction, and so forth. They had all been seen for additional (although varied) professional help, including child guidance, social/family work, and individual re-medial tuition. No progress having been made, the headteacher now felt that 'reducing the damage to the rest of the class' should be the major priority.

So, initially the definition of the problem related to certain 'difficult' children. However, discussion with the class teacher and preliminary observation in class revealed a number of problems of organization. The 'problem five' represented a focal point, but the issues raised were applicable to several other members of the class. The way their individual difficulties were expressed reflected these broader organizational issues.

The school felt strongly that they had done their best to meet the children's 'needs' in offering additional professional help, both outside the school and through extra help in special groups in school.

Certain features were apparent.

(1) They had received considerable individual and family intervention for their 'maladaptive' behaviour, but the contribution of classroom and school organization had been neglected, as had the interactive effect of individual differences and classroom organization.

(2) An observer placed in the class could not distinguish between the 'problem five' and certain other pupils in terms of the behaviour in question but could in terms of the level of negative response from the teacher.

(3) Certain children (the five) were more likely to receive an order to carry out a task when the other pupils received a request. They were more likely to be warned of the consequences of non-compliance in advance of completing a task.

(4) The level of praise available to pupils generally in the class was low, but when a task was completed, praise was more often directed to 'better behaved' children than to the 'five'.

(5) The level of attention from the teacher gained by pupils generally for non-compliance with a request/order was low, but was more often directed to the 'worse behaved'.

(6)　The class was divided into groups by ability and a wide and imaginative range of resources was available. However, budgetary considerations meant that a high degree of sharing was necessary, sometimes necessitating a frustrating wait. The materials were not well located and certain traffic lanes existed for pupils to fetch the materials they needed. The pupils who were said to be the most easily distracted were placed at the junctions of these lanes and therefore suffered the most distractions. The reasonable rationale offered was that they were close to the teacher's desk/assistance.

(7)　Several support groups for language and remedial work existed and some of the pupils (three of the five, plus a few others) spent part of the time in them. They did not all go out together, but at various times, further disrupting classroom routine. This meant that sometimes pupils had to pick up the threads of a lesson out of sequence. Little effective communication existed between the support groups and the classroom teacher. Discussion of the pupils took place, but there was no joint teaching or preparation of materials to ensure that the learning taking place in one setting reinforced or extended that taking place in the other setting.

(8)　On paper, lots of support was available to the classroom teacher. Advice—psychological, remedial, psychiatric, social, etc.—existed in abundance. In fact, this advice was unhelpful and unstructured; it offered much theoretical explanation but no realistic way to translate theory into classroom practice. Although interesting, it was not useful, for a teacher to hear about problems of sibling rivalry as a possible explanation for difficulties with peers, if no practical intervention was designed to help the teacher to deal with its impact on the classroom.

Following an analysis (primarily based on the state elements) which determined the relevant importance of the issues, various suggestions were developed to meet these difficulties, which were then initiated by the school. When followed up, it was found that the head and staff were beginning to resolve issues of organization and to define problems in more objective terms. Significantly, they had begun to look at resources available within the school to meet the problems. This contrasted with the previous pattern of assuming that children who were difficult had 'special needs requiring special help'.

In the classroom originally observed, desks and materials had been repositioned, quiet areas set aside, and the timetables of the different staff blended more satisfactorily. More effective support between remedial and classroom situations had also developed. As a result of this action *by the school*, considerable improvements in the behaviour of all the children, not simply the 'five', occurred.

Conclusion

Deviance in schools is not a product of specific deficits in the child or the school; it is an interactive, dynamic process. You cannot blame the teacher, the child, the family, or the curriculum. Schools which look at themselves and this process are often surprised at what they find and the strengths that are revealed.

Certain principles need to be applied, however, if the process by which an individual school achieves or fails to achieve perceived objectives is to be made explicit. It is argued that:

(1) Problems may be multifaceted, they exist in a context, and they are amenable to understanding only in so far as that context is understood.
(2) A framework of formal analysis is necessary for understanding without preconceptions or 'explanatory fictions' in order that the unstated may be revealed and unused skills recognized.
(3) Understanding is not enough; it needs to be followed by agreement on objectives and intervention.
(4) Planned action must follow understanding, for without action there is no significant learning.
(5) Schools are dynamic, needs and resources change, consequently programmes must be evaluated and objectives periodically challenged and, if necessary, altered.

The 'impossible child', or the difficult class, provides a challenge to the school. If the school can respond to that challenge and recognize it as part of its own construction and reconstruction, then more positive classroom behaviour will be promoted, if they so choose.

Notes

1 The Portage Project, the Bereweeke Skill Teaching System, and the Superparents Series are all available from the National Foundation for Educational Research, Windsor, Berkshire.
2 Steps to Independence: a skills training series for children with special needs. Various authors contribute to the series. Available from the Research Press, Champaign, Illinois.

References

Allsopp, G. F., and Feldman, M. P. (1974) Extraversion, neuroticism, psychoticism and antisocial behaviour in schoolgirls, *Social Behaviour and Personality*, **2**, 184–190.
Apter, S. J. (1982) *Troubled Children, Troubled Systems*. Pergamon, New York.
Berger, M. (1979) Behaviour modification in education and professional practice: the dangers of a mindless technology, *Bulletin of the British Psychological Society*, **32**, 418–419.

Berger, M., and Wigley, V. (1980) Intervening in the classroom, *Contact* (ILEA), 9 October 1980, 4–5.

Brown, B. (1984) Analysis of violent events. Association for Behavioural Approaches with Children Conference.

Brown, M., and Madge, N. (1982) *Despite the Welfare State*. Heinemann, London.

Burden, R. L. (1978) Schools systems analysis: a project centred approach. In Gillham, B., *Reconstructing Educational Psychology*. Croom Helm, London.

Button, L. (1981) *Group Tutoring for the Form Teacher*. Hodder & Stoughton, London.

Coulby, L. (1980) *Division 5 Schools Support Unit: Progress Report*. ILEA, London.

Dawson, R. L. (1980) *Special Provision for Disturbed Pupils: A Survey*. Macmillan, London.

Eysenck, H. J., and Eysenck, S. B. G. (1975a) *Manual of the Eysenck Personality Questionnaire*. Hodder & Stoughton, London.

Eysenck, H. J., and Eysenck, S. B. G. (1975b) *Psychoticism*. Hodder & Stoughton, London.

Few, J. (1978) *A Behavioural Model for Local Authority Field Social Workers*. Educational Guidance Centre/NELP.

Galloway, D. M. (1979) Application of behavioural analysis and behaviour modification in schools psychological service practice. *Bulletin of the British Association for Behavioural Psychotherapy*, **4**(6), 40–47.

Galloway, D., Ball, T., Bloomfield, D., and Seyd, R. (1982) *Schools and Disruptive Pupils*. Longman, London.

Graziano, A. M. (1971) *Behaviour Therapy with Children*. Aldine, Chicago.

Green, F. (1980) Becoming a truant: the social administrative process applied to pupils absent from school. Masters thesis. Cranfield Institute of Technology.

Grunsell, R. (ed.) (in press) Schools council disruptives in school scheme.

Hargreaves Report (1984) *Improving Secondary Schools*, Part I. Available from ILEA, London.

HMI (1978) *Behavioural Units*. Department of Education and Science, London.

ILEA Health Education Team (1984) *Contact* (ILEA), 29 June 1984.

Lane, D. A. (1970) Drugs: the role of the teacher and youth worker, *Community Health*, **1**(6), 327–329.

Lane, D. A. (1972) Education in environmental health, *Community Health*, **4**(3), 149–156.

Lane, D. A. (1973a) The problem of order, *Remedial Education*, **8**(3), 9–11.

Lane, D. A. (1973b) Individuals and systems: aspects of educational issues in drug dependency, *Educational Research*, **16**(1), 52–57.

Lane, D. A. (1974a) Reading for competence, *London Educational Review*, **3**(3), 64–69.

Lane, D. A. (1974b) Truancy and the disruptive pupil. Conference paper.

Lane, D. A. (1974c) The analysis of complex cases. Islington Educational Guidance Centre, ILEA.

Lane, D. A. (1975) Dealing with behaviour problems in school. Kings Fund Centre, London. Reprint.

Lane, D. A. (1976a) Four papers on therapy response. HMI Conference Papers.

Lane, D. A. (1976b) *Persistent Failure and Potential Success*. Research monograph. Educational Guidance Centre, ILEA.

Lane, D. A. (1976c) Limitations on counselling, *Remedial Education*, **11**(3), 120.

Lane, D. A. (1977) Aspects of the use of behaviour modification in secondary schools, *Bulletin of the British Association of Behavioural Psychotherapy*, **5**, 76–79.

Lane, D. A. (1978a) *The Impossible Child*, vol. 1. ILEA, London.

Lane, D. A. (1978b) *The Impossible Child*, vol. II. ILEA, London.

Lane, D. A. (1983) *The Impossible Child*, vol. III. ILEA, London.
Lane, D. A., and Hymans, M. H. (1982) The prediction of delinquency, *Personality and Individual Differences*, **3**, 87–88.
Leach, D. J., and Raybould, E. C. (1977) *Learning and Behaviour Difficulties in School*. Open Books, London.
Lindsley, D. (1967) See Portage Project, Note 1.
McInnes, C. (1974) The Open Way, *Times Educational Supplement*, 2 August 1974.
McWilliams, W. (1975) Sentencing and recidivism: an analysis by personality types, *British Journal of Social Work*, **3**, 311–324.
Oldroyd, D., Smith, K., and Lee, J. (1984) *School-based staff Development Activity*. Longman, London.
O'Leary, K. D., and O'Leary, S. G. (1972) *Classroom Management: the Successful Use of Behaviour Modification*. Pergamon, New York.
Olson, W. C. (1935) The diagnosis and treatment of behavioural disorders of children. In *Educational Diagnosis 38th Year Book*. National Society for the Study of Education, Public School Publication Company, Illinois.
Presland, J. L. (1980) Behaviour modification and secondary schools. In Upton, G., and Gobell, A. *Behaviour Problems in the Comprehensive School*. University College, Cardiff.
Reay, D., Lowe, M., and Bowker, C. (1984) *Before it's Too Late*. Family Service Unit, London.
Reynolds, D., and Sullivan, M. (1979) Bringing schools back in. In Barton, L. A., *Schools, Pupils and Deviance*. Natterton Books, Driffield.
Rutter, M. (1975) *Helping Troubled Children*. Penguin, Harmondsworth, Middx.
Scheff, I. J. (1966) *Being Mentally Ill*. Aldine, Chicago.
Stott, D. M. (1971) *The Social Adjustment of Children*. London University Press, London.
Topping, K. J. (1983) *Educational Systems for Disruptive Adolescents*. Croom Helm, London.
Turner, B. (1974) *Truancy*. Ward Lock, London.
Ullman, L. P., and Krasner, L. (1975) *Psychological Approach to Abnormal Behaviour*. Prentice-Hall, Englewood Cliffs, NJ.
Wakefield, J. A. (1979) *Using Personality to Individualise Instruction*. Edits, San Diego.
Wall, W. D. (1979) *Constructive Education for Special Groups*. Harrap, London.
Wheldall, K. (1984) Behavioural pedagogy or behavioural overkill, *Behavioural Approaches with Children*, **8**(2), 46–51.
Wheldall, K., and Merrett, F. (1984) Batpack, a progress report. *Behavioural Approaches with Children*, **8**(2), 58–61.
White, R., and Brockington, D. (1978) *In and Out of School*. Routledge & Kegan Paul, London.
Williams, H., Muncey, J., and Winteringham, D. (undated) *Precision Teaching*. Schools Psychological Service, Coventry.

Management of Disruptive Pupil Behaviour in Schools
Edited by D. P. Tattum
©1986 John Wiley & Sons Ltd

_____ *8*___

Interpersonal skills and conflict management

Tony Bowers

If good advice on how to handle disruptive behaviour in pupils really worked, we would see very little of such behaviour in our schools. In the 1970s we saw a proliferation of books (e.g. Poteet, 1974) and extensive manuals on behaviour modification which offered practical suggestions for encouraging 'appropriate' behaviours and reducing those seen as inappropriate; we saw, too, the embracing of this new behaviour management technology by many teacher educators and educational psychologists. There were some impressive accounts of success, though most related to individual case studies. Follow-up investigations of teacher effectiveness were less readily available; one elaborate attempt at teacher—and consequently pupil—behaviour change, reported by Hamblin et al. (1971), showed that despite the considerable effectiveness of the experimenters' intervention, as soon as it was withdrawn the teacher and her pupils resumed their earlier disruptive interactive patterns.

More sophisticated prescriptive texts, taking account of the complex nature of classroom interactions but still drawing heavily upon instrumental views of behaviour change, have subsequently arisen, such as those of Robertson (1981) and Laslett and Smith (1984). The techniques and approaches which they advocate make sense, and if followed by teachers will no doubt increase their effectiveness. At one time I would eagerly recommend such works to teachers who were experiencing aggressive outbursts from pupils and a breakdown of their own authority in classroom and school, and who were suffering from the resultant stress. They seized on them, read them, discussed tactics, made decisions—and then went on doing most of the same counterproductive things at school. What had gone wrong? After reflection, it became clear that for teachers who were already generally effective, information on such issues as giving directions to children, establishing contracts, avoiding physical intervention and using non-verbal communication, did seem to allow them to refine what they did; for their less fortunate colleagues there was a yawning gap that could only be accounted for by what their head teachers chose to refer to as 'personality' or a 'lack of style'. In their cases, the maxim that 'it ain't what you do, it's the way that do it' seemed particularly apt.

Pik (1981) has described the 'Chinese meal syndrome' in teachers attending courses entitled 'Disruptiveness', 'Behaviour Problems', 'Maladjustment', or some similar euphemism. He sees them quickly left with a hunger for effective working strategies. This is probably too simple: it is more likely that many teachers are actually unable to assimilate such strategies into their classroom behaviour.

Interpersonal skills: a two-tier view

It is a fair assumption that the quality of our interpersonal relationships, at home, at work, and in our social activities, sets the quality of our lives. An admission of ineffectiveness in interpersonal skills is likely to be as painful as an acknowledgement of incompetence at making love or driving a car. Yet we are all familiar with some people who are very bad at dealing with others, and a lot more who are at times inept.

A glance at the literature on interpersonal skills training reveals two fundamental approaches. The first is concerned primarily with providing individuals with a repertoire of techniques for dealing with other people which will increase the likelihood that the objectives of each interaction are achieved. The assumption underlying it is that interpersonal skills can be learned in much the same way as the techniques involved in carpentry, tennis, or bread making. The concentration is on the skills themselves, not on the person who acquires those skills.

The second approach, on the other hand, does not assume that the skills can be separated from the person. At its extreme it requires an individual to explore his or her fears, denials, repressions, and projections which contaminate relationships with others. Turner (1983) considers this vital, seeing personal understanding and not the skills themselves as the major focus. It is not necessary, though, to adopt a depth-psychology position to fall into this second category; even in such traditionally instrumentally-focused areas as assertiveness training we now see stress laid upon the more intrapersonal areas of beliefs and self-esteem (Kelley, 1979).

When we look at Hargreaves *et al.*'s (1975) portraits of 'deviance-insulative' and 'deviance-provocative' teachers in secondary schools, it appears that the major feature which distinguishes them is their beliefs about their pupils' motivations and about their own role in achieving change in those pupils. The deviance-provocative teacher 'sees his interaction with these pupils as a contest or battle—and one that he must win. He is unable to "de-fuse" difficult situations; he frequently issues ultimatums and becomes involved in confrontations' (p. 260). The deviance-insulative teacher, however, 'is highly optimistic, in contrast to the fatalism of the deviance-provocative teacher, and confidently assumes that pupils will behave well and cooperate with him' (p. 261). To provide a teacher fitting the deviance-provocative description with a few techniques for improving class control is not likely to have much effect, or at best it will constitute an elastoplast remedy. What would appear to be required is something more deep-seated and radical: a self-appreciation by the teacher of his or her own chosen styles of interaction with pupils, the ability to monitor the sensations that occur in challenging and confronting situations and, most importantly, a wide choice of potential behaviours in response to those of others.

Conflict: a management perspective

It is only too easy to focus upon a child whose behaviour appears provocative, disobedient, insolent, defiant or aggressive, to define that child as a problem and indeed as *the* problem, and to seek a solution which in some way removes that problem from the arena in which it is most noticeable and most challenging.

However, the idea that we need to look beyond the individual child to the school itself, and seek not to change the child but factors within the school, has been gaining steadily in stature (e.g. Galloway *et al.*, 1982; Tattum 1982; Phillips and Jones, 1983). In looking at schools and disruptive behaviour, Gillham (1981) has drawn the analogy between schools and commercial organizations, arguing that both are hierarchically structured institutions. In the second, though, problems of worker disenchantment and non-cooperation are not usually looked at in terms of individual pathology; what do come under consideration are methods of communication, the reward systems which operate, task–worker match, and so on. He sees it as 'an axiom of management practice that trouble with employees is always the fault of management' (p. 19).

It is quite easy to argue against this comparison. In many ways, schools have more in common with hospitals or prisons than with factories or offices, since the bulk of their population has little choice about its placement and receives no financial reward for being there. Hospitals and prisons are not noted for their concern with human relations (cf. Keating, 1982) between inmates and staff. Additionally, in the years since Gillham's words were written we have seen a polarizing of industrial relations practice and a tendency to ascribe covert motives to disgruntled workers in industry. Nevertheless, it is a line worth pursuing. Bird *et al.*'s (1980) study of London comprehensive schools revealed characteristics of schools with large numbers of disaffected pupils which bear a close relationship to those of industrial concerns with poor worker–manager relations. A scrutiny, too, of Hargreaves *et al.*'s (1975) description of deviance-provocative and deviance-insulative teachers reveals strong similarities between these and McGregor's (1960) 'Theory X' and 'Theory Y' management styles and their associated belief systems; the Theory X manager sees people as fundamentally disliking work and therefore needing to be coerced, controlled and directed, whereas the Theory Y manager believes that people want to work, dislike being lazy, and are capable of generating their own interest and motivation to complete a task.

DeCecco and his co-workers (DeCecco and Richards, 1977; DeCecco and Schaeffer, 1978) have extended the industrial relations model to the management of conflict in schools. Defining conflict quite narrowly as one or more incidents in which one person or group is seen by another as threatening or taking action against them, they have looked in some detail at the processes of issues clarification, negotiating and bargaining between teachers and pupils. While potentially useful, it presents one particular approach to coping with conflict which, by its very nature, is time consuming and appropriate only to certain situations. In this chapter, I will attempt to explore some of the applications of the broadly based literature on conflict management in human and industrial relations which may be made by teachers in our schools, and to look at implications of this both for in-service training and for the overall ethos of the school.

Conflict or confrontation?

A useful working definition of conflict has been provided by Thomas (1976), who sees conflict as a process which begins when one of the parties in an interaction perceives that another has frustrated, or is likely to frustrate, one of his or her needs or concerns. Viewed this way, we can see that conflict pervades practically every aspect of our lives. It occurs when there is one television and two people want to watch different channels; it happens when you feel like going out for a meal with someone close to you and then discover that they have made plans to stay in instead; it occurs all the time in schools between pupils, between teachers, and between teachers and pupils. The child who wants to go outside but is told to finish a piece of work, the teacher who wants to go on with the next part of a lesson but is asked a seemingly irrelevant question, the deputy head who wants to chat in the staffroom but has to quell a disturbance in the corridor: each is in conflict with another party.

The existence of conflict does not necessarily mean that what Pik (1981) and Laslett and Smith (1984) refer to as 'confrontation' will necessarily occur. For these authors, a confrontation apparently means a situation in which a teacher and one or more pupils openly challenge one another's power. Indeed, Pik defines it as a 'showdown' in which a pupil demonstrates open defiance to what a teacher considers a reasonable request. Before putting forward their guidelines for avoiding such confrontations, Laslett and Smith (1984) actually acknowledge the multiplicity of factors at work in teacher–pupil interaction which make it impossible to suggest ways in which teachers can avoid unproductive or regrettable confrontations. They then go on to suggest them.

Conflict management in schools embraces far more than confrontation avoidance or successful confrontation management. Indeed, Jamieson and Thomas's (1974) survey of American high school students revealed that they showed a marked preference for avoidance or opting-out behaviour when experiencing differences with a teacher. Such behaviour is in no way confronting, but still represents one method of managing conflict between individuals. Confrontation, then, may be particular means of conflict management, but conflict management itself encompasses a far wider spectrum of styles and behaviours.

Self-esteem, stress, and teacher assertiveness

Practically all the teachers that I have met whose coping strategies, in the classroom or outside, are ineffective or inadequate appear to possess a low level of self-esteem. This can manifest itself in a number of ways, but typically it presents as a defensive inability to look critically at one's own practice, a tendency to criticize others and to blame them for the problems that one experiences, to rationalize and justify one's own behaviour, to become irritable at the least adversity, and to be disillusioned with both job and school. Low self-esteem may lead to a failure to be assertive with potentially confronting pupils, or to the adoption of an overbearing manner. Seldom is it accompanied by assertive behaviour in the sense of standing up for one's own rights whilst acknowledging the rights of others and not endeavouring to 'put them down'. Linton and Russell (1982) have outlined the importance of staff who deal with what they term 'antisocial' adolescents demonstrating clear-cut expectations in an assertive way. Pik (1981) has referred to the feelings of fear, anger, and embarrassment in teachers after experiencing confrontations with pupils, all of which are in their way self-punitive. He has also drawn attention to children's increasing awareness of themselves as people with rights, power, and an entitlement to respect.

A recent study by Petrie and Rotherham (1982) has demonstrated that assertiveness and self-esteem are closely connected in the workplace, and that both of these are inversely related to stress. In other words, it is likely that a teacher who has low self-esteem will not be assertive or will be aggressive and will experience considerable stress. In their turn, as one might predict, high stress and anxiety have been linked to such a teacher's experience of children as uncooperative or aggressive (Pratt, 1978) and to a fear of violence, theft, harrassment, and damage to property (Block, 1977). We have, then, a close link between these variables and the teacher's perceived lack of control of his or her working environment—the classroom and the school as a whole.

Power and the classroom

Conflict, as Chin (1976) has pointed out, is 'in' any system. It is certainly prevalent within any school, yet some teachers manage it effectively, appearing to drift easily through the day in an unstressed manner, while others struggle continually with the challenges that it presents. The ability to cope successfully with conflict is among the most important social skills that anyone can acquire; it has particularly critical implications for teachers at a time when their sources of position power (Etzioni, 1961) are less potent and likely to become increasingly so. 'Position power' refers to the ability to influence others' behaviours—in this case those of pupils—by dint of one's formal position; it links easily with French and Raven's (1960) concepts of legitimate, reward, and coercive power.

　　Legitimate power is based on the internalized values of one person that another has a right to prescribe certain behaviours for him or for her. Legitimate power equates closely with authority, since this (cf. Tattum, 1982, chapter 5) rests on an assumption that obedience is given voluntarily when commands come from a source which is justified in giving them. A teacher using it relies on influencing children simply by virtue of being a teacher. This may be enough for some children; for many it is not. Beyond this, reward and coercive power refer to the extent to which a teacher can muster resources to make good things happen to pupils or to make things unpleasant for them. Jamieson and Thomas's (1974) high school students rated their teachers' power bases as high in terms of legitimacy and coercive potential, but very low in terms of their ability to provide rewards. Theirs was a representative sample, and it is highly likely that pupils who are characterized as difficult to teach would have an even more polarized view. What then, it is necessary for teachers to ask, can they do to make outcomes more potentially rewarding for pupils?

　　Beyond these three sources are two of personal power: referent and expert. The first is based on one individual's (the pupil's) desire to maintain or establish a friendly relationship with the power source; the second on the individual's preception that the other person has some special knowledge or ability that is valued or useful. For many teachers, in relation to particular pupils with whom they have difficulty, these power sources are very limited. It is necessary, therefore, for teachers to review in some detail the nature and extent of the power that they can call upon in interactions with given individuals. Mr Jones, for example, was quite a successful history teacher in terms of examination results. He was not well liked, tending to be aloof and rather critical of most pupils, but he was tolerated by his O-level and CSE groups. However, he found himself working with one group of 15–16-year-olds, some of whom were low attainers in most areas of the curriculum and saw what Mr Jones had to teach as largely irrelevant. One in particular, Darren, took little notice of Mr Jones; he was a large lad who looked older than his years and he seemed to prefer talking to two of his friends. Mr Jones spent the first couple of weeks telling Darren and his friends to be quiet, each interjection having an effect for 2 minutes at the most, and each successive request for quiet being accompanied by greater signs of frustration in Mr Jones, more grins from Darren and his companions, and progressively more noise and inattention from the rest of the class. A feeling of losing his grip crept over Mr Jones.

Mr Jones actually lost sleep on the Sunday night before the third week of term. At three in the morning he was mentally playing through what he would do on the Monday; then he dropped into a fitful sleep and awoke tired. He made a point of being in his room to receive the class when it arrived after the mid-morning break. Darren was among the last to enter, shouting remarks at two girls in front of him. Before he reached his seat, Mr Jones called to him from the front of the room, beckoning him to sit near to his own desk. Darren looked at him, grinned at his friends, then sat in his usual place at the back of the room. His face had an air of what Mr Jones took to be mock innocence, his teeth moving almost imperceptibly over the gum in the corner of his mouth. The class went strangely quiet and Mr Jones felt himself become tense, his heart beat faster and he became conscious of his more rapid breathing.

Had Mr Jones possessed the ability to 'decentre' at this stage, he might have made an objective appraisal of the options open to him. DeCecco and Schaeffer (1978) see this as a vital capacity in handling conflict. It fundamentally concerns separating self from environment, or personal involvement from the impersonal analysis of the divergent commitments of all parties to a conflict. When decentred it is not only possible to appreciate others' points of view, but to look dispassionately at the types and extent of power possessed by oneself and by others.

Having stepped outside his personally preoccupying position, Mr Jones might have noted that with this group of pupils, and with Darren in particular, his legitimate power was not having much impact. His coercive potential might have been worth testing but there was a strong chance that it would turn out to be ineffectual. He is not a big man; in fact Darren is a little larger than he is. He could draw on sanctions such as detention or reporting to the year head, a deputy head, or the head teacher. He could set Darren additional work; he could set everybody a routine and mundane task such as copying from their books. These might very well prove unimpressive to Darren and his friends and could indeed be quite rewarding. His actual reward power is probably very low. Because of the constraints imposed by the timetable and because Mr Jones feels that pupils should not need 'bribing' to do what he expects them to do, he has not established any procedures whereby particularly enjoyable or valued activities occur in his lessons. He does have an assessment function in their work for the CSE examination, but not many members of this group expect good grades and few of them would see these as something to strive for anyway.

Referent and expert power are also low for Mr Jones. He has expertise, but not in anything that is presently significant. His earlier relationships with Darren and others have given them little to try to maintain and little to lose by his displeasure. In short, his bases of power were generally neglected and in need of underpinning. What is apparent is that in any confrontation with Darren he will have little option but to rely on his legitimate and coercive powers.

In contrast, an analysis of Darren's power on the same dimensions would probably yield a very different picture. Mr Jones would have to look at Darren's power not only in relation to himself but also in relation to other group members. With them he was strong on reward power, coercive power, referent power, and, in the present potential confrontation, expert power also. In relation to Mr Jones, as with many of his other teachers, he had a high level of coercive power.

Styles of conflict management

For anyone whose job involves them in managing other people, the ability to cope successfully with conflict is a vital social skill. For a teacher, involved as he or she is in managing the behaviour of others throughout the day, it is of critical significance. As people mature both personally and professionally, they develop particular behaviours for dealing with conflicts which are usually modelled on the behaviour of others rather than acquired in any guided or systematic way. There is evidence (Ross, 1982) that each individual develops a preferred style—or fairly restricted range of styles—to employ in coping with interpersonal conflict. If a person is fortunate enough to have had good models, and also to be in situations in which the modelled style is effective, then he or she is likely to experience success. Such good fortune does not always occur, however; often our approaches to conflict management become 'locked into' one particular mode which is in fact ineffective or unproductive in the circumstances in which it is used.

There would appear to be five distinct styles which can be employed in coping with situations in which interpersonal conflict occurs or is likely to occur. First introduced by Blake and Mouton (1964), they have subsequently been elaborated by Thomas (1976).

A *competitive style* of dealing with conflict reflects a desire to meet one's own needs and concerns at the expense of those of the other party. It fundamentally involves a win/lose strategy, since one person expects to come out well from an interchange while the other will do badly. Hardly surprisingly, in view of the emphasis upon competition which most teachers have experienced throughout their own education and in their appointments to jobs, and which permeates their social lives through such activities as sports and games, a competitive style is likely to develop and to be used readily and frequently.

If Mr Jones were to continue in his attempt to move Darren by, say, threatening him with further consequences, fetching a senior member of staff, or even using physical force, he would be adopting a competitive mode. In such a case, each party is likely to strive not to be the loser by being the winner. A further escalation by Mr Jones would probably cause Darren, with the unacceptable prospect of capitulation and loss of face in front of the rest of the class, to raise the stakes and thus force Mr Jones to go to even greater lengths to avoid appearing to lose.

Such win/lose conflict management attempts are often in actuality lose/lose. Even if Mr Jones were to emerge as a 'victor' after the intervention of colleagues, his credibility and status in their eyes would probably be lowered. Additionally, once it has erupted, open competitive conflict is difficult to control. Lippitt (1983) points out that it tends to polarize groups, to create suspicion and distrust, and to destroy morale and decrease productivity. Continued competitive conflict strategies in a classroom are likely to do all of these things and to make it increasingly necessary for the teacher to use a competitive style.

Despite an assumption by many teachers that a competitive style is forced upon them by pupil behaviour, Jamieson and Thomas (1974) actually found this to be the least preferred mode on the part of their sample of high school students. The most commonly found style was that of *avoidance*. Avoidance of conflict is characterized by both uncooperative behaviour and lack of assertion; by continually evading the issue or withdrawing from a potential conflict, each party is conveying the message that it is indifferent to the other's needs and concerns. As an interim measure it can, though, be helpful. It may be useful to allow the other person to cool down emotionally, to analyse a problem in more detail, if an issue is relatively unimportant or where there is insufficient time to achieve a successful resolution to a conflict. Mr Jones might have chosen to use avoidance before he arrived at his classroom; he might even have been able to shift into an avoidance mode by ignoring Darren's response or by creating a diversion such as the cracking of a lighthearted remark.

As a permanent strategy, though, there is little possibility of satisfying anyone's needs if avoidance is used. Mr Jones would continue to experience discomfort and probably have sleepless nights. Yet persistent avoiders are still found at all levels in schools, their avoidance sometimes disguised as a denial that any conflict exists or might exist.

The user of *accommodation*, on the other hand, acknowledges that a conflict exists—and then gives way. An accommodative style can be appropriate and effective if one person is not as concerned as the other; then it may build goodwill and lead to cooperative relationships. It may also be useful when one party has a great deal more power than the other. Mr Jones considers that he has until now accommodated to Darren; Darren may well feel that he has accommodated to Mr Jones's uninteresting and irrelevant material and unsympathetic manner. So often in a conflict each party may view itself as having given more ground than the other.

Jamieson and Thomas (1974) view pupil avoidance of conflict, and by inference accommodation to conflict, as passive-dependent behaviours which are likely to shape subsequent development of initiative and acceptance of authority. Arguably, such behaviours may be modelled by those pupils' own teachers. Minimizing one's own needs reduces the possibility of issues being addressed openly; in contrast, a *collaborative style* involves acknowledging that there is a conflict and identifying and recognizing the other's concerns and goals.

This sounds all very well in theory. How, though, could Mr Jones possibly collaborate with Darren? In the situation in which we left him, collaboration would in all likelihood call on more resources than he possessed. Collaboration requires more commitment than other styles and takes more time and energy. Mr Jones should ideally have developed the opportunity for open dialogue with his pupils which could lead to openly facing the disagreement between himself and Darren and negotiating around their respective positions. DeCecco and Schaeffer (1978) provide a detailed account of this collaborative process between teacher and pupils. Ideally, if properly carried through, it can lead to a win/win solution, with both sides meeting their respective needs.

It might still be possible for Mr Jones to use a collaborative approach, provided that he first practises avoidance of the existing conflict which both he and Darren have recently escalated. Pik (1981) recommends that the teacher set up the opportunity for private discussion of major issues before the next scheduled 'public' meeting. For him, the message that should be conveyed is 'let us not try to force each other into a difficult position again' (p. 141). However, it is necessary for both parties to have access to this style;

if Darren has not himself seen collaborative skills modelled, he would be likely still to adopt another mode—probably the competitive or the avoiding—in response to Mr Jones's approach.

Compromise falls somewhere midway between the last four styles of conflict management. Its aim is a partial fulfilment of both parties' needs. Often teachers reach a tacit compromise with particular pupils, particularly those with coercive power, each giving some ground in exchange for concessions from the other. Where an effort to collaborate has failed, compromise may be seen as a good second best, but ideally it should be explicit. While compromise is actually a lose/lose resolution strategy, the losses are potentially smaller for each party than would arise from unsuccessful competition. The idea of the teacher ensuring that the pupil has a gracious way out, and that he or she has too, is a good example of preparing for a compromise solution.

Laying the foundations

The conflict management workshops with which I have recently been involved are directed largely at secondary school teachers, although some social services staff working with adolescents in community homes have also taken part. Our first concern is to assist participants to examine their preferred approaches to coping with conflict, thus enhancing self-awareness—sometimes a mildly painful process. This is done through structured questionnaires which ask for preferred responses to particular situations, and through games, such as Prisoner's Dilemma, which place participants in potentially competitive situations but which still allow creatively collaborative solutions.

From this, we can look at the extent to which the particular styles outlined in the last section come into play, and can provide a rough index of the flexibility of choice of mode displayed by participants. There is also the opportunity to look at tendencies towards an assertive or an aggressive management style, or alternatively an avoiding or a conciliatory style. The flexible individual will not come close to these extremes but, interestingly, large numbers of our self-selected workshop members do veer sharply towards one or another.

Our programme then sets out to increase each individual's repertoire of styles through a variety of means which include role play, playing games, and simulated events in the classroom and elsewhere. Pomerantz (1983) has recounted in some detail the use of behavioural rehearsal and dramatic improvization to change teachers' behaviours and to alter their understanding of the effects of those behaviours on others. We go beyond this sometimes, encouraging role reversal which can lead more easily to attitude change;

at times, identification by teachers with their pupils' needs is so close that they need to be carefully 'de-roled'.

Some pointers to conflict management

Whilst it is the contention of this chapter that there is no 'golden rule', that successful conflict handling requires flexibility and the assessment of what best suits a situation, there are none the less some principles which are worthy of expansion. That flexibility is important and that formulae should be viewed with caution become only too evident when we look at methods of handling conflict within different cultures. Laslett and Smith (1984) counsel the teacher to avoid public denigration of a child and to practise 'planned ignoring' of confronting or provocative behaviour—wise advice in many overt conflict situations. However, a recent study by Garner (1983) of a predominantly black community shows that the competitive use of verbal insults provides a channel for conflict resolution within that culture. 'Walking away' or other attempts at non-participation are viewed as an acknowledgement of defeat. There is, though, an underlying value system which requires hostilities to be brought into the open, which generates highly charged emotional relationships and which encourages people to 'tell it like it is'. For a teacher to use the more suppressed approaches advocated by Laslett and Smith would probably not lead to much success in such surroundings.

There is a way around this which we have attempted to work on during our training sessions. Bandler and Grinder (1979) refer to a technique which they term 'pacing': essentially, matching one's own tempo to that of the other in terms of breathing, body posture, tone of voice, and so on. Once the ability to pace has been achieved, it should be possible to work effectively in most new interpersonal situations such as the one which Garner (1983) has described. From pacing springs 'leading': changes in your behaviour will start to elicit changes in the other person's behaviour provided that a paced rapport has been achieved. So calming the voice, relaxing the body posture, beginning to smile, and similar de-escalating behaviours will be matched by the other. Without initial pacing, though, their effectiveness is much less certain.

In the effective management of conflict, the ability to recognize emotional states in oneself such as anger, jealousy, or fear is important and necessary. This does not imply that these emotions should be suppressed or discounted; they are natural and therefore legitimate. But if they go unrecognized, then it is easy to slip naturally into patterns of behaviour that may be counter-productive in the circumstances that prevail. Recognizing emotions in oneself also helps one to be more sensitive to those in others and therefore to appreciate their point of view.

Where, as is sometimes found, a person's style is predominantly one of competitive conflict resolution, it may be very difficult for them to alter that mode in response to particular situations; their reflexive emotional response may be too powerful to allow it. There are, though, certain guidelines that can be followed within a competitive framework which will ensure that it does not become destructive. Indeed, Karp (1983) has argued that provided these become established as norms of behaviour, argument and open conflict can actually be productive. This would appear to run counter to the values of many schools and many schools and many teachers. Jamieson and Thomas (1974), however, point out that the predominance of conflict avoidance which they discovered in schools actually prevents any creative change occurring.

Essentially, a teacher who wants to employ and encourage a useful competitive approach to conflict should first establish with the pupils that it is legitimate to question one another's actions and indeed to disagree with one another. Having done this, it is important to deal with one issue at a time rather than bring up unresolved arguments from the past. Never raise old transgressions or misbehaviours to back up your present points. Choose the arena carefully, too; catching a pupil off guard or at a time when he is unprepared may actually lead to defensive aggression. Avoid reacting to unintentional remarks made by the pupil in the heat of the moment; stay with the issue and accept that sometimes things will be said which are best left alone. Avoid cornering a pupil, either physically or by proving that you are 'right'. Such an approach may provide short-term satisfaction but lead to long-term retaliation and an attempt to regain lost face. Finally, throughout any competitive conflict, it is important that one should try to maintain a sense of humour and to avoid the temptation to become progressively more righteous.

Bolton's (1979) conflict resolution principles are also worth considering. He calls it the 'one-two-three' process, since it involves a sequential application of three steps. While we have taught it to teachers, there would seem to be no reason why it should not be taught to pupils as part of any life skills programme. Step one involves treating the other person with respect in the way you listen to them, look at them, in your tone of voice, and in the type of reasoning you use. Talking down to the other, talking at them, talking past them, snapping at them, treating them paternalistically, or looking at them disparagingly, all contribute to an undermining of self-worth which will only increase hostility. The second step involves attending until you 'experience the other side'. Try to understand the content of any verbal utterance, the meaning that the conflict has for the other person and the feelings generated in them. Thirdly, one should state one's own views, needs, and feelings as briefly as possible and without the use of loaded words or threats. Although these may appear to be relatively simple guidelines, each can need considerable practice to produce an adequate performance when under stress.

Coping with potential violence

For sheer survival, it is necessary for teachers to possess the skills to recognize a potentially violent interpersonal conflict, to prepare themselves for the possibility of violence, and to possess the resources for preventing its escalation. Some people are sensitive to the cues and situations which can mark potentially violent confrontations, others are not. Some areas can be dealt with during training but perhaps the most important one—paying attention to one's own intuition—is hard to prescribe for. If things don't 'feel' right, beware. Look also for undue agitation in the other person, assess their tone of voice and body posture, look for flared nostrils, clenched fists, wide open eyes, and the obvious non-verbal signals. Be aware, too, of onlookers; depending on the circumstances, they may inhibit or provoke violence. Finally, look for evidence of what Robert (1982) terms 'psychic modifiers'. The use of alcohol, glue, or other drugs can have an unpredictable and uncontrollable influence on conflict-related behaviours. Signs of their use should make one very wary.

To prepare oneself for potential violence, it is wise first to slow down your pace of activity and then mentally to design a safety plan. Think, too, of how many options are available to you. How risky is each one? Is each risk a worthwhile one? Expect anything to happen. That way you will not be taken by surprise, either by verbal or physical abuse.

If all else appears to be failing, it may help to use injunctions such as 'Stop!' or 'That's enough!' said startlingly and very firmly. I have known that be effective when violence was about to ensue. In the final event, when you see your resources spent, be prepared to leave the scene with as much dignity as you can muster. Then look very carefully at what personal resources you should have had to handle things better—and acquire them as soon as possible.

In Conclusion

The development of access to effective conflict management styles for teachers is a relatively new departure in teacher in-service education, which has been largely knowledge- or techniques-based. In industry, where an insensitive manager can generate considerable unrest and cause significant cost to his organization, the development of both awareness and flexibility of style have received rather more attention. We have now reached a time of greater accountability in the public services, with the efficiency of non-profit-making organizations coming under greater scrutiny than ever before, and many of the expectations that middle managers in industry have had to face are increasingly likely to be placed upon teachers and other members of the 'caring professions'.

It has been the basic premise of this chapter that the complex interaction of events within groups of pupils, and between pupils and their teachers, makes it difficult to prescribe specific strategies to be followed. Even when such prescriptions are given, though, the manner in which they are followed — or whether they are adhered to at all — will be greatly influenced by the earlier learnings of the teacher and the set of beliefs and expectations that he or she brings to any perceived or real interpersonal conflict. It is a common observation that some teachers appear to cope with 'problem' pupils and to avoid difficult situations quite effortlessly, whilst others seem to attract difficulties wherever they go. The assumption, then, is that members of this last group need more than techniques: they need to be assisted in appraising their successes and failures and their usual approaches to coping with potential interpersonal conflict, and in understanding the ways that their own internal states influence their external behaviours.

Whilst our evaluation of results is only in a preliminary phase, it appears that conflict management workshops of this nature at least raise teachers' confidence to enter previously anxiety-provoking situations and make them feel that they now have increased personal resources. Although longer-term outcomes in the areas of teacher and pupil behaviour, symptoms of stress, and categories of critical incidents have yet to be assessed, there is every reason to suspect that the self-reported changes will themselves generate and sustain new and more flexible approaches to conflict management.

References

Bandler, R., and Grinder, J. (1979) *Frogs into Princes*. Moab, Utah, Real People Press.

Bird, C., Chessum, R., Furlong, J., and Johnson, D. (1980) *Disaffected Pupils*. Uxbridge, Brunel University Educational Studies Unit.

Blake, R. R., and Mouton, J. S. (1964) *The Managerial Grid*. Houston, Tex., Gulf.

Block, A. (1977) The battered teacher, *Today's Education*, March/April **1977**, 56–59.

Bolton, R. (1979) *People Skills*. Englewood Cliffs, NJ, Prentice-Hall.

Chin, R. (1976) The utility of systems models and developmental models for practitioners. In Bennis, W. G., Benne, K. D., Chin, R., and Corey, K. E. (eds), *The Planning of Change*, 3rd edn. New York, Holt, Rinehart, & Winston.

DeCecco, J. P., and Richards, A. K. (1977) Can teachers use a workshop in conflict resolution? National Association of Secondary School Principals Bulletin, **61**, 70–75.

DeCecco, J. P., and Schaeffer, G. A. (1978) Using negotiation to resolve teacher-student conflicts, *Journal of Research and Development in Education*, **11**, 64–77.

Etzioni, A. (1961) *A Comparative Analysis of Complex Organizations on Power, Involvement and their Correlates*. New York, Free Press.

French, J. R. P., and Raven, B. (1960) The bases of social power. In Cartwright, D., and Zander, A. F. (eds), *Group Dynamics*, 2nd edn. Evanston, Ill., Row, Peterson.

Galloway, D., Ball, T., Blomfield, D., and Seyd, R. (1982) *Schools and Disruptive Pupils*. London, Longman.

Garner, T. (1983) Playing the dozens: folklore as strategies for living, *Quarterly Journal of Speech*, **69**, 47–57.

Gillham, B. (1981) Rethinking the problem. In Gillham, B. (ed.), *Problem Behaviour in the Secondary School*. London, Croom Helm.

Hamblin, R. L., Buckholdt, D., Ferritor, D., Kozloft, M., and Blackwell, L. (1971) *The Humanization Processes*. New York, Wiley.

Hargreaves, D. H., Hester, S. K., and Mellor, F. J. (1975) *Deviance in Classrooms*. London, Routledge & Kegan Paul.

Jamieson, D. W., and Thomas, K. W. (1974) Power and conflict in the student–teacher relationship. *Journal of Applied Behavioral Science*, **10**, 321–336.

Karp, H. B. (1983) The art of creative fighting. In Goldstein, L. D., and Pfeiffer, J. W. (eds), *Annual Handbook for Group Facilitators*. San Diego, University Associates.

Keating, J. M. (1982) Re-humanizing our institutions: a correctional prescription, *Journal of Intergroup Relations*, **10**, 11–23.

Kelley, C. (1979) *Assertion Training*. San Diego, University Associates.

Laslett, R., and Smith, C. (1984) *Effective Classroom Management*. London, Croom Helm.

Linton, T. E., and Russell, W. P. (1982) PROVE: an innovative high school program for educating anti-social disturbed adolescents, *High School Journal*, **66**, 18–25.

Lippitt, G. L. (1983) Can conflict resolution be win-win? *School Administrator*, **40**, 20–22.

McGregor, D. (1960) *The Human Side of Enterprise*. New York, McGraw-Hill.

Petrie, K., and Rotherham, M. J. (1982) Insulators against stress: self-esteem and assertiveness, *Psychological Reports*, **50**, 963–966.

Phillips, P., and Jones, R. (1983) Individual maladjustment or systems failure? A process of negotiation and redefinition, *AEP Journal*, **6**, 38–41.

Pik, R. (1981) Confrontation situations and teacher support systems. In Gillham, B. (ed.), *Problem Behaviour in the Secondary School*. London, Croom Helm.

Pomerantz, M. (1983) Problems of some abnormal conduct in comprehensive schools and what can be done about them. In Lindsay, G. (ed.), *Problems of Adolescence in the Secondary School*. London, Croom Helm.

Poteet, J. A. (1974) *Behaviour Modification*. London, London University Press.

Pratt, J. (1978) Perceived stress among teachers: the effects of age and background of children taught. *Educational Review*, **30**, 17–23.

Robert, M. (1982) *Managing Conflict*. Austin, Tex., Learning Associates.

Robertson, J. (1981) *Effective Classroom Control*. London, Hodder & Stoughton.

Ross, M. (1982) Coping with conflict. In Pfeiffer, J. W., and Goldstein, L. D. (eds), *Annual Handbook for Group Facilitators*. San Diego, University Associates.

Tattum, D. P. (1982) *Disruptive Pupils in Schools and Units*. Chichester, Wiley.

Thomas, K. W. (1976) Conflict and conflict management. In Dunnette, M. D. (ed.), *Handbook of Industrial and Organizational Psychology*, vol. 2. Chicago, Rand McNally.

Turner, C. (1983) *Developing Interpersonal Skills*. Bristol, FE Staff College.

Management of Disruptive Pupil Behaviour in Schools
Edited by D. P. Tattum
©1986 John Wiley & Sons Ltd

9

Counselling in the treatment of disruptive pupils

Anthony Bolger

Introduction: The emergence of school counselling

Counselling is a relatively recent phenomenon in British education. It originated in the early 1960s as a way of encouraging positive mental health, began to move forward with the establishment of training courses in the universities of Keele and Reading, gathered momentum with the appointment of full-time counsellors in schools, and for 10 years or more, became a new force in education, a source of controversy, a source of inspiration for some, a source of theoretical understanding, a source of practical skill. Then with recession and cuts in public spending, development slowed down, training courses closed, counsellors moved back into teaching posts and new counselling appointments almost ceased. But all the gains were not lost—'counselling' had become an accepted term in the educational vocabulary, counselling had been established as a desirable skill for teachers, 'pastoral care' had developed in schools, inspired and informed by a counselling viewpoint, and teachers trained in counselling had become widely distributed in educational administration and training.

By the time the National Association of Schoolmasters completed its survey of disruptive and violent behaviour in schools (Lowenstein, 1975) counselling had become something of a cure-all. In fact, there is some research evidence that counselling can produce positive results with difficult pupils (e.g. Lawrence, 1971; Maguire, 1971; Thompson, 1970; Connor, 1979). The largest-scale research into the effectiveness of counselling in schools was reported by Rose and Marshall (1974). The work of school social workers and school counsellors was measured and quite a marked improvement in delinquency and non-attendance rates was reported.

Towards a definition of counselling

One of the difficulties in appraising the effectiveness of school counselling has been the very wide target area aimed at by counsellors. From the beginning there have been two main threads in school counselling. The first, with its origin in the guidance philosophy of the 1950s (Morris, 1955), was aimed at the total school population, expressed itself through the curriculum, vocational guidance, and school organization, and had a preventive objective. The second, derived from the client-centred therapy of Carl Rogers (1951), emphasized individual and group counselling and therapeutic outcomes. On the one hand the emphasis was upon prevention (Daws, 1973) and on the other upon cure (Maguire, 1975).

Counselling is a helping process which depends on the development of a relationship between people which is sufficiently supportive to enable one of these people, the client, in this case the pupil, to explore aspects of his life more freely and to arrive, possibly, at more adequate ways of coping. The counselling relationship, it seems, is based upon the early attachment that is formed between a baby and its mother or mother-substitute. This relationship is essential to the healthy development of the baby and nourishing relationships — 'human nourishment' — continue to be essential for healthy development throughout life (Carkhuff, 1969).

Counselling should be progressive, developing through stages, as the counsellor increases his understanding of the client, and the client develops his understanding of himself, and this makes a useful model for the counselling of disruptive children. The model being suggested here is three-stage, expanding Hamblin's (1974) model following the assumption that 'counsellors and their clients should focus on goals relating to experiencing, thinking and acting, in that order' (Nelson-Jones, 1982). I call this the affective-cognitive-behavioural (or a-c-b) model, since these are key words describing the main emphasis at each stage. It is an eclectic model, drawing its rationale from a number of sources on the assumption that each theory has something to offer to an understanding of human nature. The central approach is humanistic, owing much to Rogers's client-centred theory but drawing upon psychoanalytic and related theories, rational-emotive and other cognitive approaches, and behavioural techniques based upon learning theory. This model is appropriate for school counselling since it can apply to formal and informal situations and can be applied to all kinds of pupil needs — educational, vocational, personal — and to the difficulties of disruptive pupils. Initially, the description will emphasize formal, one-to-one counselling situations, although some mention will be made of informal counselling.

The affective-cognitive-behavioural approach

(1) The affective stage

The initial or affective stage is appropriate to all counselling situations in schools. It is basically a client-centred approach which emphasizes the development of good relationships between teacher and pupil. The qualities of relationship which have been found to be important may be summarized under three headings:

(a) the attitude of the counsellor towards the pupil;
(b) the attitude of the counsellor towards himself;
(c) the quality of communication between pupil and counsellor.

I shall look at each of these aspects in turn.

The attitude of the counsellor towards the pupil Two main qualities are needed in the attitude of the counsellor towards his pupil: *warmth* and *respect*.

The quality I have described as *warmth* is one which most people are able to recognize among their acquaintances. It consists of an ease of relationship, a sense of relaxation in other people's company which comes from liking other people and being happy with oneself. It is, it seems, related to extroversion, that is, an outgoing, sociable type of personality, but it is not restricted to extroverts and may be developed in those of more introvert personality. This approachability comes at least partly from developed social skills, from responding appropriately to emotional cues given by other people, and from ease of emotional expression. The person who is perceived as warm responds in an appropriate way to the tone of voice, the smile, the eye contact, the gestures, the posture, and the touch of another. If he should respond inappropriately, avoiding eye contact, staring too hard, shifting eye contact too rapidly, avoiding reasonable physical contact or over-using touch, using stereotyped gesture or posture, he will be seen as rejecting overtures of friendship, unwelcoming, cold, distant. As others react to this perceived coldness the person learns to perceive himself as cold and behaves appropriately. This learning process has usually taken place over a long time and is often difficult to un-learn, although people can be helped to modify their verbal and non-verbal responses.

This quality of warmth is not simply a matter of social skills, however, it is also concerned with attitudes towards other people—what is perhaps best expressed by Rogers's (1951) term, 'unconditional positive regard'. The term sums up what is involved—concern, caring, acceptance, being non-judgemental, giving non-possessive love. It also introduces the other main aspect of the counsellor's attitude towards his client, *respect*, which communicates regard and helps the recipient to feel self-respect. Many children in school have had little practice in self-respect. They come from homes in which little value is placed on them as persons and they begin school with a poor self-image. Having little confidence with which to tackle the new tasks before them they experience failure in reading and writing, and this reinforces their negative self-image. By the time they have reached secondary school such children become deviant, through a process of attribution and labelling. One way of helping these disruptive and disrupted pupils is by giving them back some self-respect. Counselling is not the only activity through which respect may be conveyed, education provides many opportunities for shared activities and the achievement of success, but counselling is a particularly powerful way of improving the self-concept since it consists of giving someone undivided attention and this is a rare commodity for many disruptive pupils.

The attitude of the counsellor towards himself   It is important, too, that the counsellor has positive attitudes towards himself. He needs to have self-respect and conviction in the value of what he is doing. If he has this conviction then he will feel genuine in what he is doing, and this will help the client to feel that he is sincere. Rogers talks of this quality as congruence, that is, the counsellor should feel the same inside as he seems on the outside. This is not always easy; self-consciousness in playing a role, conflict between being both warm and sincere, negative emotions, all prevent the counsellor from acting naturally. Some clients, too, are more difficult to warm to than others, and, if the counsellor should try to simulate warmth, then he is likely to be perceived as insincere. Beginners in counselling, like beginners in any skill, feel awkward and self-conscious; they feel 'phoney' and, as a result, may appear insincere to their clients. This is where training is an advantage. Practising counselling in safe situations, role playing and co- counselling for example, helps beginners to move through the stage of self-consciousness.

For the teacher-counsellor one awkwardness which may arise comes from a perceived discrepancy between the kind of teaching role he normally plays and his new counselling role. For some teachers, whose style is 'traditional', that is, didactic and authoritarian, the discrepancy is wide and difficult to bridge; for others whose style is 'progressive', that is, child-centred and non-authoritarian, the transition is less difficult and the counsellor feels little lack of congruence. For all counsellors at some time, however, problems may arise when they find themselves unable to remain warm or respectful towards a client. This may happen, for example, if they find themselves violently at odds with the values being expressed. At such times it may be useful to acknowledge these feelings, to try to understand their source and, if it should seem appropriate, express their feelings about bullying or extortion, for example, to a pupil who is boasting about his exploits. A counsellor is client-centred but not ethically neutral.

The counsellor at such a time preserves the genuineness of his encounter with the pupil at the risk of losing, temporarily, some of the warmth which he has built up between them. In my experience these occasions are very rare in school counselling. The very act of relating warmly to a pupil and entering into his life can be a rewarding experience, and very soon the counsellor finds that his expectations of counselling are all positive and, just as a teacher can find himself warming to even the most unlikeable children if they are his special responsibility in school, so he can find himself in an interview responding with warmth even to an aggressive or cynical client.

The communication between counsellor and pupil   Finally, we need to look at the quality of the communication which develops between the counsellor and the pupil. At this first stage of the counselling interview the aim is to achieve 'primary accurate empathy' (Egan, 1975), and we should be careful not to hurry the client by presenting him prematurely with startling or unexpected insight.

At the beginning of an interview it is important to set the mood; a feeling of friendliness can be achieved by arranging the furniture in an informal manner, making sure that the traditional distance between teacher and pupil is reduced, by greeting in a friendly manner, by preserving eye contact, by giving open invitations to talk. Empathy is achieved by close attention to what the pupil is saying and how he is behaving while he is saying it. The counsellor responds to what the pupil is saying by encouraging him to go on talking. He does this by giving him the minimal amount of encouragement which he needs, that is, through eye contact, nods, neutral monosyllables, rather than questions or comments. The counsellor tolerates silences, preserving eye contact but allowing the pupil to take his time to find words to express himself. When the pupil appears to have finished talking, or has said something which seems to need comment, the counsellor responds by reflecting back to him key words and ideas or brief summaries of what the pupil has said. Sometimes he will ask for clarification although he will avoid direct questions whenever possible.

At the same time as listening to the words the counsellor will be attending to the tone of voice, facial expression, gesture, eye movement, and posture, and all these cues tell about the emotional state of the pupil. He will respond to this emotion, recognizing it, acknowledging it, allowing its expression. The emotions aroused by disturbing circumstances are often repressed and many pupils find it difficult to express their anger, resentment, sorrow, gratitude, or even joy. Such repression may prolong any distress. An example of this would be the process of grieving following bereavement or other loss which may leave 'unfinished business' or blocked emotion. If this stays unresolved for long, then the person's capacity to cope with the circumstances of his life is diminished and he may become depressed.

One of the aims of counselling, therefore, is to help a person to express emotion, to feel that such expression is legitimate (not unmanly or something to be ashamed of), and to help him to understand the source and nature of his emotions. These two processes, catharsis and insight, are two of the ways in which counselling may be particularly useful to disruptive pupils; but, in order to use these approaches, the counsellor must develop an understanding of both the inner world of the pupil and the circumstances in which he lives. The nearer he gets, however, to sharing in this inner world, the more he needs to add something else to his empathic understanding.

He will need to help the pupil to be concrete rather than abstract, specific rather than general, to deal with the 'here and now' rather than the 'there and then'. It is this quality of *concreteness* which will determine how far he is able to help the pupil to improve his understanding of himself and the circumstances of his life. Many young people have little insight into themselves, and, in fact, find it very difficult to think of themselves sufficiently objectively to be aware of their own thoughts and how and why they react in various ways. The counsellor can help by enabling his client to be more precise in his descriptions, keeping to specific episodes, giving, as far as possible, verbatim reports: *not* 'I don't get on with my Dad'; but rather, 'The other night when I was watching the telly with my sister, my Dad came in and said . . .'.

Sometimes, such self-exploration will need to be stimulated in other ways: focused descriptions (e.g. 'Tell me everything you did last Saturday, starting from when you woke up'.), diaries, checklists, timetables, self-report forms, drawing, modelling in plasticine. In fact, with younger or less sophisticated children, counselling may be very similar to play therapy. It must be noted, however, that in this first stage we are seeking to encourage self-exploration, and more detailed, more specific, exploration is appropriate in the second stage.

(2) The cognitive stage

By this time the client may be ready to move into the second or cognitive stage. He has begun to accept the counsellor as trustworthy, he has begun to understand rather more about his own difficulties, and he has begun to have some confidence in his own ability to change. Now, the timing of this will vary considerably in any counselling relationship, and never more so than in school counselling. Some clients are already well-known to their teacher-counsellor, who can move very quickly into the second stage, while other pupils, equally well-known perhaps, may need to stay indefinitely in the first stage. As will be explained later, most informal counselling will stay at the first level, since it is in the security of unhurried privacy that cognitive exploration can commence.

When the counsellor judges the time to be right, he begins to adapt his style to a more active one. It is now that advanced accurate empathy can be developed as the counsellor begins to acknowledge less obvious aspects of his client's behaviour. He will maintain his client-centredness, his concern and his respect, but these will lead him to a respect for his client's ability to face all aspects of his own behaviour, even the not so nice aspects. This will mean drawing attention to what is implied as well as what is stated, to contradictions and anomalies, to recurring themes and to what the client is denying as well as what he is admitting. All this will mean that the counsellor will, at times, adopt a more confrontative stance, but this should never be perceived by the pupil as personal criticism but rather as a reflection of his own emerging insight.

This stage is cognitive because it shifts the emphasis from feeling to thinking, that is, from the affective to the cognitive domain. A person's first reaction to difficulties is likely to be emotional and we need to deal with this emotion, but it is important to go on from there to look at underlying thought processes. The ways in which we perceive our lives, the incidents which occur to us, the strains to which we are subjected, are what determine our reactions. In the first instance, there is our perception of our lives as a whole. We may perceive ourselves in many different ways, as rebel or victim, as helpless or invincible, as perfectionist or failure, for example, and this frame of reference determines the way in which we interpret what happens to us. Such interpretations are given expression in our internal dialogues, the 'self-talk' in which we go over events in our lives, past and future. The way in which we conduct these dialogues, and what we tell ourselves about the event and about ourselves, largely determines the way we act. If, for example, we tell ourselves that an event is stressful, then it is likely to appear so and, the more we tell ourselves that, then the more stressful it will be. Our bodies will respond accordingly, hormones will be secreted, our heart-rate will go up, our blood pressure will increase, our digestive system will be interrupted. These body changes, in turn, are likely to alarm us and to increase the feeling of being under stress. The same chain of events is likely to occur in most other situations, e.g. a pupil's perception of himself as incompetent, no good at school, not much good at anything. His self-talk is likely to include many negative statements: 'I can't do that!' 'Why bother.' 'They don't care about me!' 'It's a waste of time.' 'It serves them right.' This will ensure that he goes into most situations with the expectation of failure and a 'them and us' attitude to authority, which is likely to develop into an antisocial view of life. The boredom and alienation he feels will translate into a body state of irritability, restlessness, hyperactivity, which will increase his disruptive behaviour and decrease his chance of coping with school work.

Since people are, above all else, language users, behaviour is very largely mediated by language, and it is important that counsellors encourage clients to identify the actual words they use to themselves about themselves, the significant people in their lives and the events that connect them all together. Once some idea has been gained of these words then clients can begin to be helped to change negative statements into positive ones. This can be done by working with the client to list negative statements, then listing alternative positive statements, going on to rehearse their use in the interview, getting the client to practise their use in everyday life and, finally, evaluating progress in succeeding interviews. Understanding the nature of self-talk is an important step towards client self-control. Clients may achieve further self-control by examining the basic life positions which they adopt, or the various philosophies which affect their response to everyday events.

It is possible to help clients to change their whole orientation towards life. This process is called cognitive restructuring. Although it calls for considerable skill and sensitivity, this skill is very largely part of the repertoire of good teachers, and when a relationship such as that described in the first stage has been built up, then teacher and pupil can work together to try to understand the ways in which the pupil's thinking is creating the problems he wishes to solve. Under such scrutiny it is possible to distinguish the irrationality of many of the statements that the pupil is making to himself. Ellis (1962) has pointed out, more clearly than anyone else, the link between reason and emotion; the ways in which our interpretation of what is happening to us creates the actual feelings which we attribute to the event itself. Some of the common irrationalities that we all employ at some time or another, but which may be particularly crucial in understanding the pupil's behaviour, are dealt with in Table 9.1.

What we are trying to do, then, in this second stage of counselling is to help the pupil to reach a level of understanding, objective and realistic, which will enable him to follow effective plans of action. The way in which he thinks about his world and the words he uses, internally and externally, to express his attitudes and responses have been concentrated upon in this description, but it is also necessary to help the pupil to examine what lies behind his overt behaviour and to understand what prevents him changing. This means that counsellor and client together will study any discrepancies in the client's account, such as distortions, evasions, games, strategies, and help him to modify these.

The counsellor will need to understand many details of his client's life and, because of this, may need to ask him to describe some aspects very thoroughly. He will need to form an overall picture as well as achieve a detailed understanding of relevant aspects. He will also need to satisfy himself about the client's actual commitment to change.

I have been emphasizing that it is the client who has to change and

Table 9.1 Common irrationalities

Common irrationalities: expressed in the kind of self-statements that pupils make

---

Exaggerating the consequences:

> 'It's awful! My friends won't speak to me.'
> 'If I don't go on the school trip life won't be worth living.'

Overgeneralization:

> 'I hate teachers!' 'Lessons are boring.'
> 'Boys are crap.'

Belief in efficacy of worry:

> 'I must think of all the terrible things that might happen and if I do I can stop them.'
> 'If I keep on thinking about that terrible thing that happened last week then perhaps it won't have happened.'

Need to punish:

> 'He shouldn't get away with it!'
> 'One day I'll get him for this.'

Need to be perfect:

> 'I'll never make the first team so I won't play any games.'
> 'What's the use! I'll never be good enough.'

Feeling of powerlessness:

> 'Nobody cares.'
> 'No matter what I do, it won't get better.'

Need to be loved:

> 'If he doesn't like me it will be awful.'
> 'I must have your attention whatever I have to do.'

---

that it is impossible to impose change against his will. This means that the teacher-counsellor, from the beginning, will match his own growing understanding of the pupil with the pupil's own capacity to understand and accept such insight. This pacing is an important part of the counsellor's skill and means that he does not move too quickly, which would confuse and disturb his client, or move too slowly, which would be too cosy or boring. If this pacing has been sustained, the client will continue to want to extend his self-knowledge so that he not only understands the source of his difficulties but wants to go on to solve them—this means change. Of course, it may be that, as he realizes the implications of the proposed change he will decide that the cost is too high and he does not really want to do it. For example, someone who wants to give up a bad habit, smoking or over-eating perhaps, may consult an expert for advice upon how to go about it. Together they explore the nature of the habit, its effects, the motives to change, the lifestyle that sustains it, the steps that need to be taken to eliminate it and the implications of the change. About this time he may decide that he does not wish to change as much as that and declines the treatment, or he may begin it but in an attitude of mind that ensures its failure. Many pupils will come to the same conclusion, and the counsellor will need to test out the degree of their commitment and to ensure that it is the pupils who wish to change and not just the staff who wish them to change.

Many teacher-counsellors find it useful at this stage to draw up an explicit contract. This will spell out the behaviour that the pupil wishes to change and what he and the counsellor and other significant people involved intend to do to change it. This *behavioural* contract may be verbal or written, but should be specific. The behaviour specified should be sufficiently limited to make the expectations of change realistic and the steps to be taken should be small enough to make successful change visible. It may be necessary to negotiate with parents, other teachers, even the pupil's peer group, in order to ensure that the conditions are favourable to change.

The behavioural contract is one way of deciding upon the goals for stage three. With some pupils, however, it is better to keep goal setting informal and tentative, but it should always be overt in that it needs to be shared between counsellor and pupil and should not remain as a hidden agenda in the counsellor's mind.

(3) The behavioural stage

We assume, then, that during stage two issues will have been clarified, plans will have been discussed, and commitment to change established. Thus the ground-work for various kinds of action will have been done, and counsellor and client will work together towards the accomplishment of one or more of the goals set in the previous stage. This will be in the context of a continuing client-centred relationship. At this stage, this means keeping the client's needs to the fore—above, for example, the need for the counsellor to prove his competence or the demand to prove the efficacy of a particular programme. As suggested earlier, goals should be limited, expressed clearly, with set time limits and established methods of evaluating progress. For example, if a pupil is having difficulty in controlling his temper, then a situation in which he is likely to lose control is chosen. He has already been helped to develop more positive self-talk, now he is helped to develop a way of coping with the stresses of that situation, is coached in the method, is rehearsed in it and then he goes on to try it out. In subsequent interviews he will report on the degree of success he has experienced and the counsellor will use this feedback to modify or extend the approach, perhaps establishing new goals.

Certain phases can be determined within this stage, although the approach should be kept flexible and the phases may not necessarily occur in the order they are described here.

Phase One: Learn Ways and means are decided, methods are taught, demonstrations are given, rehearsals are held.

Phase Two: Practice The 'homework' phase, when the new skill is practised in real life. The pupil tries it out in some situation for which he has been prepared.

Phase Three: Monitor The reporting-back stage, when the pupil returns to the counsellor to report on what happened in the practice phase, and is reinforced for success, consoled for failure.

Phase Four: Evaluate Assessment of progress, establishment of new goals, or a decision to end counselling.

The counsellor, following this kind of approach, is not restricted to a passive role but has a whole range of methods at his disposal as indicated in Table 9.2.

Table 9.2 Counselling methods

(1) *Life skills:* identify and practise new or improved life skills, e.g. rehearsal, role play, remedial teaching, study skills.

(2) *Reinforcement:* find out what rewards and incentives work for the individual pupil and help him to practise using them.

(3) *Cognitive restructuring:* help the pupil to develop more control over his own self-talk by stopping negative thoughts and thinking more positively.

(4) *Self-monitoring:* use diaries, checklists, etc., to help the pupil to understand more clearly the circumstances surrounding his behaviour.

(5) *Relaxation:* training in simple methods of relaxation (perhaps PE and drama time could be used for practice).

(6) *Desensitization:* gradual adjustment to situations or ideas until they no longer produce anxiety, particularly useful in school and other phobias.

(7) *Social drama:* best in group counselling, but role play can be used with individuals to rehearse and practise social skills.

(8) *Behaviour contracts:* using individual plans and contracts to help pupils keep to a programme of change.

(9) *Tender loving care:* supportive counselling where it is judged to be necessary to a deprived pupil.

Counselling disruptive pupils

Throughout most of this chapter the emphasis has been on formal counselling, assuming that the teacher-counsellor is able to find the time and the place for private interviews with individual pupils. This has been done not only because of the belief that such individual sessions are particularly valuable, providing the pupil with essential care and attention, but also because it is easier to describe the counselling model under such conditions. It is clear, however, that these are ideal conditions and that many teachers coping with disruptive pupils have to make do with more hurried and less private contacts. I believe firmly, however, that whenever teachers are urged to employ counselling as one of their skills they should demand the conditions necessary to practise those skills, just as they would demand the correct conditions for teaching science or cooking.

Given, however, that even in an ideal world many contacts between staff and pupils are informal, then teachers must be prepared to give what counselling help they can at such times. The question then becomes, how may we adapt the counselling approach to (1) everyday contacts with pupils in the classroom, (2) crisis situations around the school—confrontations between teachers and pupils, pupils and pupils, for example—and (3) brief interviews with children in public and semi-public places? The first point to stress is the importance of taking our attitude of *unconditional positive regard* with us at all times. This is not always easy, faced with unruly classes and disruptive pupils, and does not mean that teachers become saints overnight but that, believing firmly in the essential worth of each pupil, they avoid cynical and denigrating remarks and persist in a pupil-centred rather than a subject-centred response to their problems. This will mean that the counsellor will bring the same sensitivity which is developed in the counselling interview to everyday contacts, realizing the complex causes of all problems and seeking, from observation of verbal and non-verbal behaviour, some understanding of what makes each individual behave in a particular way. In other words, many of the aims of stage one of the counselling model may be accomplished within the classroom, with class teacher or pastoral care tutor establishing a firm relationship of trust and a basis for understanding individual difficulties. Teachers will obviously encounter difficulties in maintaining a caring, non-punitive attitude at all times, and there will be a continuing need for asserting authority and apportioning responsibility. This is true, too, of the parent role, but modern parents manage, albeit with some difficulty, to be accepted in both a democratic and an authoritarian role.

Inevitably, however, there will be crises. Disruptive children will need to test out the limits of the relationship being offered to them; to find out how far they can still be accepted when they are rude and aggressive.

Additionally, the coping mechanisms they have developed in early childhood may well include attention seeking and power seeking, and the closer they get to a teacher the more they will feel impelled to use on him the methods they have evolved with their own parents. Here the teacher must be on guard against responding in kind; giving the attention seeker the attention he wants by punishment or expostulation, or locking into a power struggle with the power seeker. He must also be able to deal with the immediate behaviour as it occurs without prejudicing the long-term treatment that is required. Redl and Wineman (1957) have described the 'first aid' treatment of deviant behaviour in the classroom and there is no space to repeat it here, although this has been done elsewhere (Bolger, 1975). Basically, it consists of recognizing the situations in which individuals are likely to be disruptive or the first signs of disruptive behaviour, and acting quickly, in a preventive way if possible, to stop contamination of others in the group. The teacher should act calmly and firmly and, whenever possible, keep the pupil informed of what is happening and why, so that it does not become a personal confrontation.

Opportunities should be given for 'cooling off' and for expressing anxiety and distress, and these brief counselling sessions may often move into stage two or stage three if the necessary ground-work has been done. This, particularly, is the role which middle management in pastoral care will adopt. In addition, the vigilant teacher-counsellor will spend time around the school observing particular pupils and will provide frequent opportunities for informal counselling—a few words inquiring about the situation at home, an inquiry about health or state of mind, a check on school progress. If this is done within a scheme which allows for in-depth formal counselling then the best environment for helping disruptive pupils has been provided. Teachers working in units—either on-site or off-site—for disruptive pupils are in a position to employ counselling at all levels, i.e. in enhancing the general climate within the unit, in informal counselling contacts, and in formal counselling interviews. Trained school counsellors have a valuable part to play in working with disruptive pupils in such units.

Formal and informal kinds of help should be available to all pupils as an integral part of the pastoral care provision of a school, to help them with the normal difficulties of growing up in a complex and changing society and with the exceptional problems that arise from time to time in everybody's life. Disturbed and disturbing pupils, however, require not only access to counselling when they feel they need it but also interviews on a routine basis. These interviews and the group work that may stem from them should be maintained with the basic objective of dealing systematically with the problems in living that pupils are experiencing.

Counselling as described here is, therefore, not merely a synonym for talking nicely to pupils, but is a powerful and effective method for changing the kind of behaviour which is disturbing both to the young people themselves and to all those who associate with them.

References

Bolger, A. W. (1975) *Child Study and Guidance in Schools.* Constable, London.

Bolger, A. W. (1982) *Counselling in Britain: A Reader.* Batsford, London.

Carkhuff, R. R. (1969) *Helping and Human Relations,* vol. 1. Holt, Rinehart, & Winston, New York.

Connor, M. P. (1979) School counsellors and school attendance: an investigation into the work of counsellors with pupils who are poor attenders. Unpublished MA thesis, University of Keele.

Daws, P. P. (1973) Mental health and education: counselling as prophylaxis, *British Journal of Guidance and Counselling,* **1** (2), 2–10.

Egan, G. (1975) *The Skilled Helper: A Model for Systematic Helping and Interpersonal Relating.* Brooks Cole, Monterey, California.

Ellis, A. (1962) *Reason and Emotion in Psychotherapy.* Lyle Stuart, New York.

Hamblin, D. H. (1974) *The Teacher and Counselling.* Blackwell, Oxford.

Lawrence, D. (1971) The effects of counselling on retarded readers, *Educational Research,* **13** (2), 119–124. (Also in Bolger, 1982).

Lowenstein, L. F. (1975) *Violent and Disruptive Behaviour in Schools.* National Association of Schoolmasters, Hemel Hempstead.

Maguire, U. (1971) The effectiveness of short-term counselling on secondary school pupils. Unpublished PhD thesis, University of Keele.

Maguire, U. (1975) The school counsellor as a therapist, *British Journal of Guidance and Counselling,* **3** (2), 160–172.

Morris, B. (1955) Guidance as a concept in educational theory. In Bolger, 1982.

Nelson-Jones, R. (1982) *The Theory and Practice of Counselling Psychology.* Holt, Rinehart, & Winston, London.

Redl, F., and Wineman, D. (1957) *The Aggressive Child.* Free Press, Glencoe.

Rogers, C. R. (1951) *Client-centred Therapy.* Houghton Mifflin, Boston, Mass.

Rose, G., and Marshall, T. F. (1974) *Counselling and School Social Work.* Wiley, London.

Thompson, A. J. M. (1970) An investigation into the work performed by some trained counsellors in English secondary schools. Unpublished report to SSRC, University of Keele (mimeo).

Management of Disruptive Pupil Behaviour in Schools
Edited by D. P. Tattum
©1986 John Wiley & Sons Ltd

_____ *10*___

Social learning approach to the analysis and modification of violent behaviour

Barrie J. Brown

Introduction

Thinking about ways to deal in the classroom with anger and face-to-face interpersonal aggression appears not to have been a priority for teachers. Instead, more interest has been shown in directing young violent pupils to resources outside the school (Mortimore *et al.*, 1983). Yet, there is no shortage of interest in approaches to the management of violence amongst other professions, and the wide range of methods derived from the social learning perspective is a significant contribution. For example, in non-educational settings, there has been a growth in the use of specific approaches based on cognitive-behavioural principles to help violent people control their anger. Such approaches have become widely used in mental health services for adults and for children (Graziano and Mooney, 1984), but their application to the management of anger and violence has not been explored in the school setting with children and adolescents.

Teachers themselves, however, seem to have been more interested in a second area of interest: in finding out about the relationship between the style of the teacher and disruptive and violent behaviours in the classroom. The work of Kounin (1970) has demonstrated how episodes of teacher — pupil interaction are related to difficulties in the management of pupils. Further analysis of the impact of teacher behaviour on violence in the classroom has been reported by Hargreaves (1982). A third focus of interest in the education field has been on the use of behavioural techniques to manage the behaviour of specific children and adolescents in the classroom in such a way as to have indirect (and sometimes direct) effects on disruptiveness in that setting. Broadly, these approaches have combined behavioural methods which increase on-task or classroom appropriate behaviour with punishment to eliminate disruptive behaviours. Much of

171

this work appears to have developed from the specific difficulties presented by hyperactive children (Ayllon *et al.*, 1975). Practical behaviour modification techniques are now widely used in special schools (Presland, 1977) and by specialist support services (Lane, 1978), but with relatively little extension to ordinary secondary schools (Presland, 1982), in spite of some successful applications (e.g. see Long and Williams, 1973).

What these foci on disruptiveness and violence in the classroom share is an analysis of problem behaviours in the classroom derived from a range of suggestions which themselves emerge from the social learning perspective. Each assumes that violence is a behavioural response associated with individual deficits in such interactive social skills as being able to argue or negotiate without getting angry. Traditionally, the deficit model has focused on the child, but the teacher, too, can be the target of analysis. Each focus places emphasis on the importance of cognitive processes in the development and maintenance of disruptiveness. The teacher or the child attaches personal meaning to situations in which they find themselves in the classroom, as well as to the kinds of expectations they have regarding probable consequences of using this or that particular strategy. Each focus allows that violent behaviour may serve the function of enabling the perpetrator to achieve an instrumental outcome, thus encouraging future violence.

This chapter deals with practical application of each focus in turn. It suggests some general tactics that can be adopted by the teacher to reduce the overall frequency of classroom management problems. It describes the use of behavioural approaches with individual children and adolescents in the classroom, and the use of therapeutic techniques aimed at reducing disruptive and violent behaviour, having to be 'delivered' elsewhere than in the classrooms, normally by specialist or advisory worker, but perhaps capable of adaptation to the classroom setting.

General teaching style

Teaching is a public activity, but it takes place in the private world of the classroom. Rarely can the teacher enjoy the benefit of constructive feedback about success and failure in dealing with problems. The isolation is, perhaps, encouraged further by the high value placed by teachers on classroom and curriculum autonomy, as well as on the widely shared view that being a good teacher, and perhaps maintaining good discipline, is a matter of 'personality' rather than of explicit knowledge, tactics, or learned skills. Thus, few researchers have penetrated the secrets of the classroom. Those who have, however, have suggested that, as Hargreaves (1982) put it, it is possible to 'de-intuit' the 'mysterious art' of classroom teaching.

An early example of this can be found in the work of Kounin (1970), who analysed sequences of teacher—pupil interaction and examined the relationship of these sequences to problem behaviour. Two particular sequences occurred frequently—'flip-flops' and 'dangles'. A flip-flop occurs when a teacher completes an activity, introduces a new activity to the class, but then returns to the first activity. For example, the teacher may tell the class to put away their arithmetic exercise books, and take out their English books (the 'flip'). When the pupils have done this, the teacher then asks who got all the test questions right in the arithmetic lesson (the 'flop').

A dangle occurs when a teacher sets up and introduces an activity to a class but then leaves it floating in mid-air whilst dealing with another matter. Kounin (1970) observed teachers in ordinary elementary schools and encountered a number of flip-flops and dangles. There was a clear relationship between general disruptiveness in each class and the frequency of flip-flops and dangles. Unintentionally, the teachers appeared to be actively contributing to the emergence of this behaviour. Kounin (1970) was able to show how, once individual teachers were made aware of their use of flip-flops and dangles, they could exercise direct control of them and reduce both their frequency and the frequency of management problems.

More recently, Hargreaves *et al.* (1975) have examined 'switch-signalling'. They give as an example of this the word 'right'—to intervene in an activity, to stop it, or to signal the start of a new activity. Analysis of the use of such switch-signalling in secondary school classes indicated that teachers who gave clear signals of activity phases had fewer classroom misbehaviours. Teachers who gave no switch-signals or gave them ambiguously had significantly more behavioural problems in their classes. Other researchers have suggested that a wide range of very subtle classroom behaviours may be associated with the frequency and intensity of difficult behaviour. Torode (1976) has shown that teachers who present rules as independent of the teacher or the pupils (e.g. by using the pronoun 'we' to spell out the rule) avoid personal confrontation between the teacher and the pupil.

More recent research has attempted to isolate teacher behaviours associated with disruptive pupil behaviour. An analysis of violent episodes in an educational resource centre for difficult secondary pupils has shown that physical assaults on teachers are closely associated with non-compliance (Brown and Drinkwater, 1984). In a study of 140 such violent episodes, more than half the incidents were preceded by a compliance demand made by a teacher either generally or to a specific child, and a similar proportion of the incidents included a refusal to accept the demand. Extending this research into a secondary school classroom, Abbott (1984) examined teachers' use of compliance demands with individual children in the class, and found that teachers tended to use only a narrow range of methods of asking pupils to carry out an action. Each teacher also had a clearly recognizable style of compliance bidding. Some teachers made very frequent demands in their classroom, others hardly any at all. Some teachers signalled that they were about to ask for compliance, and waited until the pupil looked towards the teacher before completing the request, whereas others jumped straight in with a compliance bid. Some teachers did not wait for the pupil to comply before adding further instructions, urging the pupil on to comply or intruding in some other way into the pupil's response, whilst others made their compliance bid and did not intrude. Abbott (1984) found that significant associations could be found between styles of compliance bidding and frequency of non-compliant responses. Compliance was associated with low frequency of compliance bidding, absence of intrusion by the teacher, and orientation towards the teacher by the pupil. In contrast, teachers who used frequent compliance bids, intruded into the compliance interaction, and did not wait for orientation from the pupil, had much higher frequencies of disruptive and violent responses as well as a much lower level of compliance in their pupils.

Much of this research is tentative and exploratory in nature, but one firm conclusion can be drawn from these few studies. It is that the presence of external observers who can give useful feedback to the teacher is vital to the development and understanding of the relationship between teacher behaviour and classroom disruption. Whilst it would not be true to say that disruptive classes have disrupting teachers, the work of Kounin, Hargreaves, Brown, and Abbott does suggest that teachers may, unwittingly, play a part in the development and maintenance of management problems. The difficulty is to find ways of analysing teacher behaviour which are not too intrusive in the classroom and do not disrupt the teaching process itself.

Working with individual children in the classroom

An underlying asumption of all three foci on managing disrupting and violent behaviour in the classroom is that undesirable outcomes of high levels of disturbed behaviour are reduced academic productivity, less focused or on-task behaviour, and reduced sense of fulfilment and enjoyment on the part of the pupils. It is the second of these—'on-task' behaviour—that has received most attention.

What is meant by on-task behaviour varies from study to study, but a common element tends to be the relative frequency or the percentage of completed work assigned by the teacher within a standard lesson time. Pursuing this approach to managing disruptive and violent behaviour, a number of examples of the use of explicit reward for completing assigned tasks have appeared, generally under the label of 'good behaviour game' techniques. An example of this approach in a highly disruptive class has been described by Fishbein and Wasik (1981). The class was divided into teams and each team awarded points by the teacher for 'good behaviour'.

Unambiguous criteria for good behaviour were written down and displayed in the classroom. The winning team was reinforced with a desirable activity at a designated time during the school week, whilst the losing team continued usual academic work during the same period. When both teams earned enough points to reach the criterion of good behaviour a tie was recorded and both were reinforced with the reward. Further examples of this approach have been described with infant through to secondary age children (Graziano and Mooney, 1984).

In another example of encouraging on-task behaviour (Marlowe *et al.*, 1978) the teacher was trained to use attention (verbal praising) to on-task behaviour, accompanied by ignoring of disruptive behaviour, in a primary class with difficult, aggressive children. Results from this pairing of reinforcement of on-task behaviour and ignoring disruption were remarkable. Teacher's differential attention was found to be more effective than behavioural counselling sessions or extra attention after class, suggesting that advisory and specialist staff in schools might perhaps be more effective in helping to deal constructively with disruptive and aggressive behaviour in school if they were to focus on the classroom environment instead of providing extra-class counselling or therapy.

A number of difficulties in the use of behavioural techniques in the classroom, however, have been documented by Presland (1982), who has shown how successful application of these principles in primary and special education settings has been widely taken up (Presland, 1977). Yet, as Presland (1977) shows, organized workshops involving large numbers of secondary school teachers resulted in a very low take-up of the use of behavioural management methods in comprehensive classroom settings. Little is known about why, precisely, methods so successful in primary and special school settings appear not to be usable in secondary and comprehensive schools. One possibility is that the use of reinforcement strategies by the classroom teacher for individual pupils in classes numbering 20 or more pupils imposes excessive demands on the teacher's time, attention, and energy. In an attempt to identify minimally demanding reinforcement strategies, a series of studies (Shirodkar and Scherer, 1984; Scherer and Brown, 1984; and Scherer, Shirodkar and Hughes, 1984) has now been reported by practising teachers and supportive staff into methods of reducing very difficult behaviours, such as violence and extreme disruptiveness, in an educational resource unit for delinquents.

In the first of these studies (Shirodkar and Scherer, 1984) an attempt was made to identify natural occurring reinforcers in a classroom containing violently disruptive adolescents. Four pupils were chosen from this class and arrangements made for them to attend a local college during lunchtime where they could engage in a leisure pursuit of their choice as a potential reinforcer. One of the pupils was also allowed to assist the home economics teacher in school during the lunchtime as a potential reinforcer, these reinforcers being chosen by the youths themselves. The study involved three stages: (1) baseline, (2) teacher monitoring, and (3) pupil self-monitoring. Teacher monitoring consisted of placing a mark on the blackboard against the name of the pupil engaged in a disruptive or aggressive act. Self-monitoring consisted of the pupil carrying out the same procedure. The marks were added up and, when he reached a certain number, the youth was given access to the reinforcer on the next available day. Results showed an immediate increase from (1) to (2) from around 0 to 25 per cent on-task to 80 to 100 per cent on-task for all pupils. This level of on-task behaviour was maintained during stage (3).

In the second study (Scherer and Brown, 1984) a more direct approach to violent behaviour was employed in a secure unit for adolescents. The unit contained two classrooms, a lounge, a dining room, a kitchen, and a bathroom, and each of the eight residents had his own individual bedroom. Incidents involving physical aggression or physical damage to persons or objects were categorized as either: (1) instantaneous violence which did not continue, or (2) violence which persisted beyond a single blow or assault. The study took place over a period of 6 months and comprised three conditions. In stage A, category (2) violence was responded to by using time-out—the violent youth was physically removed to a time-out room, bare of any furniture or dangerous objects for a period of 15 minutes. He remained there alone (but under close supervision at 5-minute intervals), but was allowed to leave if calm after a minimum of 5 minutes. Results showed that during this period the number of time-outs used per week varied from none to twelve, with an average of around five per week.

During stage B, non-exclusion time-out (NETO) was introduced for category (1) behaviours. NETO consisted of issuing the boy with a 'red card' and suspending him from the token economy programme which operated in the unit. On the 'red card' was recorded the boy's name and the dates and times at which the 'red card' commenced and ended. Also recorded on the card were two targets which the boy would have to achieve before being permitted to return to the token economy programme or to consume any back-up reinforcers. These targets were selected so as to teach alternative behaviours to the kind of violence or disruption which had led to the use of the 'red card'. During stage B there was a significant decline in the number of time-outs used, but the frequency of the use of 'red cards' remained at a very high level—more than fifteen per week.

During stage C, an attempt was made to increase the punitive effect of the 'red card' by removing any limits to the number of points which could be earned by the youths on the token economy. In stages A and B, the youths had a maximum number of points they could earn in each classroom session. In stage C this limit was removed so that, in theory, an infinite number of points could be earned if the youths worked infinitely hard. The results showed that during stage C not only did the use of time-out remain virtually at zero (actually, only one time-out was used in 10 weeks) but also the use of 'red cards' declined from approximately fifteen per week to fewer than three per week.

The Scherer and Brown (1984) study has been able to show that even very high levels of violence and aggressive behaviour can be managed without frequent recourse to extensive extra-classroom facilities such as a time-out room. NETO, in the form of a 'red card', was found to be a practical and successful procedure with delinquent adolescents in a secure setting. The study was not able to show, however, whether the NETO procedure would have operated so successfully without the use of a token reinforcement system which focused on encouraging on-task and academic behaviours. There was also some suggestion in the study that extensive training and close support enhanced the speedy application of the 'red card' procedure by the teaching staff.

In the third of these studies (Scherer, Shirodkar and Hughes, 1984) the use of varying conditions of reinforcement in a secondary classroom was evaluated. Two procedures for delivering points reinforcers for on-task behaviour were examined. During the first condition, points were delivered at the end of the lesson on the basis of subjective recall by the teacher. During the second condition, the teacher observed the class at variable intervals selected randomly, and each of the pupils in the class received a '1' alongside his name on the blackboard if he was on-task at the observation point. Each '1' represented ten points, exchangeable for desirable leisure activities later in the school day. Results showed that immediate points delivery for on-task behaviour was more effective than delayed points in reducing the rate of off-task behaviour, and in the frequency of disruptive and violent episodes. The teaching staff involved in this study also commented that the procedure made minimal additional demands on them, and the management of the school commented that inexpensive back-ups could be found easily in an educational setting.

The burgeoning literature on the use of contingent reinforcement techniques by teachers in primary and special education settings is a tradition quite separate from that described by Hargreaves (1982) on teaching style or general classroom teacher behaviour. What both approaches share, however, is a focus on analysis, monitoring, and experimentation in the behaviour of the teacher in the classroom. What both approaches assume is that the teachers' behaviour is a significant cause of disruption on the part of pupils in classrooms. The unspoken assumption that the term 'disruptive behaviour' labels only the functioning of children has to be abandoned.

The more recent studies quoted above are beginning to explore practical methods which can be used in classrooms with very difficult adolescents, and this work represents an advance on the more limited focus of earlier behavioural applications which paid little heed to the practicality of resource demand. The next 5 years or so should see further development in the use of specific behavioural techniques which pay close attention to the descriptive work on teacher interaction styles, thereby helping to develop further positive and practical approaches in the classroom which will not appear to be dauntingly complex, excessively specialized, or ethically obnoxious.

Other approaches

Although on most occasions an experienced teacher can deal with misbehaviour, disruption, and perhaps occasional violent episodes so as to ensure that a productive, happy atmosphere is maintained in the classroom, there is widespread acceptance that, occasionally, the cause of the breakdown in relationship between teacher and pupils is so serious that either the pupil must be removed from the ordinary classroom or outside help must be offered to the pupil to ameliorate the situation. Moreover, for the vast majority of teachers in ordinary schools, some balance has to be found between the needs and rights of pupils and those of teachers. It is crucial for schools to be organized so that such behaviour is reduced, and certainly both pupils and teacher have the right to dignity and freedom from bullying, sarcasm, and abuse of legitimate or coercive authority. In such situations, two additional approaches remain for the school and the teacher to use to manage disruptive and violent behaviour. One approach is the use of procedures introduced by the teacher (or a pastoral care specialist in a secondary school) which focus on self-management by the *pupil* of the difficult behaviour. The second approach is to refer the child to a specialist therapist, say, a clinical or educational psychologist or a schools counsellor, for one or other of the variety of cognitive behavioural therapeutic approaches now developed in clinics, hospitals, or other settings for children and adolescents.

Self-management techniques

There has been a growing interest by educational and child development researchers in the effectiveness of procedures to teach children to regulate their own behaviour (Graziano and Mooney, 1984). These research workers have tended to define self-management as a sequence of three activities to be carried out by the child — self-monitoring, self-evaluation, and self-reinforcement. Self-monitoring is assumed to be a process in which the child keeps track of his own behaviour through self-observation and recording. The study already quoted (Shirodkar and Scherer, 1984) used a typical self-monitoring procedure—the child placing a check or mark on the blackboard against his or her own name whenever a previously defined action occurred. Shirodkar and Scherer report no difficulties in secondary age pupils in a classroom containing violently disruptive adolescents carrying out this procedure. Other techniques of self-monitoring include frequency counts, cumulative frequency counts, and day-to-day diary accounts. Recent research has shown that each of these techniques can be used effectively by junior and secondary age children (see Graziano and Mooney, 1984). Considerable help, however, has to be given to the child by the teacher in designing the self-monitoring programme and perhaps in preparing data sheets and recording procedures.

Self-evaluation simply involves an extension of self-monitoring and, again, ample opportunity for discussing progress in self-recording is required from the class teacher. Although the teacher needs to help, the children should be largely responsible for defining the specific target behaviours they wish to achieve, carrying out their own daily monitoring of progress, recording and evaluating their behaviour, and arranging for their own reinforcement. The majority of self-management programmes of this kind have used reinforcement as the end process in the self-management sequence, usually in the form of consumable back-ups or points which can be cashed in later to purchase such back-ups. In one study, however, the effects of self-regulated punishment on classroom disruption and academic behaviour has been reported (Humphrey *et al.*, 1978).

In this latter study, the teacher established a baseline measure of classroom disruption and levels of academic behaviour in a primary school classroom group. The teacher introduced a token economy in the classroom, giving points for increasing positive behaviours to one group, allowing another group to use self-managed positive token reinforcement, and requiring a third group to use self-managed response costs (i.e. self-managed removal of points when off-task or disrupting). Results obtained in the study showed that all three groups improved in academic performance and reduced the frequency of their disruptive behaviour, but the self-managed reinforcement group improved reading rates and workbook performance to a significantly greater extent. Use of self-managed punishment, although effective, was found not to be a good substitute for self-regulated positive reinforcement. It remains to be seen whether a combination of both self-regulation procedures—reinforcement and response cost—might produce an effect which is more powerful in reducing disruption and increasing academic performance than either technique alone. Other reported attempts to use self-management procedures have suggested that the process of encouraging the violent or disruptive child to engage in self-monitoring may itself be a significant factor in helping the child to maintain improved behaviour over long periods of time. In general, most of the self-management programmes described in the educational literature combine the use of self-evaluation, monitoring, and reinforcement with a well-organized token reinforcement system in the classroom similar to those described in the previous section. How effective these programmes are in the long term, however, is as yet unclear.

Cognitive-behavioural intervention

In recent years a number of intervention strategies for dealing with individual pupils exhibiting extreme anxiety, anger, impulsive and aggressive behaviour have been developed under the general rubric of cognitive-behavioural approaches. There is no one theory of cognition which accounts for all of these approaches, and each tends to be employed for a limited range of presenting problems. What they have in common, however, is a focus on the use of verbal mediation in the form of cognitive skills, strategies, and self-instruction as a means of influencing feelings and behaviour. They also share the use of verbal mediation to enhance problem solving, reduce destructive and unpleasant emotions, evaluate alternative plans of action in social situations like the classroom, change beliefs, and increase the range and effectiveness of social interaction skills. There is rapid growth of interest in these approaches, so that advisory and specialist staff such as psychologists, school counsellors, and social workers will in future years have increasing opportunities to use each of the particular techniques described here. At the present, however, the development of these techniques is at an early stage, and teachers and other staff may need to explore them in order to seek out how valuable and useful they are in the classroom.

Interpersonal cognitive problem solving (ICPS)   Interpersonal cognitive problem solving (ICPS) is discussed elsewhere in this book (chapter 5 by Laing and Chazan). It derives from the work of Spivack *et al.* (1976) who explored how children and adolescents solve problems in interactions. Their assumption was that, if behaviour is to be changed, the specific cognitions that mediate the behaviour must also be affected. In particular, the child must be taught how to take different perspectives, generate alternative solutions, work out solutions step-by-step, think through a problem, and make connections between causes and effects. The ICPS approach focuses on changing *how* the child should think rather than *what* the child should think.

Evaluation of the use of ICPS (Spivack and Shure, 1974) suggests that, for children in infant school classes, alternative solution thinking is the best predictor of longer-term good social adjustment. Later, in the junior school classroom group, the inability to articulate spontaneously the sequence of steps needed to carry out solutions to interpersonal problems is associated with the use of physical or verbal force as a means of reaching personal goals. In adolescence, deficiencies in perspective taking, alternative solution thinking, and means–end thinking, are all prominent in pupils described as impulsive in ordinary classrooms (Spivack and Levine, 1963). More recent research evaluating the effectiveness of ICPS skills training has produced mixed results (Weissberg and Gesten, 1982), with a general conclusion suggesting the need to improve the instruction and supervision of trainers in ICPS skills. Neither is there any evidence available yet of the effectiveness of ICPS training methods in classroom groups, although a full scripted programme for teaching alternative solutions and consequential thinking to 4- or 5-year olds in small groups has been published by Spivack and Shure (1974). For teachers who want further details of this technique, Weissberg and Gesten (1982) have described how ICPS training can be used in the classroom, including role play and reflecting techniques.

Cognitive social skills training Most social skills training has aimed to increase social behaviours likely to promote positive interactions between the pupil and peers or between the child and adults. Well-developed programmes for use in the classroom, for example, have been published by Goldstein *et al.* (1980), but more recent developments have focused not so much on the skills training as on the use of covert verbalization. Such interventions are designed particularly for children and adolescents who are aggressive in such settings as the classroom. The use of covert self-statements to mediate the acquisition and generalization of social skills has been given support by recent research evaluating behaviourally orientated social skills training (Halford, 1983). This research shows limited generalization unless booster sessions, varied *in vivo* practice, and the use of self-statements are introduced into the skills training approach.

Assessment of the use of covert self-instruction has been developed by Meichenbaum (1979), who has described several useful approaches to assessing such cognition—e.g. the use of self-report in conjunction with a videotape of the child's behaviour such that the child watches the tape and says what he was thinking, and the use of imagery to describe thoughts and feelings he had at the time. Procedures involved in cognitive social skills training consist of the teaching of new self-statements using teaching methods such as modelling, rehearsal and feedback, sometimes with self-instruction. Typically, over a period of 10–12 weekly sessions of up to 1 hour, the child learns how irrational beliefs encourage and develop strong emotional arousal; how to examine self-statements in social situations; and how to acquire new rational beliefs modelled by the therapist and rehearsed by the child. With the continuing use of self-instruction, later sessions enable the child to progress through graded steps of challenging maladaptive beliefs, learning new self-statements and then matching them sequentially to non-verbal and verbal assertive behaviours, such as relaxed posture, good eye contact, and serious expression, at the same time as using voice control and slow speech.

There is need for caution in the use of CSST since there is, as yet, a paucity of research evaluating it, and little evidence that the approach is usable except by counselling and other specialist support staff outside the classroom setting.

Stress inoculation Stress inoculation has been developed by Novaco (1978, 1979) to help people cope with anger. Its focus is on the emotional reaction inside the person rather than on interpersonal control and interaction. The term draws on concepts borrowed from engineering and medicine, emphasizing as it does the use of controlled exposure as a means of building-in coping mechanisms. Stress inoculation has been developed as an approach primarily with adults experiencing uncontrollable anger and anxiety. Its development for children and adolescents presenting with disruptive or violent behaviours in the classroom setting is in the very early stages, but some practical methods for teachers to try have been published (see, for example, Brown, 1982).

Assessment tends to involve an analysis of the emotional components of outbursts of anger or violence in terms of their frequency, intensity, duration, mode of expression, and effects on performance, health and personal relationships. Thus a link is formed between maladaptive thoughts or beliefs and emotional overreactions on the part of the child, and what ideas, thoughts, and experiences are associated with outbursts of anger. Stress inoculation involves several phases. In the first, an educational phase, the child is taught to understand the physiological and cognitive aspects of strong emotional reaction such as extreme temper loss. The child is encouraged to keep a diary or a log. In the second phase, coping skills are taught to the child. *Coping* is defined as the linking of maladaptive thoughts and feelings to new adaptive statements. Thoughts and feelings which previously led to explosive temper are now the signal for cognitive coping statements. These skills are rehearsed, with a particular focus on confronting and handling stresses, coping with feelings of being overwhelmed, and the use of reinforcing self-statements. Finally, the child is encouraged to practise these newly acquired coping skills, first of all in role rehearsal with the therapist and later in *in vivo* training. Basic relaxation is often used in conjunction with this rehearsal and practice. Graphic examples of this approach to working with angry and aggressive children have been published by Segrave (1979).

'Think Aloud' programmes   The 'Think Aloud' programmes developed by Camp and Bush (1981) are of particular interest to teachers, both because they are well-developed packages and because they combine and integrate a number of the approaches already described in this chapter. The programme is designed to teach self-verbalization skills to young, violent children. The children are taught to ask four questions out loud themselves—What is my problem? What is my plan? Am I using my plan? How did I do? Cue cards are used to signal to the child to think aloud as a series of increasingly complex problems are presented by the teacher. With frequent practice, the children acquire cognitive skills to plan action and use these to guide performance. The methods have been found to be useful with children of up to 8 or 9 years of age, but no research data are currently available relating to older children. Complete and explicit instructions are available to teachers in the Camp and Bush (1981) publication.

Summary and conclusion

In a recent report on improving secondary schools, Hargreaves (1984) identifies four objectives for educational achievement: remembering and using facts, using practical and spoken skills, the ability to communicate and cooperate, and dealing with setbacks and difficulties. In this chapter, the wide variety of social learning approaches available to teachers and other advisory and supportive staff have been described. What can be achieved with the use of these approaches is a step in the direction of two of these four objectives—communicating and cooperating and dealing with setbacks and difficulties. It is not intended, however, that the chapter should be understood as providing a menu of solutions for the teacher who is face to face with violence in the classroom. It is, rather, an attempt to suggest a number of approaches derived from the social learning perspective which may be useful. What is evident in this review is the limited extent of our knowledge of the impact that general teaching style and specific individual approaches in the classroom by the teacher can have on disruptive and violent behaviour. Yet, the general theme of research suggests that, whilst teaching style and specific behavioural interventions are necessary for dealing constructively with disruption and violence, they are not sufficient to ensure the development and persistence of the child's self-controlled behaviour. The recent development of cognitive behavioural approaches has perhaps provided an additional range of interventions which can help to augment the use of teaching style and direct intervention in the classroom. The extent remains to be seen to which these methods can be adapted to the resources available to the teacher in the mainstream classroom. Whether teachers *should be expected* to deal with such problems remains an important question.

Neither is the intention of the chapter to try to persuade teachers that they have many new tricks to learn. As Hargreaves (1982) suggests, teachers in ordinary classrooms know more than they sometimes think they know, and they ought, perhaps, to be considerably more sceptical of 'experts'. The use of improved technique may well be a necessary condition for some teachers to deal more effectively with violence and disruption in their classes but, in the end, as is shown in *Fifteen Thousand Hours* (Rutter *et al.*, 1979), it is the teachers' and the school's philosophy and basic assumptions about children and education, rather than specific technique, which will have the most lasting and significant effect. It is the basic social learning orientation of the range of approaches described here that is of significance—an orientation which assumes (1) that behaviour of children and teachers is related systematically to its circumstances; (2) that problems for children and teachers in the classroom are associated with deficits in interactive social skills; (3) that thinking and feeling processes are important in mediating the development and use of those skills; (4) that the philosophy of the staffroom for the teacher and the pressure of the peer group for the child are significant influences. Although there is nothing new about this general philosophy, in this chapter some of the practical methods of carrying out that philosophy have been outlined. What is now needed is a thorough evaluation of those practical methods.

References

Abbott, K. (1984) An analysis of compliance and non-compliance in the classroom. Unpublished MPhil thesis. Institute of Psychiatry, University of London.

Ayllon, T., Layman, D., and Kandal, H. (1975) A behavioural-educational alternative to drug control of hyperactive children, *Journal of Applied Behavioral Analysis*, **8**, 137–146.

Brown, B. J. (1982) Dealing with violence: a multi-level approach with young people, *Orchard Lodge Studies of Deviance*, **2**, 15–31.

Brown, B. J., and Drinkwater, J. (1984) A method of recording violent episodes in residential care using behavioural analysis, *Orchard Lodge Studies of Deviance*, **4**, 3, 185–200.

Camp, B. W., and Bush, M. A. S. (1981) *Think Aloud: Increasing Social and Cognitive Skills—A Problem-solving Program for Children*. Research Press, Champaign, Ill.

Fishbein, M., and Wasik, B. (1981) Effect of the good behaviour game on disruptive library behaviour, *Journal of Applied Behavioral Analysis*, **14**, 89–93.

Goldstein, A. P., Sprafkin, R. P., Gershaw, J. J., and Klein, P. (1980) Social skills through structural learning. In G. Cartledge and J. F. Milburn (eds) *Teaching Skills to Children: Innovative Approaches*. Pergamon Press, New York.

Graziano, A. M., and Mooney, K. C. (1984) *Children and Behaviour Therapy*. Aldine, New York.

Halford, K. (1983) Teaching rational self-talk to help socially isolated children and youth. In A. Ellis and M. E. Bernard (eds), *Rational-Emotive Approaches to the Problems of Childhood*. Plenum Press, New York.

Hargreaves, D. H. (1982) Teachers' knowledge of behaviour problems. In G. Upton and A. Gobell (eds), *Behaviour Problems in the Comprehensive School*. University College, Cardiff.

Hargreaves, D. H. (1984) *Improving Secondary Schools*. ILEA Publications Unit, London.

Hargreaves, D. H., Hestor, S., and Mellor, F. J. (1975) *Deviance in Classrooms*. Routledge & Kegan Paul, London.

Humphrey, L., Karoly, P., and Kirschenbaum, D. S. (1978) Self-management in the classroom: self-imposed response cost versus self-reward, *Behaviour Therapy*, **9**, 592-601.

Kounin, J. S. (1970) *Discipline and Group Management in Classrooms*. Holt, Rinehart, & Winston, London.

Lane, D. A. (1978) *The Impossible Child*, vol. 2. ILEA Publications Unit, London.

Long, J. D., and Williams, R. L. (1973) *Classroom Management with Adolescents*. MSS Information Corporation, New York.

Marlowe, R. H., Madsen, C. H., Jr, Bowen, C. E., Reardon, R. C., and Logue, P. E. (1978) Severe classroom behavioural problems: teachers or counsellors, *Journal of Applied Behavioral Analysis*, **11**, 53-66.

Meichenbaum, D. (1979) Teaching children self-control. In B. Lahey and A. Kazdin (eds), *Advances in Child Psychology*, vol. 2. Plenum Press, New York.

Mortimore, P., Davies, J., Varlaam, A., and West, A. (1983) *Behaviour Problems in Schools: An Evaluation of Support Centres*. Croom Helm, London.

Novaco, R. W. (1978) Anger and coping with stress. In J. Foreyt and D. Rathjen (eds), *Cognitive Behaviour Therapy: Therapy Research and Practice*. Plenum Press, New York.

Novaco, R. W. (1979) The cognitive regulation of anger and stress. In P. C. Kendall and S. D. Hollon (eds), *Cognitive-behavioural Interventions: Theory, Research and Procedures*. Academic Press, New York.

Presland, J. (1977) Behaviour modification in day (ESN(M)) schools, *AEP Journal*, **4**, 33-37.

Presland, J. (1982) Behaviour modification in secondary schools. In G. Upton and A. Gobell (eds), *Behaviour Problems in the Comprehensive School*. University College, Cardiff.

Rutter, M., Maughan, B., Mortimore, P., and Ouston, J. (1979) *Fifteen Thousand Hours: Secondary Schools and their Effects on Children*. Open Books, London.

Scherer, M., and Brown, B. J. (1984) Time out: an alternative to rooms. Paper presented at the ABAC Annual Conference, Bulmershe College, Reading, July 1984.

Scherer, M., Shirodkar, H., and Hughes, R. (1984) Reducing disruptive behaviours: a brief report of three successful procedures, *Behavioural Approaches with Children*, **8**, 53-57.

Segrave, J. (1979) Stress inoculation program for children. Unpublished manuscript. Department of Education, University of Melbourne, Australia.

Shirodkar, H., and Scherer, M. (1984) Development of appropriate classroom behaviour by positive reward and maintenance by pupil self-evaluation in a special school classroom, *Orchard Lodge Studies of Deviance*, **4**, 25-36.

Spivack, G., and Levine, M. (1963) *Self-regulation in acting out and normal adolescents*. Report No. M4531. National Institute for Mental Health, Washington, DC.

Spivack, G., Platt, J., and Shurer, M. (1976) *The Problem-solving Approach to Adjustment*. Jossey-Bass, San Francisco.

Spivack, G., and Shure, M. (1974) *Social Adjustment of Young Children: A Cognitive Approach to Solving Real-life Problems*. Jossey-Bass, San Francisco.

Torode, B. (1976) Teachers' talk and classroom discipline. In M. Stubbs and S. Delamont (eds), *Explorations in Classroom Observation*, Wiley, London.

Weissberg, R. P., and Gesten, E. (1982) Considerations for developing effective school-based social problem-solving (SPS) training programs, *School Psychology Review*, **11**, 56–63.

Management of Disruptive Pupil Behaviour in Schools
Edited by D. P. Tattum
©1986 John Wiley & Sons Ltd

_____ *11* ___

Psychiatric aspects of problem behaviour: a consultative approach

Derek Steinberg

When is a problem a psychiatric problem? The philosophical issues surrounding this question are endless and controversial, but for the purposes of this chapter I would like to deal with the more specific and practical issue of when to refer a boy or girl for psychiatric help, and what sort of help to anticipate. On this basis the problems that children present in school can be divided, very broadly, into three groups.

Firstly, there are those problems which the school staff will be able to manage with some outside advice and help, even if it is not clear at first that they will be able to do so. Teachers and other school-based staff already manage a wide range of very difficult behaviour, and one way in which help can be provided by a specialist psychiatric team is by offering advice, or by providing consultation rather than by direct clinical intervention. The term 'consultation' is used in a special sense in this chapter, and is discussed below (p. 200).

Secondly, there are many problems where a psychiatric team can make a significant direct contribution to the boy or girl's management, but where it makes sense for much of this management to be based in the school, usually indeed in the same classroom, and where collaborative work between teachers and psychiatric team is needed.

Thirdly, there are some problems where the psychiatrist and his or her colleagues need to spend rather more time on specialist clinical work with the child, so that while liaison with the school remains important, a major focus for the psychiatrist is the work which goes on with the child in the clinic. For example, the child and family may be seen regularly for family therapy, or the young person for individual psychotherapy or counselling. Less commonly, the child may be prescribed medication. At the end of this spectrum of degrees of psychiatric intervention is the relatively rare need for the boy or girl to be admitted to a psychiatric hospital unit.

Of course, these three broad approaches—consultative, collaborative, and clinical—are by no means mutually exclusive. Nevertheless they represent three fundamentally distinct approaches to psychiatric difficulties, and reflect the reality that children's behavioural problems are extremely variable, that psychiatric disorders are not easily defined, that major mental illness is rather rare, and that the experience, skills, and interests of different professionals who work with children overlap a good deal (Steinberg, 1981, 1983). For such reasons psychiatrists and their colleagues do not limit themselves to clinical diagnosis alone, but tend to respond with a more broadly based assessment of the child and the circumstances, and to invite negotiation about which worker in school, clinic, or elsewhere is in the best position to do what.

Psychiatric teams and their approach

For complex historical reasons (Steinberg, 1983) psychiatric services for children are based in a variety of settings, e.g. in local authority premises (as child guidance units or clinics), in general hospitals as part of the outpatient services, and in psychiatric hospitals. In most areas there will be inpatient facilities for adolescents and for younger children, with outpatient and sometimes day patient services too. The traditional nucleus of the child psychiatric team is psychiatrist, social worker, and psychologist, and there is a tendency for the latter to be an educational psychologist in local authority services or a clinical psychologist in health authority services. The team may also include a child psychotherapist.

Each clinic has its own way of assessing a child's problem. Most are variants of the following basic approach: an individual diagnostic (physical and psychological) assessment of the boy or girl; a meeting with the parents (and often with the whole family) to build up a picture of the child's development and behaviour so far, and of current family relationships; and a request (with the family's permission) for a school report on the child's academic and social performance and on the special problems, if any, evident in school. Areas of success and competence are, of course, as important as symptoms and problems.

The incidence of psychiatric disorder

In a study of the 10–11-year-old child population of the Isle of Wight, carried out in the mid-1960s, Rutter and his colleagues found an incidence of psychiatric disorder of around 7 per cent (Rutter *et al.*, 1970). These included neurotic (emotional) disorders, antisocial (conduct) disorders, mixed (emotional and conduct) disorders, personality disorders, psychosis, and the hyperkinetic syndrome. The latter three were quite rare. These workers defined *psychiatric disorders* as abnormality of behaviour, emotions, or relationships which was continuing up to the time of assessment and was sufficiently marked and sufficiently prolonged to cause handicap (in the broad sense of some degree of disability) to the child himself and/or distress or disturbance in the family or community. *Abnormality* was judged in the broader context of the child's development, since transient fluctuation in function and performance is part of normal development. The abnormality had to be persistent and handicapping or distressing. The researchers stressed that this definition did not mean that if expert help were needed psychiatrists were necessarily the appropriate workers to involve. That, as we have seen earlier, depends on wider factors than the description of the child's problem alone.

Since Rutter *et al.*'s (1970) study, there have been further surveys of mental health in childhood in other settings and other age groups, some by the Isle of Wight team and some by others. The overall picture that emerged included the following: firstly, among children of the same age, psychiatric disorder, as defined above, was found to be twice as common in Inner London as in the Isle of Wight; secondly, in adolescence the rate rises to around 10–15 per cent (Graham and Rutter, 1973; Rutter *et al.*, 1976). Some studies, which have included parents' and teachers' ratings as well as assessment of children, have found a rate of psychiatric symptomatology as high as 21 per cent in some adolescent populations (Leslie, 1974), including distressing symptoms of which parents and teachers were unaware (Rutter *et al.*, 1976). This latter study was important in affirming that, at least in the younger adolescent, serious rebelliousness about major issues is *not* common—the 'generation gap' is largely mythical—while distressing inner feelings of sadness and over-sensitivity are not uncommon. This is not to say that aggressive rebelliousness on the part of adolescents is rare; teachers know it happens, and in some settings it is common. However, whatever its origin, there is no reason to regard serious, persistent rebelliousness and misbehaviour in adolescence as 'normal', to be expected, or to be taken for granted.

In this respect schools vary considerably in their rates of behaviour problems and of psychiatric referral, and this has been shown in studies that were designed to allow for possible differences from area to area and from school to school. The differences found between schools was a real one (Gath *et al.*, 1977), and this is paralleled by other studies which have demonstrated major variations between schools in terms of other sorts of behaviour, e.g. absenteeism (Galloway, 1976; and see Rutter *et al.*, 1979). When we consider high levels of problem behaviour in the context of this degree of possible variation between schools, the distinction between individual disorder on the one hand, and problematic behaviour resulting from the way the child is handled on the other, becomes unclear and open to argument. It will not be taken further here.

Psychiatric treatment

A child psychiatric team will ordinarily have most or all of the following types of approach at its disposal.

Psychodynamically based psychotherapy

The essence of psychotherapy is to bring about a change in the patient's feelings, attitudes, and (as a result) behaviour by way of the therapist–patient relationship. To put a complex and indeed contentious issue briefly, the principles underlying psychotherapy are based on the three following assumptions.

Firstly, the patient brings into the therapeutic relationship an aspect of himself that, for someone, is a problem; e.g. the naughty child misbehaves in the therapeutic setting, perhaps being defiant towards the therapist because anger and sadness about his parents make him angry and fed up with most adults.

Secondly, the therapist, by trying to understand *why* the child acts that way, is able to get it into perspective himself, and then try to handle the child in such a way that alternative ways of feeling and behaving become possible. Thus, by the therapist's persistence with the child despite his defiance (but not necessarily being permissive about it) the child might learn a wider range of feelings and behaviour towards the therapist. Protest, sadness, and defiance become accompanied (not replaced) by feelings of acceptance, trust, optimism, and friendliness. This is not based on the therapist simply being 'nice'; on the contrary, the therapist may be quite demanding. But the therapist manages the relationship so that as far as possible the child 'sticks with' the therapy and is not so destructive, physically or metaphorically, that the possibility of treatment ceases. Such changes for the better as occur take place gradually, in fits and starts, accompanied not by dramatic changes of mind but by the gradually developing capacity in the child to tolerate mixed feelings, experience new ones and explore new attitudes.

Thirdly, it is expected, or hoped, that any changes for the better that occur in the psychotherapeutic sessions will generalize to other relationships. The child, behaving more constructively and in a more age-appropriate way with the therapist (e.g. an adolescent may argue where he used to have infantile tantrums), now begins to behave this way in other relationships and settings.

To understand what he is doing, the psychotherapist will use a psycho-dynamic frame of reference that informs the assumptions he makes about the child, guides the strategies he adopts, and indeed sustains the psycho-therapist in what can be demanding work with few early rewards. Which frame of reference he uses depends on his experience, training, and taste; there are an enormous number of variations of the basic Freudian, Jungian, and other sets of theory.

There are also many variations in practice. For example, a psychotherapist may see the child individually, in a group, or regularly with his family. He may use play (with sand, clay, or other materials), art, drama, or music as an active basis for therapy; hence the play, art, drama, and music therapists (see, for example, Alvin, 1966; Millar, 1973; Brown and Pedder, 1980; Kahn and Wright, 1980; Warren, 1984; Dalley, 1984; Steinberg, 1986).

Among the many criticisms of psychotherapy have been the length, frequency, and intensity of *psychoanalytic* psychotherapeutic sessions; its reliance on the patient's 'self-expression' during which the psychoanalytic psychotherapist, traditionally, was supposed merely to listen, accept, and nod his head from time to time; and the selection for psychotherapy of the most articulate, reasonably behaved patients who were most likely to improve anyway. It is important to appreciate that recent developments in child psychotherapy are moving away from strict psychoanalytical orthodoxies and towards briefer, more understandable and more practical approaches. There has been increasing use of other methods as adjuncts (e.g. dealing with actual social problems, or using ideas drawn from behaviour therapy), more attention is being devoted to how the child actually behaves with parents, teachers, and therapists rather than to speculation about what 'must be' going on in his head, and there is a greater willingness to consider for psychotherapeutic treatment the more deprived, disturbed, destructive, and indeed less articulate boys and girls (e.g. see Boston and Szur, 1983).

It is true that much of psychotherapy remains obscure, difficult to describe, and of uncertain value. However, it is not true to suggest, as some do, that it has remained fixated along the Freudian classical psychoanalytic lines of the 1920s and 1930s. It has developed many quite different methods and, although they still await proper evaluation, the persisting notion that some troubled young people gain something from regular conversations with a mature, experienced professional worker skilled in psychotherapy is a compelling one.

Psychotherapy, then, is not to be dismissed. However, it is not a panacea, nor is it always practicable. It is not uncommon for psychiatrists and psychotherapists to be referred wildly misbehaving, defiant, and self-destructive children for whom 'all else has failed' and who are deemed to be 'deeply disturbed' and in need of 'deep treatment'. Often there is no way such young people can be engaged in psychotherapy, at least until they are a little more self-contained, and until that time there may be no alternative to being 'contained' in a more pragmatic way, by firm limit setting at school and in the family through authoritative adult controls, and in extreme situations in residential schools or homes. Some of these operate as *therapeutic communities*, that is to say they help a boy or girl by social means to attain a greater sense of security, self-esteem, and responsibility. It is, in a sense, psychotherapy delivered by the social group of staff and peers rather than by an individual therapist (Lennhoff and Lampen, 1968; Lampen, 1978).

Family therapy

Family therapy is worth distinguishing from psychodynamic psychotherapy even though many of its principles are derived from it. Some distinguish the *psychoanalytic approach*, which postulates and uses (e.g. by interpretation) shared unconscious material within the family, and the *systems approach* which regards the family as a whole interacting system in which individuals play parts which may include the development of symptoms (Bruggen and Davies, 1977). Thus a child's conduct disorder may be a focus for both family and professional attention, serving as a diversion from mother's depression, father's infidelity and alcoholism, and an older sibling's promiscuity as she strives to seek comfort away from the family. The younger child's misbehaviour may be bad enough but, so the systems theory argument runs, everyone in the family has an emotional investment in keeping things the way they are lest even more unmanageable issues have to be tackled. Family therapy is a developing field and many therapists use strategies derived from both psychoanalytic and systems perspectives (see Walrond-Skinner, 1976; Skynner, 1976; Dare, 1986).

Casework

'Casework' is a term used by social workers to describe much of their work. It may involve seeing the child, one or both parents, or the family as a whole (family work) to deal with primarily social issues. For example, parents may be given the task of getting a misbehaving child's behaviour under control (perhaps using a psychologist's advice) if they can, or, if necessary, going on to enlist statutory support by seeking a care order for the child. This may sometimes seem a ponderous approach to a child's problem; none the less misbehaving children can cause chaos, anxiety, and inconsistent behaviour on the part of the adults looking after them and a firm, systematic, step-by-step approach may be needed. For example:

(1) A 13-year-old child's angry misbehaviour, including walking out of school when confronted, is beyond the school's control and the parents are asked to seek help for him.

(2) A psychologist or psychiatrist offers assessment and treatment but the child will not attend the clinic and truants from school. Nor will he stay in the house when a domiciliary visit is attempted; indeed he often stays out all night. Sympathetic attempts to engage the child's cooperation are met with evasion and defiance.

(3) The parents remain responsible for their child but, it seems, cannot control him. Not only can they not establish reasonable behaviour; they cannot get him to attend for appropriate help.

(4) The situation is a serious one with wider implications for the child's wellbeing than school attendance and reasonable behaviour alone. Assuming the problem remains intractable despite efforts to help in other ways, seeking a care order under the Children's and Young Person's Act or the Education Act may prove a necessary precondition to helping the boy, whether by psychiatric or psychological treatment or simply by reestablishing legitimate and appropriate adult controls.

Casework, of course, is by no means concerned only with statutory matters, but also with the clarification of problems (as opposed to diagnosis — see Ragg, 1977), and the reestablishment and affirmation of adult responsibility and authority and, indeed, the proper roles of all family members, even when invoking child care legislation is not relevant.

As a member of a psychiatric team, the social worker often acts as an advisor on social legislation, providing information about children's and parent's rights as well as the rights and responsibilities of the workers on the team. He or she may also undertake family therapy or psychotherapy.

Behavioural therapies

Dynamic psychotherapy sets out to understand behaviour and the motivation behind it. In the behavioural therapies the question is not 'why' but 'what': *In what precise circumstances does particular behaviour occur; what makes it worse and what makes it better; what behaviour is to be discouraged and what behaviour encouraged, and by what strategy?* (See, for example, Brown and Christie, 1981.)

On this basis there is a wide range of behavioural treatments, including *reinforcement* of desired behaviour, e.g. by social encouragement or specific rewards; *desensitization* to feared situations; *response prevention* for the extinction of troublesome behaviour (e.g. obsessive-compulsive habits). These and other methods are discussed more fully elsewhere (chapters 5 and 10). Although behaviour therapy was once considered to be quite distinct from psychotherapy, the process by which a patient or family is helped to clarify desired aims and develop new skills represents a learning process which straddles psychotherapeutic, behavioural, and educational approaches. Behaviour therapy has been regarded by some as inhumane, with notions of people being treated as Pavlovian animals; in fact, for many behavioural approaches the patient is more able to understand and share in the essentially commonsense therapeutic process than would be the case with some of the more interpretative dynamic psychotherapies.

Social and occupational therapies

These therapies involve the systematic use of individual and group activities to develop self-esteem as well as improve skills in these activities (e.g. games, work, interviews).

Medication

Medication has a limited but, for a minority, important place in the treatment of some disorders. Children may be prescribed major or minor tranquillizers, antidepressants, and, rarely, lithium carbonate or the stimulant drugs, while young people who also have epilepsy will be on anticonvulsants. Two important features of medication are that clarity is needed about what drugs the child should be taking, in what dosage, and when; and that many drugs have side-effects that may be troublesome (see Steinberg, 1981, 1983).

Residential treatment in hospital

This is rarely needed and should be distinguished from the need for other forms of residential care and training (Steinberg, 1981, 1982).

Psychiatric disorders causing problem behaviour

Practically any psychiatric or physical health disorder could cause disruptive behaviour; a child with an unrecognized anxiety or phobic state, a pupil with undiagnosed hearing or sight problems or one of the epileptic disorders or general ill-health may well misbehave. Most, if not all, such physical problems will have been diagnosed by the school's medical screening arrangements, and experienced teachers soon recognize the irritable, apathetic, unwell child with a major or minor health problem. In this section the psychiatric disorders most likely to cause disruptive behaviour will be outlined. They are:

(1) *Conduct disorders*, and *mixed disorders of emotion and conduct*.
(2) *Hyperactivity* and the *hyperkinetic syndrome*. Overactivity is common, but the latter syndrome relatively rare.

(3) *Abuse of chemical substances* including solvent abuse and drug taking and the misuse of alcohol.
(4) *The major disorders of personality development*, which are relatively rare.

Other disorders are:

(5) *Obsessive-compulsive disorders*. Minor obsessive behaviour is quite common but handicapping disorder is relatively rare (see Bolton *et al.*, 1983).
(6) *Affective illnesses* (depressive and manic-depressive psychoses) occur rarely in children and adolescents (see review in Steinberg, 1983).
(7) *The schizophrenic psychoses* which are also rare (review in Steinberg, 1983).

Conduct and 'mixed' disorders

A child may misbehave because the rules for conduct have not been made clear, or are not enforced, or both, and because he or she has not been encouraged or stimulated to take part in constructive activities. To this extent misbehaviour in children who are inadequately brought up, trained, and taught is to be expected. Some children, because of individual characteristics or the accumulative effect of experience, or more commonly both, develop a pattern of antisocial behaviour which is sufficiently persistent, intractable, and pervasive to be identified as conduct disorder, although the unsatisfactory aspects of this term are acknowledged. Certainly, children identified in this way tend to have many factors in common: they are often boys; are often from lower socio-economic families which are large and crowded; have commonly experienced marital discord, family disruption, and separation; tend towards the lower end of the normal range of intelligence and have educational and particularly reading problems, although the latter is true only of those whose problems begin in pre-adolescence. There may be evidence of brain damage in some, a history of always having been impulsive and intractable, and of having been exposed to punitive, overpermissive, or inconsistent discipline, and poor (i.e. aggressive and antisocial) adult example. This is, of course, a stereotype from the individual child's point of view, but statistically there is no doubt that such characteristics and circumstances tend to cluster in these children.

The form the misbehaviour takes may be broadly categorized into:

(1) *Solitary misconduct* such as lying, stealing, absconding, or being physically and verbally abusive; when it is confined largely to the family the outlook is not so poor as for other categories.

(2) *Group misconduct*, in which a gang of youngsters misbehave in a group which generally includes normal children, and in which the child with conduct disorder may be a leader or a follower.

(3) *Conduct disorder accompanied by significant emotional problems* such as anxiety, misery, or outbursts of rage. In fact, children with apparently 'pure' conduct disorder are often unhappy about what they get away with and commonly have sad and fearful feelings and low self-esteem. In this respect the experienced adult has little difficulty in distinguishing children with normal mischievousness and high spirits from troubled, misbehaving children. Another characteristic of the latter is that while they are difficult much of the time, there is often an individual who is able to elicit reasonable behaviour and constructive activity from them, and this is often a matter for puzzlement and frustration.

Epilepsy as such does not cause misbehaviour (except in rare cases where the fits themselves include neurologically determined antisocial behaviour), but a minority of children with epilepsy have some of the disadvantages mentioned above (e.g. brain injury, learning problems) and this plus social stigma and the effects of medication can cause problem behaviour (Shaffer, 1977; Werry, 1979).

For a minority of children with conduct disorder, individual psycho-therapy, family therapy or casework, helps resolve the emotional problems behind the misconduct or reasserts proper parental care and control. For a very small number, medication (e.g. antidepressants for the depressed misbehaving child) is helpful. However, for the majority, collaborative work between clinic, family, and school, including systematic attention to the child's behaviour, and if necessary a behaviour therapy programme, is the most realistic approach. The outlook for children with conduct disorder, especially when accompanied by aggressive behaviour in the school years, when it is frequent and varied, and when it persists outside the child's immediate family and circle, is poor; many of these young people tend to become adults with psychiatric problems and difficulties with relationships and who clash with the law (Robins, 1979).

Hyperactivity and the hyperkinetic syndrome

In North America the syndrome of 'hyperactivity' is a common diagnosis, while in Britain the reverse is the case and in some surveys it is quite rare Shaffer and Greenhill, 1979; Sandberg *et al.*, 1978; Taylor, 1980). Many misbehaving children are overactive, or are perceived as over-active by exhausted adults. However, the term *hyperkinetic syndrome* is best confined to extreme degrees of overactivity, often accompanied by excitable, impulsive, and even dangerous behaviour, occurring in practically every situation the child enters, and with a very short attention span (measurable in seconds) and extreme distractability. Correspondingly the child has major educational problems. The hyperkinetic syndrome occurs in children who are in other respects quite normal, but is commonly associated with brain damage (including epilepsy) and mental retardation. These children may become underactive and apathetic in adolescence, and in later life have problems in social adaptation. Behaviour therapy, involving systematic training and rewards, can be effective, and some of these children benefit very considerably from stimulant drugs such as amphetamines, which in this age group and this disorder act paradoxically. These drugs are most effective when attention-span problems are particularly prominent. They have serious side-effects, including mood disorder, sleep and appetite problems, and retardation of growth, and need careful supervision. However, the syndrome is grossly disabling and psychiatrists may try these drugs if all else fails. It must be noted, however, that in the United States this medication is prescribed far more widely than in Great Britain. Occasionally major tranquillizers such as chlorpromazine or haloperidol prove useful alternatives.

Overactivity and other conduct problems are sometimes attributed to allergy by professional workers and others, and various diets are prescribed. It is difficult to evaluate this, particularly because of the extreme variation in the diagnosis of these disorders. In a helpful and well-balanced review, Taylor (1979) concludes that there is no evidence that food additives are a major cause of hyperactivity, nor diets helpful for most, and points out that interfering with diet can be risky; however, he suggests that in some cases the clinician can respond to the request for a diet by supervising what is in effect an experimental treatment for the child in question.

Lead in the child's environment and its precise relationship to his development, educational problems, and conduct disorder remains a complex issue (Yule *et al.*, 1981), but most authorities feel that the association is strong enough for urgent priority to be given to reduce the amount of lead in the environment.

Drug abuse and related conditions

The misuse by adolescents of a whole range of substances, from solvents to alcohol, and including whatever drug is currently fashionable and 'pushed' commercially, is increasing. As far as alcohol is concerned, Ritson (1981) has pointed out that proper concern about the disorder *alcoholism* has tended to detract attention from the other ways in which the casual misuse of alcohol damages family life and careers, results in criminal behaviour and accidents, and is sometimes associated with self-poisoning by other drugs. He suggests that education about alcohol should be provided in schools.

Solvent abuse involves an extraordinarily wide range of substances that are readily available in shops, including model-making cement, rubber solutions, nail polish remover, dry-cleaning fluids, typing correction fluids, aerosols, and petrol. They are usually inhaled from a soaked handkerchief or from a plastic bag or empty crisp packet. They produce a temporary, disorientating, excited state not unlike alcohol intoxication; indeed, many children who abuse solvents would use alcohol if they could obtain or afford it. Sudden death has been reported, and nausea, vomiting, and cardiac arrhythmias occur, but related accidents such as suffocation, falling from heights, and road accidents seem the greatest risk. Children who chronically abuse solvents include a high proportion with emotional and conduct disorders and delinquency, but there is little evidence of physical dependence, i.e. 'addiction' (Strang and Connell, 1985). Children who have been experimenting with these substances have a chemical smell on the breath for a time and may have a characteristic red ring around the mouth, sometimes accompanied by boils.

Major disorders of personality development

By late adolescence, some children with persisting conduct disorders seem to be entering the group who in adult life will be said to suffer from *psychopathic* (or *sociopathic*) personality disorders. (There is a whole range of other identified personality types, some coming close to the psychotic illnesses (Steinberg, 1985) and some merging with normality and whose definition is correspondingly difficult and controversial.) Nevertheless, there is no doubt that there is a hard core of severely disturbed individuals, commonly described as psychopathic, who are characterized by a disregard for social obligations, a lack of feeling for other people, and a tendency to be impulsively violent or to show lesser degrees of antisocial behaviour, e.g. deception. However, it is never clear which severely disturbed adolescents will be recruited to their numbers, nor who will respond to help, and the early recognition of major deviations of personality development, and real attempts to help, remain worthwhile.

For a proportion who are hard to contain or control in school and at home residential schooling may be appropriate, as for other young people with conduct problems. It takes time to obtain suitable places, and the need for residential schooling is best recognized early.

Therapeutic communities are helpful for some young people, and rely on social pressure and the expectation of reasonable behaviour. They usually include a highly active educational and creative programme and large group meetings to remind individuals of their responsibilities to each other and to the community. Some are primarily residential schools. They can be helpful for some youngsters who (1) stay the course, which may be for several years, and (2) have some degree of insight and wish to change their behaviour. Defiant, destructive, absconding, aggressive children may well find themselves in community homes (ex 'approved schools'), detention centres, remand centres, secure youth treatment centres, or prisons. It is difficult to know what to do for some of these young people, whose situation (and attempts to help them) has been well described by Millham *et al.* (1978), Millham (1981), Bruggen and Westland (1979), and Hoghughi (1978). Behavioural treatments have helped a number of them (Bedford and Tennent, 1981; Yule, 1978). Some young people have anomalies of personality development of a different type, and may be isolated, withdrawn, socially awkward, and sometimes behaviourally eccentric (Steinberg, 1985), and a proportion are helped by specialized therapeutic communities, e.g. those run on Rudolf Steiner lines.

A consultative approach to children's behaviour problems

If a child falls in the playground and breaks a bone, there is a straightforward procedure to follow, and there is no serious dispute about it from teachers, child, family, hospital. If, however, a child's behaviour is the issue, the most appropriate and most acceptable course of action may not be clear.

In this chapter I have tried to outline how psychiatric clinics operate, the range of treatments at their disposal, and the sort of problems broadly categorized as psychiatric in nature. Four things should be clear from this account, and all have a bearing on the issue of what to do for the child with seriously disordered conduct.

Firstly, psychiatric disorder does not constitute an absolutely clear-cut phenomenon, least of all where disruptive behaviour is concerned. It includes normal and abnormal aspects of behaviour, and social as well as individual problems.

Secondly, even where a child does have a psychiatrically definable problem (e.g. hyperkinetic syndrome), there are wider educational, social, and family requirements to be taken into account in the effective management of the problem (e.g. remedial teaching) as well as the general interests of the child.

Thirdly, the skills and experience of psychiatrists and their clinical co-workers (psychologists, psychotherapists, social workers) overlap very considerably with those of school-based workers (teachers, school psychologists, school counsellors, education welfare officers). It is exceedingly difficult to decide which profession is most suited to do what, and even to attempt discussion excites controversy (Steinberg, 1981).

Fourthly, whatever the problem and possible solution, authority to proceed with assessment and management is not invariably clear or generally agreed, and difficult issues of responsibility and confidentiality may arise. Not surprisingly, the very children who most need a clear, firm approach, namely disruptive boys and girls leading chaotic lives, are often those in whose lives adult authority and responsibility can be the least certain. Thus there may be disagreement (if not actual separation) between the parents, dispute between parents and school, and disagreement between school and clinic about how best to proceed. Moreover, all this may occur around a behaviour problem that is hard to resolve, and where the child in question gains a spurious confirmation of his or her lack of trust in adults by seeing them operating in confusion and at cross-purposes.

For these reasons, when dealing with the problem of disruptive behaviour, a consultative approach is likely to be more helpful than a traditional 'diagnostic plus prescriptive' approach on the part of the clinic. In describing what this approach entails, it is worth briefly considering what is meant by consultation in the specialized sense used in this chapter.

Consultation

It has been pointed out that 'consultation' can mean practically any professional activity, but in the sense used here it refers to the work undertaken when one professional (the consultant) helps another (the consultee) with a problem or other issue in the latter's work (Caplan, 1970). Responsibility for the matter in hand (e.g. a problem with a pupil) remains with the consultee, who may make whatever use he or she wishes of what emerges from consultation, the primary function of which is to provide a setting (e.g. a group or a discussion) in which the nature of the difficulty can be clarified and alternative ways of coping with it *using the consultee's resources* considered. This does not mean that outside expertise may not be appropriate; rather, it attempts to ensure that the skills available in the consultee's setting (in this context, the skills of the teacher and the facilities of the school) are used to best advantage. If the result is that the teacher is able, after all, to help a pupil who might have become a patient, then this is to the advantage of all concerned and is central to the rationale of consultative work (Steinberg and Yule, 1985). Further, when this happens, and it happens often enough in consultation, the consultee finds that he or she has gained in skill in a way that would not have been so likely if straightforward instruction had been given, still less if the child had simply been taken on by a psychiatric clinic.

The resources that good consultation helps to mobilize may be *personal* (e.g. helping the consultee to see the problem from a wider perspective and think up new approaches); or they may be intrinsic to the *working setting*, in this case the school. In one study of the problems brought by student counsellors to a consultative group, as time went by it became increasingly apparent that many 'client' problems were primarily difficulties in the job itself, and help with the latter corresponded with a reduction in the number of client-focused problems brought to the group (Steinberg and Hughes, in preparation). Problems in work may be material issues to do with time, space, and equipment, or to do with formal (official) and informal aspects of the way the organization operates and the consultee's role within it (see Menzies, 1974; Ryle, 1982).

In these ways consultation is distinct from direct clinical work, from supervision, and from 'therapy'. It is a problem-clarifying, problem-solving exercise, undertaken jointly with someone not too close to the work setting and the problem. Although it is not specifically a training exercise, it does have an educational function in that the style of consultative work, i.e. helping the consultee to clarify the problem for himself or herself, is one that should enable the consultee to operate more effectively in the future, and in this way consultation acts as a contribution to professional development.

In *behavioural consultation* consultative work can take on a more direct teaching function (e.g. see Yule *et al.*, 1977; Yule *et al.*, 1984; Steinberg and Yule, 1985). It differs from the Caplan model of consultation in focusing more directly on the child's behaviour, and is based on social learning theory (see chapters 5 and 10). It follows Tharp and Wetzel's (1969) proposal that behaviour modification in the natural environment would be more effective if undertaken by the adults who normally live and work with the child, rather than by workers in a clinic. Once again, the consultant does not take responsibility for the pupil, which remains with the teacher, but inquires into the teacher–pupil (i.e. consultee–client) interaction to find which aspects of the *consultee's* behaviour can be changed to bring about changes in the *client's* behaviour. In effect, the consultant helps the consultee to learn some behavioural approaches to the problems of the children in his or her care.

In the forms of consultation described here the consultant (e.g. psychiatrist or psychologist) may never see the pupil, but works through the consultee in order to help affirm the latter's role and skills. Other benefits include the fact that the teacher knows more about the school and the pupil than does the consultant, even if he or she is 'stuck' for the moment. Moreover, the client (in this case the pupil) need not become a psychiatric patient.

A consultative-diagnostic approach

Consultation is a practical art, and this model of 'pure' consultation is not invariably adhered to. Thus the consultant may see the child once, perhaps in a preliminary assessment shared with the school, and later may see the child again to review progress, meanwhile acting in a consultative capacity to the child's teachers who carry out a classroom-based management programme.

In my own view this dual approach can be used in an initial assessment that contains both diagnostic and consultative elements (Steinberg, 1983). Thus the clinician identifies individual problems in the child which may respond to individual treatment, while through consultation the wider aspects of the child's problems (social and family life; rights and responsibilities of parents, child, and school; education and, perhaps, special educational assessment and placement; monitoring of future progress) can be clarified, confirmed, and shared. The latter includes sharing responsibilities with members of the child's family too, something which can be lost in the pressure to take over and 'treat' a disruptive child.

Psychiatric treatment is not always appropriate, and when it it, it is not always effective. However, we do know that some treatment approaches are effective for some problems, and that the components of seriously disruptive behaviour in children are multifactorial and interact in complex ways. Moreover, adults cannot abandon responsibility when faced with the disruption and distress of the seriously misbehaving child, and must do the best they can to contain the child's behaviour, prevent people getting hurt, and correct what is correctible even if there is no cure. In the absence of straightforward solutions, a broadly consultative approach ensures that full use is made of the skills and experience of school staff, augments it with a psychiatric contribution when this is useful, and, of course, does not impede a transfer to full clinical care when this is helpful.

References

Alvin, J. (1966) *Music Therapy*. Hutchinson, London.

Bedford, A. P., and Tennent, T. G. (1981) Behaviour training with disturbed adolescents, *News of the Association for Child Psychology and Psychiatry*, **7**, 6–12.

Bolton, D. (1985) The clinical psychologist in adolescent psychiatry. In *The Adolescent Unit: Work and Teamwork in Adolescent Psychiatry*, ed. D. Steinberg. Wiley, Chichester.

Bolton, D., Collins, S., and Steinberg, D. (1983) The treatment of obsessive-compulsive disorder in adolescence. A report of fifteen cases, *British Journal of Psychiatry*, **142**, 456–464.

Boston, M., and Szur, R. (1983) *Psychotherapy with Severely Deprived Children*. Routledge & Kegan Paul, London.

Brown, B. J., and Christie, M. (1981) *Social Learning Practice in Residential Child Care*. Pergamon, Oxford.

Brown, D., and Pedder, J. (1980) *Introduction to Psychotherapy*. Tavistock Publications, London.

Bruggen, P., and Davies, G. (1977) Family therapy in adolescent psychiatry, *British Journal of Psychiatry*, **131**, 433–447.

Bruggen, P., and Westland, P. (1979) Difficult to place adolescents: are more resources required? *Journal of Adolescence*, **2**, 245–250.

Caplan, G. (1970) *The Theory and Practice of Mental Health Consultation*. Tavistock, London.

Coleman, J. C. (1980) *The Nature of Adolescence*. Methuen, London.

Dalley, T. (1984) *Art as Therapy*. Tavistock, London.

Dare, C. (1986) Family therapy in an adolescent in-patient unit. In *The Adolescent Unit: Work and Teamwork in Adolescent Psychiatry*, ed. D. Steinberg. Wiley, Chichester.

Fogelman, K. (1976) *Britain's Sixteen-year-olds*. National Children's Bureau, London.

Galloway, D. (1976) Size of school, socio-economic hardship, suspension rates and persistent unjustified absence from school, *British Journal of Educational Psychology*, **6**, 40–47.

Gath, D., Cooper, B., Gattoni, F., and Rockett, D. (1977) *Child Guidance and Delinquency in a London Borough*. Oxford University Press, Oxford.

Graham, P., and Rutter, M. (1973) Psychiatric disorder in the young adolescent: a follow-up study, *Proceedings of the Royal Society of Medicine*, **66**, 1226–1229.

Hawton, K., O'Grady, J., Osborn, M., and Cole, D. (1982) Adolescents who take overdoses: their characteristics, problems and contact with helping agencies, *British Journal of Psychiatry*, **140**, 118–123.

Hoghughi, M. (1978) *Troubled and Troublesome: Coping with Severely Disordered Children*. André Deutsch, London.

Hughes, L., and Wilson, J. (1985) Social work on the bridge. In *The Adolescent Unit: Work and Teamwork in Adolescent psychiatry*, ed. D. Steinberg. Wiley, Chichester.

Kahn, J., and Wright, S. E. (1980) *Human Growth and the Development of Personality*. Pergamon, Oxford.

Lampen, J. (1978) Drest in a little brief authority: controls in residential work with adolescents, *Journal of Adolescence*, **1**, 163–175.

Lennhoff, F. G., and Lampen, J. G. (1968) *Learning to Live*. Shotton Hall, Shrewsbury.

Leslie, S. A. (1974) Psychiatric disorder in the young adolescents of an industrial town. *British Journal of Psychiatry*, **125**, 113–124.

Menzies, I. (1974) Staff support systems. In *Proceedings of the 9th Annual Conference of the Association for the Psychiatric Study of Adolescence*, 13–22.

Miller, S. (1973) *The Psychology of Play*. Penguin, Harmondsworth, Middx.

Millham, S. (1981) The therapeutic implications of locking up children, *Journal of Adolescence*, **4**, 13–26.

Millham, S., Bullock, R., and Hosie, K. (1978) *Locking up Children: Secure Provision Within the Child Care System*. Saxon House, Farnborough.

Opie, I., and Opie, P. (1977) *The Lore and Language of School Children*. Paladin, St Albans.

Ragg, N. M. (1977) *People not Cases: A Philosophical Approach to Social Work*. Routledge & Kegan Paul, London.

Ritson, B. (1981) Alcohol and young people, *Journal of Adolescence*, **4**, 93–100.

Robins, L. N. (1979) Follow-up studies. In *Psychopathological Disorders of Childhood*, ed. H. C. Quay, and J. S. Werry. Wiley, Chichester.

Rutter, M. (1979) *Changing Youth in a Changing Society*. Nuffield Provincial Hospitals Trust, London.

Rutter, M., Graham, P., Chadwick, O., and Yule, W. (1976) Adolescent turmoil: fact or fiction? *Journal of Child Psychology and Psychiatry*, **17**, 35–56.

Rutter, M., Maughan, B., Ouston, J., Mortimore, P., and Smith, A. (1979) *Fifteen Thousand Hours: Secondary Schools and Their Effects on Children*. Open Books, London.

Rutter, M., Tizard, J., and Whitmore, K. (1970) *Education, Health and Behaviour.* Longman, London.

Ryle, R. (1982) Understanding organisations. In Dare, C., Ryle, R., Steinberg, D., and Yule, W. (eds). *News of the Association for Child Psychology and Psychiatry,* **11,** 1–16.

Sandberg, S. T., Rutter, M., and Taylor, E. (1978) Hyperkinetic disorder in clinic attenders, *Developmental Medicine and Child Neurology,* **20,** 279–299.

Shaffer, D. (1974) Suicide in childhood and early adolescence, *Journal of Child Psychology and Psychiatry,* **15,** 275–291.

Shaffer, D. (1977) Brain injury. In *Child Psychiatry: Modern Approaches,* 1st edn, ed. M. Rutter and L. Hersov. Blackwell, Oxford.

Shaffer, D., and Greenhill, L. (1979) A critical note on the predictive validity of 'the hyperkinetic syndrome', *Journal of Child Psychology and Psychiatry,* **20,** 61–72.

Skynner, A. C. R. (1976) *One Flesh—Separate Persons.* Constable, London.

Slater, E., and Roth, M. (1969) *Clinical Psychiatry.* Bailliere Tindall & Cassell, London.

Steinberg, D. (1981) *Using Child Psychiatry. The Functions and Operations of a Specialty.* Hodder & Stoughton, London and Sevenoaks.

Steinberg, D. (1982) Treatment, training, care or control? *British Journal of Psychiatry,* **141,** 306–309.

Steinberg, D. (1983) *The Clinical Psychiatry of Adolescence: Clinical Work from a Social and Developmental Perspective.* Wiley, Chichester.

Steinberg, D. (1984) Psychotic and other severe disorders in adolescence. In *Child Psychiatry: Modern Approaches,* 2nd edn, ed. M. Rutter and L. Hersov. Blackwell, Oxford.

Steinberg, D. (ed.) (1986) *The Adolescent Unit: Work and Teamwork in Adolescent Psychiatry.* Wiley, Chichester.

Steinberg, D., Galhenage, D. P. C., and Robinson, S. C. (1981) Two years' referrals to a regional adolescent unit: some implications for psychiatric services, *Social Science and Medicine,* **15,** 113–122.

Steinberg, D., and Hughes, L. (in preparation) The emergence of work-centred problems in consultative work.

Steinberg, D., and Yule, W. (1985) Consultative work. In *Child Psychiatry: Modern Approaches,* 2nd edn, ed. M. Rutter and L. Hersov. Blackwell, Oxford.

Stores, G. (1975) Behavioural effects of anti-epileptic drugs, *Developmental Medicine and Child Neurology,* **17,** 647–658.

Strang, J. and Connell, P. (1985) Clinical Aspects of Drug and Alcohol Abuse. In *Child Psychiatry: Modern Approaches,* 2nd edn, ed. M. Rutter and L. Hersov. Blackwell, Oxford.

Taylor, E. (1979) Food additives, allergy and hyperkinesis, *Journal of Child Psychology and Psychiatry,* **20,** 357–363.

Taylor, E. (1980) The overactive child, *Medicine,* **36,** 1866–1870.

Tharp, R. G., and Wetzel, R. J. (1969) *Behaviour Modification in the Natural Environment.* Academic Press, New York.

Walrond-Skinner, S. (1976) *Family Therapy: The Treatment of Natural Systems.* Routledge & Kegan Paul, London.

Warren, B. (ed.) (1984) *Using the Creative Arts in Therapy.* Croom Helm, London.

Werry, J. S. (1979) Organic factors. In *Psychopathological Disorders of Childhood,* ed. H. C. Quay, and J. S. Werry. Wiley, Chichester.

Wing, L. (ed.) (1976) *Early Childhood Autism.* Pergamon, Oxford.

Yule, W. (1978) Behavioural treatment of children and adolescents with conduct disorders. In *Aggression and Antisocial Behaviour in Childhood and Adolescence,* ed. L. Hersov, M. Berger, and D. Shaffer. Pergamon, Oxford.

Yule, W., Berger, M., and Wigley, V. (1977) The teacher-child interaction project, *Bulletin of the British Association for Behavioural Psychotherapy*, 5(3), 42-47.

Yule, W., Berger, M., and Wigley, V. (1984) Behaviour modification and classroom management. In *Disruptive Behaviour in Schools*, ed. N. Frude and H. Gault. Wiley, Chichester.

Yule, W., Lansdown, R., Millar, I. B., and Urbanowicz, M. A. (1981) The relationship between blood lead levels, intelligence and attainment in school children: a pilot study, *Developmental Medicine and Child Neurology*, **23**, 567-576.

Management of Disruptive Pupil Behaviour in Schools
Edited by D. P. Tattum
©1986 John Wiley & Sons Ltd

_____ *12* ___

The management of behaviour problems: a local authority response[1]

Anne West, Jean Davies, and Andreas Varlaam

In this chapter, the focus will be upon school support centres and their management arrangements. The chapter is divided into six sections. The first section describes how disruptive behaviour can be dealt with; the second section outlines the types of centre in existence, and also gives a brief account of the historical background to their establishment. The next three sections look at the performance of the centres from the viewpoint of the pupils who attend them, the schools which use them, and the staff who work in them; these sections draw upon research carried out by the authors (Mortimore *et al.*, 1984). The final section of the chapter discusses some of the implications of the research findings for a successful school support programme.

The management of disruptive behaviour

Disruptive behaviour can be dealt with in a number of different ways. Behaviourist theory, for example, advocates the reward of good behaviour; behaviour which is considered undesirable is simply ignored. This view relies on the lack of positive attention being a sufficient punishment for disruptive behaviour.

Sometimes disruptive behaviour is 'managed'—e.g. by counselling by members of the school's pastoral staff. This task is not simple, for the teachers concerned have to combine the role of friend and advisor to pupils in difficulty with that of disciplinarian to those whose behaviour is giving cause for concern.

Another method of dealing with disruptive behaviour is to punish it—e.g. by detention or corporal punishment, suspension or expulsion. Although corporal punishment is still used in some local education authorities (LEAs), its use is controversial and several LEAs have abolished it.

For pupils who are persistently disruptive, a further possibility is referral to special education. Although this might be of benefit to some pupils, for others, the compensation of skilled guidance may be negated by the removal from ordinary school, and in some cases, the dispatch to boarding schools some distance from home.

Another possible method of dealing with pupils whose behaviour is persistently disruptive is to remove them from the ordinary classroom, yet neither suspend them nor send them to special schools. There now exist several different kinds of provision for the withdrawal of pupils from ordinary clases. Tattum (1982) lists 15 types of units with educational, therapeutic, diagnostic, clinical, or disciplinary goals; the broad title for these units is 'support centres' and these are the focus of the present chapter.

Development of support centres

Support centres, disruptive units, and behavioural units are all terms which have been used to describe a special form of provision, mainly for pupils who are thought by their teachers to have behaviour problems. These centres are not part of either the ordinary school system or the special school system. They are, rather, intended to provide a short-term alternative for pupils whose relations with their own schools have reached breaking point.

It is important to distinguish the several different types of support centres subsumed in the general category. Support centres can be divided into on-site support centres, off-site support centres, voluntary agency centres, intermediate treatment schemes, and educational guidance centres. On-site centres can be seen as extensions of the ordinary school, in so far as they are staffed by regular teachers; pupils normally attend them on a part-time rather than a full-time basis. They are the only type of support centre invariably sited on school premises. The on-site centres appear to have three major advantages for the pupils in so far as access is easier, there is more continuity of teaching and curriculum, and reintegration into the mainstream is easier. There are, however, several disadvantages—change is only partial, the overall ethos of the institution remains constant, and a 'fresh start' is less feasible. A further danger is that the centre may become a ghetto within the school, with pupils clinging to the security of their small unit. Some centres might be viewed as 'punishment' centres by teachers and pupils alike; such a view is not helpful to pupils already alienated from the school.

Off-site support centres are generally situated away from the main school site and function more independently. They usually take pupils from more than one school and attendance is usually on a full-time basis; staff are appointed to the centre itself and not to a school. Voluntary agency centres, although supported by grants paid by the local education authority, are actually run by voluntary bodies. Many of these centres were originally set up to cope with pupils with attendance problems rather than those with behaviour problems. Intermediate treatment schemes are run by social services departments and were set up for pupils considered to be 'at risk'. At both voluntary agency centres and intermediate treatment schemes, pupils attend on a full-time basis. Educational guidance centres, which are supervised by the schools' psychological service, are also included in the category of support centre; pupils may attend these on a full-time or part-time basis. Off-site centres, unlike on-site centres, allow pupils a real change from the school in which they have been unsuccessful. Paradoxically, the principal disadvantage of off-site centres appears to be their very separateness which can isolate children from mainstream schooling.

Several pressures were instrumental in the development of support centre policies. The most important were the raising of the school-leaving age, rapid teacher turnover in the early part of the 1970s, the decision to abolish corporal punishment, and the ending of the 11-plus transfer examination.

The raising of the school-leaving age inevitably caused problems for schools, which now had to cope with pupils who had no desire to attend school. Urban secondary schools in the early 1970s suffered from a particularly high rate of teacher turnover; the difficulty in retaining experienced teachers is illustrated by an ILEA survey (Little, 1977) carried out in the mid 1970s, which showed that 77 per cent of men and 87 per cent of women teachers had been teaching in their school for less than 5 years. The abolition of corporal punishment in some LEAs in the 1970s increased teacher pressure for alternative methods of dealing with disruptive behaviour. The ending of the 11-plus selection examination and the abolition of selective grammar schools resulted in increased pressure from parents who were anxious to avoid their children's education being disrupted by other pupils' uncontrolled behaviour in the classroom.

It was hoped that the centres, most of which were set up in the late 1970s, would offer a flexible form of provision, where pupils would stay only for relatively short periods, without the delays and separateness associated with a system of special education, and without being labelled as deviant.

In the sections which follow, the characteristics of the pupils attending centres are summarized, and an attempt is made to gauge the success of these centres by examining their benefits and disadvantages as seen by the pupils who attend them, the staff who work in them, and the schools which use them. The information presented was obtained from an intensive study of support studies carried out in London in 1979–1981.

Pupils who attend centres

Characteristics of pupils in centres

Before discussing the pupils' opinions of centres, their social characteristics and reasons for referral will be outlined.

Reasons for referral   The pupils who attended support centres were not all there on account of their disruptive behaviour. The pupils fell into two main groups—they were either there because of their non-attendance (42 per cent) or because their behaviour was in some way disruptive (44 per cent). Some pupils combined disruptive behaviour when they were in school with periods of absence, and attendance was said to be a problem—if not the main reason for referral—for over two-thirds of all the pupils.

Age   The majority of pupils in the centres ranged from 11 to 16 years. Just over 60 per cent of the pupils were in the 14–16-year-old age group and just under 40 per cent were in the younger age groups of 11–13 years.

Sex of pupils   In off-site support centres, educational guidance centres and intermediate treatment schemes there were approximately two boys to every one girl, whilst in voluntary agency centres girls and boys were equally represented. In the on-site centres, on the other hand, girls outnumbered boys (by a ratio of 3:2).

Ethnic background   A frequently voiced criticism of centres is that a disproportionately large number of pupils from ethnic minorities are referred to them. It was found that children classified as Caribbean were somewhat overrepresented in centres, whereas those classified as coming from Bangladesh, India or Pakistan or 'other' places were somewhat underrepresented when compared with data from the *National Dwelling and Housing Survey* (Department of the Environment, 1978).

Family background   Pupils with parents in semi-skilled or unskilled occupations were also overrepresented among centre pupils (51 per cent in centres versus 33 per cent in ILEA secondary schools), while pupils with parents in non-manual or skilled occupations were underrepresented (23 per cent in centres versus 30 per cent in ILEA secondary schools).

Levels of attainment   Centre pupils were underrepresented in the top verbal reasoning group which comprises 25 per cent of all ILEA pupils at 11 years (in centres only 9 per cent were in this group) and overrepresented in the lowest verbal reasoning group which also comprises 25 per cent of all ILEA pupils at 11 (in centres 41 per cent were in this group). The proportion of pupils in the middle verbal reasoning group was almost identical to that for the ILEA as a whole (50 per cent in ILEA versus 49 per cent in centres).

Pupils' opinions of centres

Pupils attending centres were, on the whole, favourably disposed towards the centres. This was evident from their responses to a series of questions about their referral, their academic work and other activities at the centres, their likes and dislikes, and the benefits (if any) to be obtained from attending support centres.

Over half of the pupils said that their initial reactions to referral were positive. Several pupils, for example, mentioned the favourable impression of the centre they had gained from their initial visit. Just over a quarter of those whose initial reactions were positive made comments suggesting that they looked forward to referral as providing a change from school. Comments included 'It was better than school' and 'I thought you'd have more freedom'.

Again, almost half of the pupils said they enjoyed the work they were doing in the centres in English and mathematics. Many pupils also mentioned their enjoyment of other subjects, such as science, computer studies, social studies, and arts and crafts. Some pupils also made favourable comments about the pleasant atmosphere and the good relationships which existed between staff and pupils at the centres. Comments included 'It's like someone's home here', 'You can talk over problems with teachers', and 'Children are more friendly'.

On the other hand, about one in five of the pupils indicated that they had reacted negatively to their referral. They gave several reasons for this, with some being wary of the centre's reputation and others being worried about leaving their school friends. Nevertheless, only a small minority of the pupils actually mentioned any dislikes they had about life at the centres. The most common complaints were a dislike of rules and regulations, a dislike of other pupils or teachers at the centre, worries about the limited range of academic subjects available, and, on occasion, dissatisfaction with the centre's location or distance from home.

When asked about the benefits they thought they were getting from attending the centre, over half the pupils mentioned academic benefits, such as getting a better education or getting more help with their work. A quarter of the pupils mentioned the help they felt they received in learning to cope with, and solve, their own problems. A further benefit, mentioned by many pupils interviewed, concerned their future reintegration into school, indicating that for these pupils returning and settling back into their own school was an important benefit to be gained from their time in the centre.

Small proportions of the pupils made comments referring to their positive relationship with staff, to social skills and discussion skills taught at the centre, and to the preparation provided by the centre for work and life outside the centre. Only 7 per cent of those interviewed said that they had not gained anything from attending the centre.

These positive feelings held by the pupils about attendance at the centre were reflected in their attitudes to being absent from the centre. Pupils were asked how often they stayed away from the centre without a reason. The majority of the pupils said that they had never been absent. Almost a third said that they had been absent, but most of these pupils had only stayed away occasionally.

The schools which use centres

The vast majority of schools in inner London have used at least one type of centre at some time. Headteachers were asked to comment on the effects of the centres on pupils who attended them, on other pupils in the mainstream school, on the teachers, the management, and the running of the mainstream school in general.

Most headteachers thought that the centres had been of benefit at least to some of the pupils who had attended there. Benefits commonly mentioned included improved attendance and punctuality,[2] improved behaviour, and help with emotional and other personal problems. Most headteachers also noted that other pupils who remained at the school were more settled, had better relationships with teachers, and were better able to get on with their work without disturbance. As a result, classroom management and pastoral and discipline arrangements had all improved, and generally the atmosphere in the school had become more calm and relaxed.

There were, however, several headteachers who were rather critical of the effects of the centre. Many heads, for example, said that in a number of cases the centres had had no impact on the pupils who attended. Others felt that the effects of the centres had been transitory, or that the centres were inappropriate for some pupils who had been sent there. A number of headteachers focused on the problems of reintegrating centre pupils back into mainstream school. They thought that such problems arose either because pupils at the centres were not pressed to conform to the standards expected in ordinary schools, or because the pupils, while at the centres, had failed to keep up with the school curriculum.

A few headteachers expressed concern at the additional burden on teachers who had to provide work schemes especially for centre pupils, both while these pupils were attending the centres and on their return to mainstream school.

Finally, some headteachers felt that centres were viewed as a 'soft option' both by pupils and some teachers, who saw in the centres little more than an opportunity to avoid facing the problems encountered in an ordinary classroom.

Staff at centres

Characteristics of staff in centres

Before describing the views of staff who work in centres, their characteristics will be summarized briefly.

Sixty-four per cent of the staff were female and 36 per cent were male. Thirty-four per cent were aged under 30, 43 per cent were aged between 30 and 40, 19 per cent were between 40 and 50, and 4 per cent were over 50 years of age. Less than 7 per cent of the teachers had ethnic backgrounds outside the British Isles. Of the teaching staff, a quarter possessed a degree but no certificate of education, while a half had a certificate of education but no degree. The remainder (25 per cent) possessed both a degree and a certificate of education. Almost half of the teaching staff had taught for 5 years or less in mainstream or special education; 34 per cent had between 6 and 10 years teaching experience, 12 per cent had between 11 and 15 years, and 8 per cent had 16 or more years experience.

Views of the staff who work in centres

The views of staff who worked in centres were sought in the areas of centre management, referral and admissions to centres, and professional support received.

With the exception of on-site centres which are usually administered by the school's headteacher, deputy head, or teacher-in-charge of pastoral care, all centres in inner London are managed by some form of committee. These generally included representatives from the divisional office (of the ILEA) and from any schools served by the centres, together with education welfare officers and the teacher-in-charge of the centre. The committees of educational guidance centres included a psychologist; those of intermediate treatment schemes also had representatives from the local social services; the committees of voluntary agency centres usually included parents and representatives from the community. The functions of the management committees varied from centre to centre (as did those of the individuals in charge of on-site centres).

On the whole, the staff at on-site and off-site support centres and educational guidance centres were satisfied with the management arrangements. However, staff from several of these centres were concerned about the committees' lack of ability to provide adequate professional support in developing strategies for managing pupil behaviour and in devising a relevant programme of work for centre pupils. On the other hand, many staff from voluntary agency centres and intermediate treatment schemes were dissatisfied with the management arrangements. It was generally felt that the members of the management committees who had widely different professional interests were not sufficiently involved with the operation of the centres' programmes. Such close involvement was felt to be particularly important when new staff appointments were to be made. Existing staff thought that they should be closely involved in choosing new appointees so as to ensure that newcomers would be able to work alongside existing staff within the established framework of the centre, and without any friction.

Referral procedures vary according to the different types of centre. Referral procedures for on-site centres are the least formal, with the headteacher (or the deputy head) discussing the needs of a particular pupil with the centre's teacher-in-charge and a decision being made as to the best course of action.

Educational psychologists are officially responsible for initiating referrals to educational guidance centres. The school's headteacher and educational psychologist complete a standardized referral form and the educational psychologist then interviews the child and his or her parents. The director of the educational guidance centre is then contacted by the educational psychologist and, in turn, arranges to meet with the child, and a decision on whether or not to admit the child is then made.

In most off-site support centres, voluntary agency centres, and intermediate treatment schemes a similar procedure emerged. After referral by the pupil's school, education welfare officer, or some other agency, the centre staff obtained as much background information as they could before deciding whether to accept the pupil (some centres held a case conference before taking a decision). About one-third of the centres made use of a 'trial period' before admitting the pupil on a longer-term basis.

Most of the centre staff felt that referral procedures were on the whole efficient. However, suggestions for improvements were made. Firstly, it was felt that closer contact and improved communication with referring schools and agencies should be encouraged, so as to reduce the number of inappropriate referrals. Secondly, centre staff felt that headteachers should ensure that school staff understand the necessity of providing detailed background information when making referrals to centres. Thirdly, the centre staff in those centres where the management committee decided on admissions, felt that they themselves should have the right to veto admissions so as to safeguard the centre's work and avoid disruption by pupils who were not suited (in the opinion of the staff) to the centre's established programme and activities.

Centre staff were also asked about the extent of professional support available to them and the opportunities they felt they had for in-service training. Only a fifth of those questioned said that the opportunities for in-service training were adequate. Of the others, many felt that there were no training courses available which directly related to teaching in support centres. Others said that the staffing arrangements at their centre did not make it possible for individual teachers to have leave for training (in fact, only a minority of the teachers reported having in-service training opportunities during school hours).

Earlier research studies had shown that professional isolation was a common experience for teachers working in support centres. In view of this, centre staff were asked to say whether they themselves felt isolated. Half of the teachers said that they did not feel professionally isolated, but some said that they had suffered feelings of professional isolation for a considerable length of time. Staff in educational guidance centres were particularly vulnerable as they had very few opportunities to meet professional colleagues.

Implications for a support centre programme

The implications for a support centre programme arising from the findings described above fall into five main areas: the placement of pupils in appropriate centres, centre management, the aims and goals of the centre, the curriculum, and the problems faced by centre teachers.

There is considerable differentiation between the types of centres in existence (and between centres of the same type) and, as a result, a wide choice for schools seeking placement for their pupils. However, there are problems with such a differentiated system. Firstly, if pupils are to benefit fully from their placement in centres, it is vital that their needs are correctly assessed before referral. Secondly, there is a real need for efficient channels of communication between schools and centres, so that the chances of appropriate referrals being made are increased. Thirdly, care needs to be taken, both by the local authorities who are ultimately responsible for support centres and by the centre management and staff themselves, to ensure that the placement of girls is satisfactory; they must not be placed in centres where they might be in a small minority, or where they might be discriminated against in any of the activities of the centre. There is also a need to maintain a balance between pupils from different ethnic backgrounds. Centres where pupils from minority groups predominate are unacceptable for both social and educational reasons. Similarly, it is desirable for centres not to limit their intake to pupils from a single age group or any particular level of ability.

All these problems could be resolved, perhaps, by improving communication between schools and centres, by producing clearer guidelines and policies for admission, and by monitoring the operation of the support centre system on a regular basis.

A more intractable problem, however, arises out of the lack of flexibility and quick response from which any system composed of specialist centres and teachers is bound to suffer. It can be argued that one of the more important functions of a good support centre system is to provide a readily available alternative for pupils whose relations with their school have reached a crisis point. What both school and pupil need in such circumstances is an immediate respite from each other for a period of time. If the system is such that disruptive pupils cannot be placed until exhaustive assessments have been carried out and suitable centres found, then both school and pupil will suffer and their most pressing problem will remain unresolved.

This tension within the existing system—on the one hand, a pressing need to move the pupil speedily away from the school, and on the other, the need to find a suitable placement—was reflected in the relations between management committees and centre staff. Centre staff felt it was important for them to control admissions as they were in charge of the day-to-day running of centres, and had the relevant knowledge about the facilities and the programme of the centre and about those pupils already attending centres. Management bodies, however, tended to believe that as centres were introduced to serve schools, headteachers or management committees should have the final say on admissions. Centre staff also felt that they should meet applicants for vacant posts on the staff before any appointments were made, but this did not always happen. It was felt important, firstly, because the existing staff would be working in very close cooperation with anyone appointed and, secondly, because they felt that the centres had little chance of long-term success unless there was considerable agreement among staff about which pupils should be admitted, the aims of the centre, and the methods by which these could be achieved.

If the above analysis is correct, that is, if the tensions between management and centre staff arise largely from the conflicting demands put upon the system, then modifying management arrangements (e.g. by abolishing management committees) would not resolve these problems. Indeed, it might exacerbate them, as management committees have a better chance than any individual of maintaining a balance between conflicting interests.

Any long-term solutions to these problems are likely to involve a reorganization of the whole support centre programme by the LEA, with perhaps some of the support centres accepting immediate referrals from mainstream schools and acting as agents for them in supervising work set by the staff from the referring schools.

As noted earlier in this chapter, support centres are meant to provide only a *short-term* alternative facility for pupils; centres should aim to return pupils to mainstream schools and help with their reintegration. Reintegration into mainstream schooling is not, however, without its problems, as the evidence from the heads of mainstream schools has demonstrated. If such problems are to be overcome there is a need, firstly, for close contacts, an exchange of information, and cooperation with referring schools from the moment a child is referred to a centre. Secondly, methods of teaching and discipline must be such as to facilitate return to school, and not make it even more difficult for pupils to adjust to the demands of ordinary school life. Thirdly, the curriculum taught in centres must be sufficiently extensive and the syllabus must be tailored to the needs of individual pupils, so that they can fit in easily with the teaching and activities in their class on their return to school.

The limitations of the curriculum on offer in centres is an obvious cause for concern. As shown, there were serious difficulties in this area, most particularly in off-site centres where pupils were drawn from a large number of schools. From the point of view of centre management, the difficulties were mainly in finding staff qualified and experienced in specialist subjects and in attempting to duplicate courses on offer in the referring schools. One possible solution to the latter problem would be to restrict the intake to pupils from one or two schools, as duplication of courses would be simpler and closer contacts could be maintained with the schools. Another possible solution to curriculum problems would be the establishment of teacher resource centres to provide learning materials and equipment and to foster relationships between staff from different centres. In addition, arrangements should continue to be made to enable centre staff to meet and discuss ways in which the curriculum at the centres could be developed, and to exchange information on teaching methods and innovative techniques.

Whatever the limitations of the curriculum, it should be noted that in many ways centres are better placed than schools to introduce new subjects, to adopt new approaches to teaching, and to give pupils individual attention with their work and personal problems. There is little doubt that pupils could gain considerable benefits from the flexible and innovative programmes which were on offer in many of the centres studied.

The establishment of centres separate from the mainstream educational system gives rise to concern, not only for the pupils who attend, but also for the teachers who work there, many of whom feel professionally isolated. It would be helpful if, firstly, national and local facilities for in-service training and the advisory and support services offered could be expanded; secondly, if exchanges of staff between centres and ordinary schools could be arranged; thirdly, if centre staff could be allowed to participate more closely in the life and activities of ordinary schools; and fourthly, if there were a continual recognition by the teaching professsion as a whole of their collective responsibility for difficult pupils.

The problems facing support centres outlined in this section are not insuperable and the solutions suggested could be implemented without much difficulty or excessive cost. The question remains, however, whether support centres offer the best answer to the problem of disruption in schools. Educationalists have suggested a variety of other approaches, such as support for schools from peripatetic teacher teams, or the development of a range of 'alternative' schools which would give a greater degree of choice for children and their parents.

Such alternative approaches should not be dismissed lightly. Indeed, where they have been tried (in the United States, for example) they have met with considerable success. However, given the problems faced by pupils, teachers, and schools in the inner city at least, it is unlikely that the need for some sort of centre provision will disappear in the near future. The authorities responsible for education, therefore, must make the effort to reduce the problems associated with support centres and build on the existing work of teachers and centres.

Note

1. Although the authors of this chapter work in the Inner London Education Authority, Research and Statistics Branch, the views expressed are personal and are not necessarily those of the Authority.
2. A subsequent study of pupils returning to mainstream schooling showed that in most cases any improvement in attendance had not lasted for long after the pupil returned.

References

Department of the Environment (1978) *National Dwelling and Housing Survey.* HMSO, London.
Little, A. (1977) What is happening in inner city schools? In Field, F. (ed.), *Education and the Urban Crisis.* Routledge & Kegan Paul, London.
Mortimore, P., Davies, J., Varlaam, A., and West, A. (1984) *Behaviour Problems in Schools.* Croom Helm, London.
Tattum, D. P. (1982) *Disruptive Pupils in Schools and Units.* Wiley, Chichester.

Management of Disruptive Pupil Behaviour in Schools
Edited by D. P. Tattum

_____ *13* ___

School discipline plans and the quest for order in American schools

Daniel L. Duke

Duke and Jones (1983) found various indications of shifting disciplinary priorities. While concern in the late 1960s focused on collective student unrest and demonstrations, the early 1970s saw attention directed primarily at small group and individual violence and vandalism on campus. By the late 1970s educators were concentrating more on student 'off-task' behaviors in class. The early 1980s has witnessed yet another shift, this time to student absenteeism and apathy. It is difficult to determine whether disciplinary priorities change as a result of actual reductions in the incidence of certain types of misconduct or because of evolving societal values and expectations. A combination of both is the most likely explanation.

As the type of student behavior problem receiving the greatest attention has shifted, so too has the response of educators. The late 1960s were characterized by calls for greater curricular relevance and stress on human relations, conflict resolution, and group dynamic skills. When threats to property and personal safety increased during the early 1970s, school officials began to rely on sophisticated security measures, including electronic surveillance and cooperative programs with local law enforcement agencies. Educators began to focus on the quality of instruction and the consistency of rule enforcement as classroom management supplanted concerns with violence and vandalism. Currently, problems with absenteeism have caused educators to seek greater parental involvement in schooling. Parents may be notified immediately by phone when their children are suspected of unexcused absence and parent conferences may be arranged with teachers and counselors. In general, parents are expected to play a more active role in ensuring regular school attendance than may have been the case a decade ago.

Educators and parents have not been alone in their efforts to reduce student behavior problems. Since the mid-1960s many researchers, teacher educators, psychologists specializing in children and adolescents, pediatricians, and social workers have devoted increasing attention to helping troubled youngsters. When Duke and Jones (1983) surveyed 20 years of activity surrounding the quest for order in American schools, they summarized their findings in the form of twelve general observations:

1. The knowledge base in classroom management and school discipline has grown considerably since the mid-sixties.
2. Reservations exist concerning the quality of much of the data on student behavior.
3. Perceptions of what constitute priority student behavior problems vary within and between schools, among various groups, and over time.
4. The level of public and professional concern regarding student behaviour continues to be high.
5. School organization and procedures have undergone substantial changes in an effort to reduce concern over student behavior.
6. No consensus exists regarding the best or most effective way to manage classrooms, prevent behavior problems, or coordinate school discipline.
7. No consensus exists regarding the best way to train prospective or veteran educators in classroom management and school discipline.
8. Programs to improve student behavior rarely reflect a sensitivity to differences in student ability, age, level of maturation, cultural background, family circumstances, previous school experience, or handicaps.
9. Classroom management frequently is conceptualized solely as a matter of student control rather than a dimension of curriculum, instruction, and overall school climate.
10. There is little evidence of lasting, widespread improvements in student behavior as a direct result of an increased knowledge base, more staff development, and changes in school organization.
11. Isolated reports of classrooms and schools where student behavior problems are not a great concern or have been markedly reduced suggest that there is some reason to be hopeful.
12. Declining resources for schools and difficulties with the recruitment of skilled teachers threaten to exacerbate current student behavior problems.

When Duke and Jones sought examples of fairly widespread responses to student behavior that spanned the entire period from the mid-1960s through to the present day, one of the few that was found was the formal and comprehensive plan for managing school discipline. I shall henceforth refer to such school discipline plans as SDPs.

Toward the end of 1983 President Reagan addressed prominent government and education leaders who were attempting to delineate national education priorities. The president shared his own set of priorities, a list that began as follows:[1]

> First, we need to restore good, old-fashioned discipline. In too many schools across the land, teachers can't teach because they lack the authority to make students take tests and hand in homework. Some don't even have the authority to quiet down their class. In some schools, the teachers suffer verbal and physical abuse. I can't say it too forcefully! This must stop.
>
> We need to write stricter discipline codes, then support our teachers when they enforce these codes.

A naive listener hearing the presidential address may have surmised that school discipline only recently had surfaced as a national problem and that communities still were awaiting concerted efforts by educators to respond. Nothing could be further from reality. School discipline had been identified as a national concern at least since the late 1960s, and educators had poured considerable energy and resources into reducing student behavior problems over the ensuing years.

In this chapter, I initially plan to provide a sense of the range and scope of the quest for order in American schools. Subsequently I shall focus on a particular outcome of this quest, one which represents a somewhat substantial departure from traditional educational practice. I refer specifically to the proliferation of formal school and classroom discipline plans.

Shifting concerns and responses

While student conduct has absorbed considerable public and professional energy for the past two decades, the particular behaviors which have created the greatest stir have changed over the years, along with the preferred ways of dealing with them. In a comprehensive review of American efforts to cope with student behaviour problems, it has been estimated that three out of every four American public schools possess some form of SDP (Safer, 1982, p. 52).

SDPs are of interest not only because of their popularity but also because they symbolize a shift in how American educators think about and deal with discipline. Historically, educators have borrowed heavily from psychology, seeing behavior as an individual phenomenon that can be understood primarily in terms of a student's unique psychological make-up.

Concern focused on student ability and achievement, the quality of home life, and teacher–student interactions. More recently, educators have begun to acknowledge the crucial role that organizational factors play in shaping behavior. While not abandoning psychology, they look as well to sociology and organization theory. An appreciation is developing that how students behave in school may be related to the nature of rules and consequences, how decisions are made regarding their development and enforcement, and how disciplinary tasks are structured and allocated.

The remainder of the chapter will focus on the nature of SDPs and some key issues related to their adoption.

Organizing orderly schools

It is difficult to discern a single pattern of events that has lead to the development of local SDPs. The SDPs themselves vary greatly in content, organization, and tone. The purpose of this section is to capture a sense of the variety in these organizational responses made by American educators to the 'discipline problem' and to note, where appropriate, areas of similarity.

System-wide mandates

During the past 10 years many school systems (local education authorities) have captured headlines by promulgating strict discipline codes. Among these systems have been some of the nation's largest.

After Mayor Koch of New York appointed a special committee in 1981 to develop ways to combat an 'alarming' increase in school violence, the Board of Education established a policy requiring every school in the city to have a 'comprehensive disciplinary code that lists what the school considers to be misbehavior and what punishment teachers and administrators can administer'.[2] Codes were to be developed by principals in concert with parent groups and, in some cases, students. The board acknowledged that most New York City schools already possessed codes, but that they lacked specificity concerning which acts of misconduct were punishable and how. The new mandate defined the range of punishable offenses for the schools. Offenses included the use of offensive language, vandalism, gambling, drunkenness, and physical attacks.

Boston, like New York, was prompted to take action when a mayor-appointed committee recommended comprehensive efforts to reduce fear, violence, and disruption in local schools. Among the committee's specific suggestions were short and simple 'standards of behavior' for all schools, stiff penalties for serious offenses such as use of weapons, and the use of adult safety monitors on school buses.

One of the most comprehensive system-wide discipline codes was developed in Richmond, Virginia.[3] Unlike some other school systems where local schools were left with the task of generating SDPs, the Richmond School Board approved a standard code for all schools. The code was written by a committee of educators and other citizens who were influenced by reports that students experienced widely varying sets of rules in different Richmond schools. A copy of the Richmond, Virginia, 'Standards of Student Conduct' is included in the Appendix.

As indicated above, many school systems stop short of imposing a common code on all local schools. American education is wedded by tradition to the idea of local control. In addition, recent findings from school effectiveness and educational change studies strongly suggest that new policies and programs stand the best chance of being successfully implemented when they are adapted to the needs of the local school.

School discipline plans

While SDPs cannot openly contradict system-wide discipline codes any more than they can overlook state and federal laws, they may assume a variety of forms, even within the same district. Variations occur across several dimensions, including expectations for student conduct, consequences for disobedience, philosophy, and general disciplinary procedures. Each of these areas will be discussed.

Expectations   Common to all SDPs is some expression of acceptable or unacceptable student behavior. It may take a positive form, such as a list of student responsibilities or expectations for appropriate conduct. Or it may be stated more negatively, in the form of proscribed behavior or rules. The language and format may be straightforward or legalistic. The rules may cover broad categories of conduct or specify precise acts. Finally, the number of expectations may range from several essential rules to more than 40 specific injunctions.

To capture some of the variety among SDPs, it may be instructive to select one type of misconduct—disrespect or defiance of authority—and present some actual examples of behavioral expectations.

Courtesy and Respect for Teachers and Other Staff Members (Ocotillo School, Phoenix, Arizona)

'A person who insults or abuses a teacher in the presence of the school is guilty of a misdemeanor punishable by a fine of not less than fifty dollars or more than one hundred dollars, or by imprisonment in the county jail not to exceed three months.' (A.R.S, 15–210).

Pupils are to show courtesy and respect for teachers, staff members, and on-campus adults at all times.

Class Behavior Expectations (Mahopac High School, Mahopac, New York)

Students are expected to follow the directions of the teachers, which may include such items as assigned seating.

The Reasons for Students to be Disciplined (Carlmont High School, Redwood City, California)

Abuse (talking back, insolent, rude)

Guidelines for Student Behavior (Los Altos High School, Los Altos, California)

Disruptive, inappropriate and/or rude behavior on the part of students cannot be permitted at any time. This includes profanity and refusal to obey the directions of staff members, i.e. insubordination.
Rationale—Education cannot procede [*sic*] without an atmosphere of good order and discipline necessary to [*sic*] the effective learning of all students, and the successful functioning of the entire school community. Good order and discipline are best thought of as being positive, not negative, as helping the student succeed, rather than as punishment. Its purpose is to turn unacceptable conduct into acceptable conduct.

The four examples, selected from actual SDPs, indicate that schools may not share a common conception of what constitutes misconduct in a given area. In several cases, disrespect is broadened to encompass profanity and insolence. In other instances, it is regarded as failure to follow teacher or staff directions. Tone, style, and grammar vary as well from one SDP to another.

Among the general categories of expectations that tend to appear in SDPs are those related to school and class attendance, disruptive and defiant conduct, use of controlled substances such as drugs, tobacco and alcohol, fighting, and property damage. Less common, but still frequently found expectations, pertain to student respect for other students, behavior in special locations such as the cafeteria or on the school bus, gambling, possession of nuisance equipment such as radios and skateboards, and failure to do assignments. Some schools also have expectations related to acceptable dress, use of motorized vehicles, food possession or consumption, and littering. Expectations for elementary schools tend to be more precise (no pushing in lines, no 'goofing off' in restrooms, no throwing of objects in hallways) than those for secondary schools.

If SDPs consisted only of behavioral expectations, they would not represent a marked departure from traditional organizational practices in schools. As indicated earlier, however, the last two decades have found school officials taking a more comprehensive and systematic view of school discipline. Several prescriptions for SDPs have appeared in the literature as guides for administrative practice. Wayson and Pinnell (1977, p. 7), for example, contend that a complete 'discipline code' requires a list of student rights plus the following:

1. Specific limits on the length of school suspensions and provisions governing student re-admission
2. Specific guidelines concerning the consequences for misconduct
3. Guidelines concerning voluntary student transfer to another school
4. Procedures governing student hearings, including the right to review evidence
5. Provisions for staff development aimed at preventing the conditions that give rise to misconduct
6. Provisions pertaining to classroom management and teacher support

Safer (1982, pp. 51–52) provides a somewhat different list, contending that codes of conduct should clarify the following matters:

1. The right to an education for students
2. The school discipline policy relative to
   a. prohibited acts
   b. specific consequences of the commission of such acts
   c. due process entitlement
   d. types of discipline (punishment)
3. Freedom of expression
4. Police in school—searches
5. Access to student records
6. Extracurricular activities
7. Student government
8. Prohibition of racial and sexual discrimination

In my own manual for school administrators (Duke, 1980), I maintain that a 'Systematic Management Plan for School Discipline' requires seven key elements:

1. Rules, consequences for disobedience, and provisions for teaching students the rules
2. Data collection system for monitoring the effectiveness of school discipline efforts

3. Conflict resolution mechanisms
4. Team troubleshooting provisions for staff members
5. Parent involvement
6. Provisions for improving the climate for learning
7. Staff development opportunities

Given the fact that all three sets of guidelines for developing SDPs call for specification of consequences for rule breaking by students, it may be useful to examine how rule breaking is handled in different SDPs.

Consequences As with expectations, so too with consequences — variation is the norm. In fact, agreement does not even exist on how to refer to the results of rule breaking. 'Disciplinary action,' 'punishment,' and 'consequence' are among the most frequently found terms.

The actual consequences specified in SDPs tend to be fairly limited. The list of options used in the North Clackamas School District is representative (a copy of the complete North Clackamas School District Guidelines for Student Behavior is contained in the Appendix):

Informal talk
Loss of privileges
Conference with school personnel
Parent involvement
Corporal punishment
Short suspension (up to three days)
Long suspension (four to seven days)
Expulsion

In recent years school officials have been compelled to define suspension and expulsion with great care. The constitutionality of denying a student access to schooling as a punishment has been challenged in the courts. Since education is defined as a basic right, due process must be accorded students who are threatened with suspension or expulsion from school. Some school systems have created a complex array of suspension practices to give them more flexibility in dealing with the due process issue. Atlanta (Georgia) Public Schools, for example, differentiate between in-school, emergency, short-term, and long-term suspension. A formal hearing is not required for the first three categories of suspension. Emergency suspension, for example, provides for the expeditious removal of 'dangerous' students from school settings. Sequoia High School in California distinguishes between teacher-initiated, principal-initiated, and superintendent-initiated suspension.

Besides the more common consequences such as warnings, teacher conferences, and referral to the 'office', some schools utilize detention centers and 'time-out rooms' to which students can be referred during school or immediately after school. Grant High School's (Portland, Oregon) SDP explains that the purpose of its time-out room is 'for students to identify, solve, and implement the solutions to problems that have prevented acceptable classroom performance'. A few schools provide students charged with misconduct with the option of attending a special short-term class focusing on behaviour improvement or participating in a peer counseling program.

School-based consequences may be supplemented by court-ordered punishments in cases where criminal behavior is entailed. Many states require school personnel to report to police authorities problems involving possession of controlled substances or weapons, assault, arson, and vandalism. Students guilty of criminal offenses may be subject to disciplinary action by school officials in addition to court-ordered punishment.

SDPs vary in the degree of sophistication with which consequences are handled. Some simply list the options from which a school official may choose when disciplining a student. Others specify which consequence or consequences may be employed for particular behaviour problems. Some SDPs even distinguish between the consequences for a first offense and repeated violations (see the North Clackamas Guidelines in the Appendix). SDPs also may indicate which individuals are responsible for utilizing particular consequences. Invariably, consequences involving student contact with administrators are considered more serious than those calling for meetings with teachers or counselors.

Philosophy The emphasis placed on certain consequences, as well as the procedures for determining when to invoke them, often is related to prevailing attitudes in the school and community about how the young should be treated and the purpose of schooling. In some cases, these attitudes are formalized in a philosophical statement introducing the SDP.

The purpose of the Atlanta (Georgia) Discipline Guidelines, as stated by Superintendent Crim, is 'to effectively reduce negative behaviors which infringe upon the rights of others and which disrupt the educational process while at the same time guaranteeing that student due process rights are being protected'. Nothing is said about cultivating student responsibility and, in fact, the Discipline Guidelines make no direct reference to ways to encourage responsible conduct. Portland's Grant High School, on the other hand, possesses an SDP which states that its goal is to provide 'a friendly, orderly atmosphere in which students are able to learn basic academic skills and develop the self-discipline necessary to function in our society'. The Grant SDP includes various mechanisms by which students are taught how to be responsible and opportunities to demonstrate responsibility. Finding the proper balance between student rights and student obligation seems to be one of the major challenges in the development of SDPs. Some SDPs handle the matter by providing a list of student rights to accompany the list of behavioral expectations.

While many philosophical statements introducing SDPs tend to focus generally on why rules and good behavior are necessary for successful school operations, a few embody the beliefs of particular thinkers in the area of school discipline. The Liberty (Oregon) Discipline Policy, for example, derives from the work of psychotherapist Alfred Adler. The introduction to the document reads as follows (see the Appendix for the complete SDP):

LIBERTY DISCIPLINE POLICY

Some years ago, Alfred Adler developed his explanation of the structure which enables us to live as a free democratic society, and proposed a set of basic psychological premises that fit democratic principles.

1. Man is a social being and his main desire is to belong. This is true for adults and children alike.
2. All behavior is purposive. One cannot understand the behavior of another person unless one knows to which goal it is directed, and it is always directed toward finding one's place. If a person misbehaves, then it indicates they have wrong ideas about how to be significant.
3. Man is a decision-making organism. He decides what he really wants to do, often without being aware of it. He is not a victim of forces converging on him such as heredity, environment, or other outside influences.
4. Man is a whole being who cannot be understood by some partial characteristics. The whole is greater than the sum total of its parts.
5. Man does not see reality as it is, but only as he perceives it and his perception may be mistaken or biased.

Using Adler's personality structure and psychological premises as a basis to understand student behavior, we at Liberty further believe that:

1. All behavior is learned.
2. Behavior is learned from society (especially from school and home).
3. Behavior is used to fulfill needs.
4. It is important that school and society share in the development of a positive environment.
5. It is important that we be aware of an individual's perception of a situation.

6. Students, parents, and teachers will be more responsible when expectations are clear.
7. Students, parents and teachers can work cooperatively, helping each develop individual responsibility.

Procedures and other concerns In addition to statements of philosophy, sets of behavioral expectations, and lists of consequences, SDPs may contain other information, such as specific procedures by which disciplinary decisions are to be reached. As scrutiny of school disciplinary actions by courts and special interest groups has increased, so too has the importance of clearly indicating the steps to be followed in reaching disciplinary decisions. These decisions may include determining when more evidence is needed and what kind, establishing guilt or innocence, and settling on appropriate consequences in the case of guilty verdicts. Additional procedures may be needed if particular actions, such as corporal punishment, search and seizure, or suspension, are necessitated. The formalization of disciplinary procedures presumably increases the likelihood that student misconduct will be handled consistently.

An illustrative set of disciplinary procedures comes from Milwaukie (Oregon) Elementary School. Separate instructions govern the handling of 'minor inside class violations,' 'minor outside class violations', and 'major violations'. In the first instance, the classroom teacher is instructed to deal with the minor violation and then record the misconduct and action taken. In the event that a student is 'written up' three times, s/he must be sent to the office with a referral form. Minor violations occurring outside of class require staff members to handle the problem and forward a written report to the student's classroom teacher. The classroom teacher then administers punishment and notifies the referring staff member of the action taken. Major violations, as defined by the school district, must be referred directly to the school administrator. Procedures such as these assure teachers that a specific point exists beyond which they no longer have to deal with student misconduct. At the same time, however, these procedures often call for more paperwork and attention to detail by teachers.

Procedures related to suspension and expulsion may be very complex because the student's constitutional right to an education is jeopardized. Some states require special review boards to consider all cases calling for long-term suspension. Elsewhere, the local school board must grant a hearing to students threatened with suspension. Appeal procedures, instructions for notifying parents, and regulations regarding missed assignments may be specified. In most cases, suspension procedures are determined at the district, not the school, level and incorporated into school SDPs.

Besides disciplinary procedures, SDPs may include other content, such as lists of student rights, details concerning the disciplinary responsibilities of various role groups including parents, and provisions for the reinforcement of appropriate behavior. Some SDPs also indicate how students and parents are to be informed of school rules and procedures. That SDPs vary greatly in complexity is clear. What remains uncertain, though, is whether complexity is a function of efforts to prevent student misconduct from becoming a major problem or a response to already serious discipline problems.

Critical issues with SDPs

It is one thing to develop an SDP on paper and quite another to see that it is implemented systematically. Research suggests that there exist various levels of adoption for new programs, ranging from awareness of the program to full-scale implementation (Hall *et al.*, 1975). While a previously cited study estimated that three out of every four schools possess some form of SDP, no reliable data exist on the extent to which SDPs actually govern the behavior of teachers and administrators in these schools. Some reports, however, suggest that consistent school discipline is still the exception rather than the rule (Hollingsworth *et al.*, 1984; Wynne, 1980).

Two reasons why new programs may be developed but never fully implemented are lack of resources and the inertial nature of some school personnel. Another explanation may be problems with the program itself. Heretofore no attempt has been made to identify possible flaws in SDPs and problems with their implementation. At least six concerns merit attention: goal displacement, unequal beneficiaries, unrealistic expectations, overreliance on referral, inflated value of consistency, and the illusion of improvement. The remainder of the chapter is devoted to a discussion of these concerns.

Goal displacement

Researchers have noted a tendency for schools to elevate the control of student behavior to the status of a primary goal of schooling rather than merely a means to more academic ends (Tattum, 1982, p. 123). Denscombe (1980) observes that the closed classroom structure of most schools heightens concern with student control, since one teacher usually must face large numbers of students alone. The potential for disorder is ever-present. The issue, of course, is not whether order is a necessary prerequisite to learning, but whether, having achieved order, some educators feel their major responsibility has been met.

If there is already a tendency in many schools for discipline to be regarded as an end in itself, it can be argued that an SDP may only reinforce it further.

Overemphasis on student control may result in a number of undesirable by-products, ranging from the alienation of responsible students to the preoccupation of teachers with rule enforcement. Clarity about the mission of the school and the purposes of the SDP is probably the best precaution against goal displacement. Staff agreement, for example, that the main goal of the SDP is to increase the likelihood of responsible student behavior, rather than minimize the likelihood of irresponsible student behavior, can lead to a significant redirection of energies. Instead of promulgating rules to cover any anticipated infraction and removing all temptations that may induce students to misbehave, school personnel focus on teaching students how to behave responsibly and providing supervised opportunities to exercise responsibility. Research on alternative schools suggests that treating students as persons capable of responsible behavior may, in fact, reduce the need for school rules (Duke and Perry, 1978).

Unequal beneficiaries

The issue of goal displacement leads to another concern. Who really benefits from SDPs? The previous discussion suggested that school staff may benefit more than students, particularly if the maintenance of order receives greater attention than academic growth. Even if academic growth is not at stake, however, there are indications that students are not always the prime beneficiaries of school discipline efforts. For example, the discipline problems that cause the greatest concern for administrators and teachers are not likely to be the same as those that worry students the most. While administrators tend to be primarily concerned with attendance problems (truancy, cutting class, tardiness) and teachers are bothered most by class disruptions and disrespect for authority, students are apt to view fighting, theft, extortion, and related interpersonal problems as those most deserving official attention (Duke, 1978a). Administrators and teachers are likely to devote more effort to dealing with misconduct they regard as more serious. If this misconduct is different from that which bothers students the most, it is easy to see how students can come to believe that SDPs exist more for the convenience and protection of adults than for the benefit of students.

An argument assuredly can be made that students are more likely to cooperate with school personnel when they consider SDPs to represent their interests. One way to encourage this perception is to involve students in developing SDPs. Some evidence, in fact, exists that student participation in rule making and other phases of school discipline may be related to lower levels of concern with misconduct (Duke and Perry, 1978; Lasley and Wayson, 1982; McPartland and McDill, 1976). It is uncertain, however, to what extent students have been involved in the creation of contemporary

SDPs. I suspect that some student input may be solicited initially, but that once SDPs are completed and implemented, student advice is no longer sought. To be most effective, an SDP should probably be reviewed and updated periodically—by students as well as staff.

Unrealistic expectations

A tendency may exist for educators who have invested a great effort in developing SDPs to *expect* discipline problems to diminish overnight. Dramatic changes in student conduct, however, are unlikely. A certain amount of youthful challenge to authority may simply be part of the maturational process. Goodlad (1984, pp. 73-74), in his impressive study of schooling in the United States, comments on the enduring nature of student behavior problems:

> All of the groups [teachers, parents, students] rank 'student misbehavior' high as a problem. Yet, students place 'teachers' failure to discipline' relatively low; indeed, in answering another question, the majority viewed teachers' discipline as 'about right'. It appears that all three groups tend to view the misbehavior of the young as pervasive, existing as a condition apart from efforts, including teachers', to control it.

One mechanism by which educators may reduce the likelihood of unrealistic expectations is disciplinary goal-setting. If the creation of SDPs is accompanied by the establishment of specific goals related to improvements in student behavior (e.g. a 25 per cent annual reduction in tardiness to class), educators have an opportunity to reflect on what it is reasonable to expect in terms of behavior change. Progress toward goals is shared with members of the school community as a means to heighten awareness of the importance of rule-governed behavior. Few schools with SDPs, however, currently set specific behavior improvement goals.

Overreliance on referral

The spread of SDPs has been accompanied by the proliferation of new roles related to school discipline (Duke and Meckel, 1980). It is not uncommon to find schools employing the services of special deans or assistant administrators responsible for discipline, school psychologists, 'crisis' teachers, social workers, security guards, hall patrols, in-school suspension supervisors, student management specialists, and school–community liaisons. SDPs often specify the functions of these support personnel in dealing with student behavior problems. Impetus for this growing division of labor in school discipline has come, in part, from teachers' unions. The

National Education Association, for example, proposes the following language be used by school boards developing discipline policies (Dunlop, 1979, p. 29):

> The Board recognizes the responsibility to give all reasonable support and assistance to teachers with respect to the maintenance of control and discipline in the classroom. Whenever it appears that a particular pupil requires the attention of special counsellors, social workers, law enforcement personnel, physicians or other professional persons, the Board will take reasonable steps to relieve the teacher of responsibilities with respect to such pupil.

While the growing ranks of school discipline specialists is encouraging, the potential for overreliance is great. As the availability of resource persons increases, individual teachers may be less willing to exert a serious effort to understand and deal with student misconduct. Many educators and researchers feel there can be no substitute for a student's relationship with his or her teacher. Metz (1978) has noted how much students value a teacher's persistence in trying to work with their problems. Tattum (1982, p. 125) suggests that rules are invoked—or referrals are made, it can be added—when 'role fails'. In other words, overreliance on formal procedures and specialists may contribute to the deterioration of the primary relationship between student and teacher. Some SDPs attempt to reduce this possibility by requiring a discussion between teacher and student as a first step in any but the most serious disciplinary actions.

Inflated value of consistency

No more consistent educational demand has been made over the years than the cry for consistent discipline. Consistency typically is considered to be more of a virtue by civil servants than by professionals. The dilemma, of course, is that teachers and administrators are *both* civil servants and professionals. While the norms of a public bureaucracy dictate that all clients be treated alike, the norms of a profession call for each client to be treated as an individual. Should a student who rarely talks out in class be disciplined in the same way as one who chronically interrupts and answers questions out of turn? To the extent that SDPs increase the likelihood of similar treatment for different students, they may inhibit the tendency of educators to listen to student explanations and take account of extenuating circumstances. Teachers may feel so pressured to respond to a student behavior problem by invoking a rule that they fail to consider ways in which the problem may be regarded as an opportunity. Rules may begin to take precedence over relationships, thereby undermining teachers' ability to 'reach' troubled students.

The real difficulty with procedures designed to ensure consistency is that it is unlikely that all students need them to an equal extent. Many students seem to be able to cope quite well with differing expectations and inconsistent treatment. It can even be argued that, since the adult world is rarely characterized by consistency, these young people are receiving an important introduction to the complexity of life after school. The problem, though, is that *some* young people are unable to cope with inconsistency. The question, then, is to what extent does the formalization of disciplinary procedures risk adversely affecting one group of students in order to benefit another group of students?

The illusion of improvement

Certain acts have great symbolic value without necessarily making a difference to the way the world works. Creating an SDP, for example, may serve as a potent message to the public that a school has taken to heart its concern with the behavior of young people. As was discussed earlier, however, the creation of an SDP is no guarantee (1) that it will be implemented faithfully or (2) that student conduct will improve. If an SDP helps to quiet critics of disciplinary policies that continue to be unfair or causes educators to shift attention from instructional improvement to rule enforcement, it is questionable whether such a development is in the best interests of students.

Kounin (1970) advised educators not to overemphasize rules and consequences. He urged them to attend to what occurs just prior to misconduct rather than immediately afterward. In other words, a key to preventing discipline problems is improving the conditions that give rise to them rather than stressing rules and punishments. The latter strategy may produce public satisfaction that the school is 'tightening up', but will never address fundamental questions concerning the appropriateness of instruction, the relevance of course content, or the quality of teacher–student relations.

Conclusion

Is an SDP enough? The preceding discussion suggests that a formal plan for school discipline may be useful in focusing attention on the value of order, but that, alone, it is insufficient to ensure that productive learning takes place. Other efforts must accompany the creation of SDPs—staff development and teacher training to upgrade the quality of instruction, organizational redesign to reduce the size of large schools and provide alternative learning settings for certain students, and curriculum reform to increase the likelihood that students will regard schooling as a meaningful experience. In a recent study of school discipline, students who were interviewed indicated that they broke rules in some classes, but not in others (Hollingsworth, Lufler, and Clune, 1984). The implication is clear. Where teachers and teaching are regarded positively, students are more likely to behave. In the absence of caring teachers and capable instruction, no set of disciplinary practices is likely to produce harmony or effective learning. It is this fundamental lesson that American educators are beginning to acknowledge in their quest for school order.

Notes

1. Text of the President's Speech at the National Forum on Excellence, *Education Week* (21 December 1983), 11.
2. N.Y.C. to require discipline codes, *Education Week* (8 December 1982), 14.
3. School board adopts student conduct rules, *Richmond News Leader* (18 August 1978), 13 and 24.

References

Denscombe, Martyn (1980) The work context of teaching: an analytic framework for the study of teachers in classrooms, *British Journal of the Sociology of Education*, **1**. **3**, 279–292.

Duke, Daniel L. (1978a) How administrators view the crisis in school discipline, *Phi Delta Kappan*, **59** (5), 325–330.

Duke, Daniel L. (1978b) Looking at the school as a rule-governed organization, *Journal of Research and Development in Education*, **2** (4), 116–126.

Duke, Daniel L. (1980) *Managing Student Behavior Problems*. Teachers College Press, New York.

Duke, Daniel L., and Jones, Vernon E. (1983) Two decades of discipline—assessing the development of an educational specialization. Paper presented at the 1983 annual convention of the American Educational Research Association.

Duke, Daniel L., and Meckel, Adrienne M. (1980) Disciplinary roles in American schools, *British Journal of Teacher Education*, **6** (1), 37–50.

Duke, Daniel L., and Perry, Cheryl (1978) Can alternative schools succeed where Benjamin Spock, Spiro Agnew, and B. F. Skinner have failed? *Adolescence*, **13** (51), 375–392.

Dunlop, John (1979) Negotiating student discipline policy, *Today's Education*, **68** (2), 27–30.

Goodlad, John I. (1984) *A Place Called School*. McGraw-Hill, New York.

Grant, Joan (1981) The school team approach: issues in school change. Paper presented at the 1981 annual convention of the American Educational Research Association.

Hall, G. E., Loucks, S. F., Rutherford, W. L., and Newlove, B. W. (1975) Levels of use of the innovation: a framework for analyzing innovation adoption, *Journal of Teacher Education*, **29** (1), 52–56.

Hollingsworth, Ellen Jane, Lufler, Henry S., and Clune, William H. (1984) *School Discipline: Order and Autonomy*. Praeger, New York.

Kounin, Jacob (1970) *Discipline and Group Management in Schools*. Holt, Rinehart, & Winston, New York.

Lasley, Thomas J., and Wayson, William W. (1982) Characteristics of schools with good discipline. *Educational Leadership*, **40** (3) 28–31.

McPartland, James M., and McDill, Edward L. (1976) The unique role of schools in the causes of youthful crime. Report No. 216. Center for Social Organization of Schools, John Hopkins University, Baltimore, Md.

Metz, Mary Haywood (1978) Clashes in the classroom: the importance of norms for authority. *Education and Urban Society*, **11** (1) 13–47.

Safer, D. J. (1982) *School Programs for Disruptive Adolescents*. University Park Press, Baltimore, Md.

Tattum Delwyn (1982) *Disruptive Pupils in Schools and Units*. Wiley, Chichester.

Wayson, William W., and Pinnell, Gay Su (1977) Developing discipline with quality schools. Citizens Council for Ohio Schools.

Wynne, Edward A. (1980) *Looking at Schools: Good, Bad, and Indifferent*. Lexington Books, Lexington, Mass.

Appendix

Richmond (Virginia) Public Schools—Standards of Student Conduct

The Richmond Public Schools recognize the right of every student to a relevant education without disruption and a corresponding responsibility not to deny this right to any other student. It encourages acceptable behavior by working with students in an atmosphere of respect and understanding centered around freedom, firmness and consistency to build pride and confidence in the student and the school.

The Professional Senate, Student Senate, Parent-Teacher Associations and administrators have met periodically over two years for the purpose of developing a system-wide management plan in relation to student conduct that will ensure due process procedures for students and will be executed in all Richmond Public Schools. Specifically, procedures that will insure a systematic, equal opportunity for parents, students, and school personnel to understand the responsibilities of each in relation to student conduct and, likewise to understand the consequences for failing to assume these responsibilities.

In order to promote and maintain acceptable standards of behavior by all students and to promote a better understanding among parents, students and school personnel, a policy on student conduct is hereby proposed.

Standards of conduct

1. Students shall not dress in a manner that is distracting to themselves, to other students or that interferes with the orderly progress of instruction. For example; halters, tube and tank tops, bare midriffs, hats on in school, etc.

Systematic consequences

First Offense
a. Students will be counseled in relation to acceptable dress.
b. With parent knowledge, the student will go home to acquire acceptable dress and return to school.
c. If (b) is not feasible, the student will be placed in an in-house location until dismissal time.

Repeated Offenses
a. All of the above and in-school suspension will be ordered for two days.

2. Students shall not take another's property under duress, threats, or by any other means.

First Offense
a. A hearing will be held to determine facts.
b. Restitutions will be encouraged.
c. Parent or guardian will be notified.
d. In-school suspension will be ordered for two days.

Repeated Offenses
a. All of the above with the extension of in-school suspension to not less than five days.
b. Referral will be made to Pupil Personnel Services.
c. Referral to legal authorities will be encouraged.
d. Out-of-school suspension for five days.
e. Expulsion recommended to the School Board.

3. Students shall not use profanity or abusive language.

First Offense
a. A conference will be held to determine the facts.
b. Parent or guardian will be notified.
c. In-school suspension will be ordered for two days.

Repeated Offenses
a. A conference will be held with parent or guardian, student, and the accuser.
b. Referral will be made to Pupil Personnel Services staff.
c. Out-of-school suspension will be ordered for five days.

4. Students shall not have in their possession or on their person guns, knives, explosives, or other types of dangerous articles.

All Offenses
a. A conference will be held to determine the facts.
b. Parent or guardian and police will be notified.
c. Out-of-school suspension will be ordered for five days.
d. Services of the Pupil Personnel team will be requested.
e. Students will be suspended from that school for the remainder of the school year.

Repeated Offenses
All of the above and expulsion will be recommended to the School Board.

5. Students shall not have in their possession or on their person illegal drugs or alcohol.

First Offense
a. A conference will be held to determine the facts.

b. Parent or guardian and police will be notified in cases of illegal drugs (including marijuana).
c. In-school suspension will be ordered for five days.
d. Parent or guardian conferences will be held in cases involving alcohol.
e. Referral will be made to Pupil Personnel staff.

Repeated Offenses
a. All of the above and out-of-school suspension for five days.
b. Pupil Personnel Services team will involve community resources in treatment process.
c. Expulsion will be recommended to the School Board.

6. Students in high schools shall not use tobacco in any form except in such places and at such times as the principal designates. Smoking is not permitted in elementary and middle schools.

First Offense
a. Conference to establish the facts.
b. Parent or guardian will be notified.
c. In-school suspension will be ordered for two days.

Repeated Offenses
All of the above and in-school suspension for five days will be ordered.

7. Students shall not fight or display aggressive behavior that is disruptive or dangerous.

First Offense
a. Conference will be held to establish facts.
b. Parent or guardian will be notified.
c. In-school suspension will be ordered for three days.

Repeated Offenses
a. All of the above and a Pupil Personnel Services team will make an evaluation.
b. In-school suspension will be ordered for eight to ten days.
c. Out-of-school suspension will be ordered for five days as a 'cooling off period'.
d. Expulsion will be recommended to the School Board.

8. Students shall be regular and punctual in attendance at school and in all classes unless interrupted by conditions of health or unavoidable circumstances.

First Offense
a. Conferences will be held to determine facts.
b. Parent or guardian will be notified.
c. Missed class assignments will be completed.
d. After-school detention will be ordered.

Repeated Offenses
a. All of the above and a conference will be held with parent or guardian.
b. Pupil Personnel Services team will be consulted.
c. In-school suspension will be ordered for three to five days.

9. Students shall not behave in a disruptive manner while riding school buses. Refer to The Official Bus Operator's Handbook.

First Offense
a. A conference will be held to determine facts.
b. Parent or guardian will be notified.

Repeated Offenses
a. A conference with parent or guardian will be held and suspension from riding the bus for one to five days will be ordered.
b. Privilege will be denied to ride school bus for remainder of the school year. Parent or guardian will be notified to provide transport to and from school.

10. Unauthorized persons shall not trespass on school property.

All Offenses
a. Persons will be asked to leave school property.
b. Police will be notified.

11. Students shall not deface or cause destruction to school property.

All Offenses
a. Students will be counseled.
b. Parent or guardian will be notified.
c. Students or parents will be required to restore or pay for any defacement or destruction of school property.
d. Legal action will be taken in extreme cases.

12. Students shall not have in their possession pornographic material, obscene or indecent literature.

First Offense
a. Teachers will confiscate questionable material.
b. Parent or guardian conference will be held and questionable material returned to parent.

Repeated Offenses
All of the above and in-school suspension for two days will be ordered.

CODICIL

It shall be incumbent upon each administrator or supervisor to ensure the orderly, systematic implementation of the Standards of Conduct and Systematic Consequences as set forth in this document.

It is imperative when infractions occur, that procedures are followed in the order presented. In addition, every effort must be made to utilize appropriate support services to facilitate actions taken in resolving disciplinary matters.

It is recognized that the Standards of Student Conduct do not embrace all possible examples of student behavior; therefore, each principal will exercise good judgment in keeping with the intent implicit within the Standards and Consequences in the maintenance of a proper educational environment.

North Clackamas School District Guidelines for Student Behavior

Elementary School

School is a place where students come to get an education. We think they should be able to learn in a school that is safe and orderly. In North Clackamas, we insist on this because we want the best for your youngster. Open, honest communication with you is the best way we know to achieve this goal.

Students, parents and school must share the responsibility for creating the best possible school setting. The school must provide a quality staff and programs to help youngsters succeed in a complex world. Parents must help their children learn to take responsibility for their actions. Students must respect themselves, the school staff members, and their classmates. The North Clackamas School District has set the following guidelines to insure consistency in discipline at all schools.

Actions and responsibilities

Disciplinary actions are taken with the aim of correcting behavior patterns. Most behavior problems can be handled routinely with properly organized school and classroom programs. Nearly all students respond satisfactorily to friendly encouragement, firm direction and understanding guidance. For those students who do not, and to protect the rights of all our children, it is important that parents and students understand the consequences of misbehavior. There are certain responsibilities we all share in helping the students overcome behavior problems. If a student's misbehavior is directly related to an identified handicap, the school staff will take such conditions into account. A student who becomes involved in areas of problem behavior will be subjected to certain disciplinary actions. Depending upon the seriousness of the behavior problem, one or more of the following actions will be taken by the school staff. *In the case of severe violation of rules, the disciplinary action taken may extend beyond these guidelines.*

Informal talk　A member of the school staff will talk with the student to reach agreement regarding the student's behavior.

Loss of privileges　The school administrator may notify the parent of privilege suspension. These privileges may include removing the student from playground, cafeteria, media center, and/or class participation.

Conference A conference will be held with the student, the teacher, the administrator and other appropriate staff members, to develop a plan for improving behavior. The parent may be contacted.

Parent involvement The parent will be informed of the problem area. A conference with the student, the parent, and appropriate staff members may be scheduled. If a plan is developed to help improve the student's behavior, copies will be given to the student and the parent.

Corporal punishment The school administrator will notify the parent when corporal punishment (spanking) will be given in accordance with school board policies.

Short suspension The student is excluded from school and related non-public activities for a period of up to 3 school days. In these cases parents will be notified and a conference between the administrator, student, parents and other school staff will be conducted. Recorded in student behavioral file.

Long suspension The student is excluded from school and related non-public activities for a period of 4 to 7 calendar days. Parents will be notified and a conference between the administrator, student, parents and other appropriate school staff will be conducted. Recorded in student behavior file.

Expulsion The principal, through the Superintendent, may recommend that a student be expelled. the student is suspended pending a hearing and/or action by the Board of Directors. Through this action the student is excluded from school and all non-public activities for the remainder of the current semester. Under special cases exceptions in the length of the expulsion may be recommended to the Board of Directors by the school staff. The student and parent are notified of charges by telephone and certified letter. The procedure for expulsion follows in accord with the rights of the student within due process. Recorded in student behavioral file.

Bus rules

The following rules and regulations apply to all students riding District operated school buses. These rules and regulations were established to assist the drivers in assuring that you are afforded the safest possible ride to and from school. The school bus driver is responsible for the enforcement of the regulations.

1. Students being transported are under authority of the bus driver.
2. Students shall stay in their seats and keep hands and feet to themselves.
3. Students must have permission from parents and/or school to leave bus other than at regular stop.
4. Students shall converse in normal tones; profane language is prohibited.
5. No animals can be transported on the bus.
6. Students who refuse to obey may forfeit their privilege to ride the bus.

Automatic suspension of bus privileges will result for following infractions:

- Use of tobacco or creating a fire hazard
- Fighting
- Possession of alcohol or drugs
- Throwing hazardous objects in or from the bus
- Interference with the safe operation of the bus
- Flagrant insubordination/defiance
- Vandalism

When rule violations occur, a conduct report is given to the student and building administrator. The administrator will attempt to resolve the problem with the student and/or parents. The parent is expected to assume major responsibility to counsel the student as to acceptable behavior while riding the school bus.

The bus driver has the option of recommending a suspension from the bus and in severe cases a loss of bus riding privileges will result. However, every effort is made to correct minor situations through a conference, parent involvement, or an administrative action.

Your right of due process

This booklet has explained the major disciplinary problem areas and the actions that may result for those students who will not follow the rules. All students are entitled to due process. This means that no action will be taken against a student until the facts have been presented by everyone involved, and a judgement has been made. There are certain procedures which school officials must follow prior to taking appropriate disciplinary action. There are also procedures which students and parents must follow if they do not agree with the school's actions.

Hopefully, students will never be in a situation where they need the protection of due process. If, however, a student does become involved in a suspension or expulsion, both the student and his/her legal guardian, upon request to the principal, will be given a more detailed description of the due process procedure.

PROBLEM AREA	STUDENT RESPONSIBILITY	PARENT RESPONSIBILITY	SCHOOL RESPONSIBILITY	DISCIPLINE ACTIONS	
VIOLATION OF BUS RULES	Students are required to follow the rules for bus riding.	Parents are requested to review bus rules with student and encourage appropriate behavior at all times.	The school will instruct students to obey bus rules and will assist students and bus driver with problems that occur.	Minimum	Informal talk
				Maximum	Loss of bus privileges

PROBLEM AREA	STUDENT RESPONSIBILITY	PARENT RESPONSIBILITY	SCHOOL RESPONSIBILITY	DISCIPLINE ACTIONS 1st OCCURRENCE
ATTENDANCE/ TARDINESS	Come to school each day and be in class when the bell rings.	Help children get up in the morning and arrive at school on time.	Keep records of student attendance/tardies.	Minimum Informal talk Maximum Conference
DEFIANCE OF AUTHORITY	Respect staff members and other adults in the building at all times, even when they are telling you that you have made a mistake.	Support school staff in helping children develop a sense of respect for authority.	Show respect for students and reinforce those that demonstrate good behavior.	Minimum Informal talk Maximum Short suspension
DISORDERLY CONDUCT	Be well-mannered during school day. Use good language, walk in the halls, bring only items that belong in school, and show respect for other students.	Impress upon children that school is a place to learn. Pay attention in class and play only during recess.	Plan structured activities and model appropriate behavior that creates an orderly learning environment to help students behave and use their time properly.	Minimum Informal talk Maximum Short suspension
THEFT*	Keep all personal items in proper places, and use adults' or other student's items only with their permission.	Support the idea that taking what doesn't belong to the child is wrong.	Keep classrooms neat and orderly, limiting the temptation for the students to take things that don't belong to them.	Minimum Informal talk Maximum Parent involvement
TOBACCO	Bringing tobacco to school in any form is not allowed.	Teach and discuss good health habits with your child concerning the use of tobacco.	Encourage students to participate in a program of good health and physical fitness, and discourage the use of	Minimum Parent involvement Maximum Short

PROBLEM AREA	STUDENT RESPONSIBILITY	PARENT RESPONSIBILITY	SCHOOL RESPONSIBILITY	DISCIPLINE ACTIONS
	classmates.	themselves and others.	students feel safe and comfortable.	Maximum Short suspension
FIGHTING	Seek alternative ways to resolve conflicts.	Help children to develop alternative methods of resolving conflict and to seek assistance from staff when necessary.	Establish an atmosphere of open communication for students to seek help from staff members.	Minimum Informal talk Maximum Short suspension
POSSESSION* OF ALCOHOL & DRUGS PHYSICAL* ASSAULT POSSESSION* OF WEAPONS OR EXPLOSIVE DEVISES ARSON* VANDALISM*	Avoid disrupting the educational process at school by realizing the severity of these problem areas.	Explain to the children the harm to themselves and to others when they are involved in any of these problem areas. Support the school rules at home by providing sufficient consequences for such misbehavior.	Report and identify all violations of these problem areas and contact parents.	Minimum Parent involvement Maximum Expulsion

PROBLEM AREA	STUDENT RESPONSIBILITY	PARENT RESPONSIBILITY	SCHOOL RESPONSIBILITY	DISCIPLINE ACTIONS REPEATED OCCURRENCES
REPEATED VIOLATIONS	Learn from their first mistake and not to become involved in misbehavior again.	Cooperate with the school staff to improve their child's behavior and help children understand that continued misbehavior disrupts the educational process.	Deal with repeated violations by developing a behavior plan that uses appropriate resources.	Minumum Conference Maximum Expulsion

Liberty Discipline Policy

Some years ago, Alfred Adler developed his explanation of the structure which enables us to live as a free democratic society, and proposed a set of basic psychological premises that fit democratic principles.

1. Man is a social being and his main desire is to belong. This is true for adults and children alike.
2. All behavior is purposive. One cannot understand the behavior of another person unless one knows to which goal it is directed, and it is always directed toward finding one's place. If a person misbehaves, then it indicates they have wrong ideas about how to be significant.
3. Man is a decision-making organism. He decides what he really wants to do, often without being aware of it. He is not a victim of forces converging on him such as heredity, environment, or other outside influences.
4. Man is a whole being who cannot be understood by some partial characteristics. The whole is greater than the sum total of its parts.
5. Man does not see reality as it is, but only as he perceives it, and his perception may be mistaken or biased.

Using Adler's personality structure and psychological premises as a basis to understand student behavior, we at Liberty further believe that:

1. All behavior is learned.
2. Behavior is learned from society (especially from school and home).
3. Behavior is used to fulfill needs.
4. It is important that school and society share in the development of a positive environment.
5. It is important that we be aware of an individual's perception of a situation.
6. Students, parents, and teachers will be more responsible when expectations are clear.
7. Students, parents, and teachers can work cooperatively, helping each develop individual responsibility.

The following are expectations at Liberty:

1. Awareness of School Rules and Schedules
   STUDENT
   Right: To be made aware of school rules and schedules.
   Responsibility: To follow School rules and schedules.
   PARENTS
   Right: To be made aware of school rules and schedules.
   Responsibility: To review and periodically check their child's under-
   standing of the rules and school procedures.

STAFF

Right: To expect students to cooperate with all school rules and schedules. To expect parent support in working with students.

Responsibility: To keep students, parents, and other staff informed of the rules and schedules. When necessary, to involve students and parents in the development or modification of school or room rules.

2. Attendance and Punctuality

STUDENT

Right: To have an uninterrupted education at their level.

Responsibility: To attend school and to arrive at school on time with the required materials.

PARENTS

Right: To have knowledge of individual student attendance and punctuality.

Responsibility: To see that children attend school punctually and with needed materials.

STAFF

Right: To have all students in class on time with adequate materials to complete work.

Responsibility: To encourage students to attend class and to monitor and inform parents of attendance or punctuality violations.

3. Proper Use and Supervision of School Facilities

STUDENT

Right: To be made aware of the school facilities and designated areas they are to use for various activities. To use the facilities for their good.

Responsibility: To be with their assigned supervisor and in the designated area for each activity. They are expected to get permission before leaving any group or area.

PARENTS

Right: To be made aware of the rules and to be made aware when their child continues to disobey.

Responsibility: To work with the school in correcting a persistent problem.

STAFF

Right: To have student and parent cooperation in this matter.

Responsibility: To have their assigned students under their supervision at all times. To inform parents of persistent problems.

4. Student Behavior Coming to and from School and at After-school Activities
STUDENT

Right: To be made aware of rules traveling to and from school. To travel to and from school free of harassment.

Responsibility: To follow all school/bus rules while travelling to and from school, to be respectful of people and property, and to travel safely. Students should also follow school rules at after-school or evening activities.

PARENTS

Right: To be made aware of rules and to be made aware of persistent problems.

Responsibility: To help their children learn safe and respectful behavior in traveling to and from school. Parents should also assume responsibility for their child's behavior when they are with their children at evening activities.

STAFF

Right: To have students who cooperate in an appropriate manner coming to and going home from school.

Responsibility: To teach and reinforce safety and respect in the area of traveling to and from school. Staff members are expected to deal with inappropriate behavior of students during nonschool hours, when appropriate.

5. Human Respect
STUDENT

Right: To have their rights and feelings respected by other students and adults. To be helped to achieve maximum success and self-worth.

Responsibility: To be polite and cooperative with supervising adults, and students, respecting their rights and feeling.

PARENTS

Right: To have their rights as a parent respected and to have their rights and feelings respected by their children, other children, and adults.

Responsibility: To instill in their children a respect for others and to help them develop a good feeling about themselves. To be cooperative with staff and to encourage children to be polite to adults and students. To deal directly with staff members about their questions or concerns.

STAFF

Right: To have their rights and feelings respected by students, parents, and staff.

Responsibility: To encourage respect for adults and students by modeling and providing guidance. To help each child achieve success and self-worth.

6. Respect for Building and Property.
    STUDENT
    Right: To have personal property respected.
    Responsibility: To be responsible for their personal property and to take care of any borrowed property. To respect the school building and school property and the ownership of other student's personal property.
    PARENTS
    Right: To have their personal property and public property respected.
    Responsibility: To help develop an attitude of respect for the school building, school property, and personal property of others.
    STAFF
    Right: To have their personal property respected.
    Responsibility: To promote responsible behavior toward the school building, personal property, school property, and the personal property of others.

7. Attitude Toward School and Learning
    STUDENT
    Right: To express their attitudes and feelings in a constructive way, to be encouraged and supported in their learning efforts, and to be provided an environment supportive to learning.
    Responsibility: To understand their responsibilities in the learning process. To cooperate in the completion of learning activities. To develop a positive and eager attitude toward the learning process.
    PARENTS
    Right: To be included in the learning process. To be aware of their role in that process.
    Responsibility: To support their children in their learning by being encouraging, positive, and understanding. To work cooperatively with the teacher and the child in assisting the child's learning and in building positive attitudes towards learning and school.

STAFF

Right: To have a classroom uninterrupted by misbehavior. To help each child reach maximum learning.

Responsibility: To be clear about their expectations for children's behavior. To maintain a positive, nurturing, learning environment and to assist the child in building positive attitudes towards learning.

Management of Disruptive Pupil Behaviour in Schools
Edited by D. P. Tattum
©1986 John Wiley & Sons Ltd

_____ ***14***___

The management of disruptive behaviour in Western Europe

Jean Lawrence, David Steed, and Pamela Young

The chapter is devoted to six European 'cameos' which are brief accounts of ongoing work or processes of particular relevance to the teacher-practitioner, and pointing to possible developments in the United Kingdom. They are reflections on violence in the French nursery school, the French preventive psycho-pedagogic groups, the Danish and Dutch response to disruptive behaviour, the Belgian research on the close relationship between delinquency and disruptive behaviour, and an Austrian scheme for in-service teacher education.

The cameos are part of a larger study reported elsewhere (Lawrence *et al.*, 1984, 1985) which gathered comparative information about disruptive behaviour in European schools through a questionnaire sent to European educationalists, psychologists, and others working in the field. At the time, it was not possible to sample classroom teachers' opinion. This part of the study showed, for example, that 'off-site' units as we know them in the UK are rare in Europe. The advisory service is much more developed in the UK than in other countries in Europe. Teachers' centres are almost non-existent in Europe. Thus the European patterns of support for teachers in their work in the classroom are different and well worth exploring for the ideas they can offer us.

Our first cameo is about violence in the French nursery school, and is based on the work of Liliane Lurçat (1980), head of research at the preschool education psychology laboratory of the University of Paris.

Violence in the French nursery school

One perturbing feature of the returns from the European psychologists to our questionnaire was the impression that the current disruptive scene is spreading progressively downwards to children of younger age. If the limited survey of assistant teachers' opinions conducted by the Assistant Masters' and Mistresses' Association in 1984 is to be accepted, then a similar phenomenon may be observed in some English schools.

In some French nursery schools, children's relationships with adults, according to Lurçat, are seen as different today from what they were 10 or even 5 years ago. Children are less intimidated by adults, whose reactions they learn to anticipate through television, and perhaps also in their daily lives through, in particular, the style of the modern home. Teachers are no longer the same: they support children less, though they wish to come closer to them. Sometimes they develop less conventional attitudes than their predecessors, but they are also more vulnerable.

Many children are brought up in an urban environment where often the play group is the only place in which they can get any exercise. Their confinement in tiny flats can lead to violence, fed by the violence of the society they live in and violent models at home and in the street. It is from this environment that children learn racism, sexism, and brutality towards those smaller and weaker than themselves. In addition, nursery school teachers often feel inadequate to cope with the mix of nationalities of their immigrant children. Children simply being together is not necessarily an educative experience: it can have the effect of crystallizing the most negative attitudes.

In these schools the problem can be thought of as principally one of moral education, of tackling 'moral' teaching in a situation where psychology and medicine have replaced morality and have eliminated the responsibilities of pupils, parents, and teachers. Lurçat believes that teachers have been given too much power in relation to the selection and labelling of pupils, and this prevents them from teaching morality, because they believe in (or allow for the possibility of) behavioural determinism.

The problem of the French school is mainly a moral problem, at three levels:

— at the level of the transmission of knowledge and values;
— at the level of the teacher and his responsibility for each of his pupils;
— at the level of the school as the whole; that is, to provide for each child, with his right to acquire basic knowledge and also to have the joy of learning, that which is not strictly utilitarian.

These levels are abstractions and need to be viewed in terms of their practical implications for teachers' work in the classroom. If we follow Lurçat, then the classroom needs to become a place where moral issues arising from behaviour are raised and discussed with children, and where, through role playing and the modelling of 'good' teacher behaviour, this teaching of morality is reinforced.

Our second 'cameo' deals with preventive work with those of regular school age.

A preventive approach by the Groupes d'Aide Psychopédagogique (GAPPs)

In France, as in Britain disruptive behaviour (*troubles de compartement*) has been perceived as a matter of considerable concern. At the time of writing (1984) there are concerted efforts in France to develop GAPPs beyond the Rouen area from where this account is derived.

A GAPP is a team consisting of a psychologist and one or several remedial teachers who are invited into the school. It is responsible for one or more groups within the school and looks after the remediation of pupils by taking part in continuous observation and discussion with the class teacher. The group intervenes through educational-psychological or psychomotor remedial help given to an individual child or a small group, at the first sign that a child has need of such support. It refers to the appropriate school medical service any of those pupils who, because of the nature, seriousness, or pathology of the difficulties which they present or which are suspected, require an in-depth multidisciplinary examination and techniques beyond those possessed by the group. This definition is the official one (see Circular IV, 70–83, 9 February 1970, in the B.O. de l'Éducation Nationale no. 8, 19.2.1970, on the prevention of maladjusted behaviours).

The GAPP offers a team setting for psychological and educational help, and tries to control and understand the situational variables of maladjustment, in order to prevent it from developing. The GAPP provides a resource and a place where one can be listened to, whether one is a child or a parent; a place where some situations can be defused, where all sorts of information is gathered and where an attempt is made to get the child and the school to adjust to each other. At the same time, personnel try to respond to the child's needs, to his potential, and to the demands of the school by intervening in different ways with the child, his parents, and the teachers closely involved in his behaviour. The GAPP is part of the school, which in a way it changes so as to avoid intolerance and the segregation and exclusion of children in difficulties. Because the GAPP is inside the school, it shortens delays between request and response, and it can intervene early and flexibly. This is its characteristic and undoubted advantage.

On the other hand, the remedial teachers, in addition to their educational-psychological training, are specialist teachers, which means that, like the school's psychologist, they have a first-hand knowledge of what being a teacher involves. They are trained for work which is close to teaching. The GAPP is thus in contact with centres with a mainly therapeutic stance like a psychiatric clinic. In no way do GAPPs attempt premature rehabilitation in the medical sense of the term: this is beyond the limits of their intervention. Medical cases are passed on to one of the appropriate agencies with which the GAPP will of necessity cooperate. A GAPP is a team working with individual pupils and a change agent group working with a class or school.

The Danish experience

Food for thought and possibly action on the part of teachers and others concerned with disruptive behaviour may be sought in Denmark. The experience of Danish educators may be increasingly relevant to concerns and pressures created by secondary reorganization and the integration of pupils with 'special needs' into British schools. Teachers in Denmark seem to be less of a beleaguered profession and less defensive than those in the UK (Steed, 1982) where pupils with problems connected with learning or behaviour are perceived as failures of the school or the teacher, and not of the pupil alone.

In Denmark, whilst local responses vary as in other countries, they do so within parameters established by the Ministry of Education and by a pervasive child-centred philosophy which takes an optimistic view of the possibilities of environmental planning. National guidelines emphasize equality of treatment between classes and sexes, and choice and participation at every level for pupils and parents (Danish Ministry of Education, 1977a, b; 1978).

The existence of 'free schools' — alternatives to ordinary school provision and largely financed by the state — is important in understanding why teachers appear to be more relaxed about disruption and less sensitive regarding challenges to their authority. It is acknowledged that the same regime may not suit all pupils. If all else fails, then there is the possibility of transfer elsewhere without incurring stigma. Free schools thus signify the importance attached to parental and pupil choice, and act as an important safety valve so that neither the teacher nor the pupil is forced into an organizational cul-de-sac where neither has a way out without loss of face.

Most ordinary schools have, in addition, access to the specialized welfare and psychological services. The difference between this situation and that in the UK lies in the degree to which these services have been systematized — there is a team of doctor, nurse, dentist, psychologist, educational welfare worker, and counsellor to each pair of schools, and the expectation is that they will be regularly available and used by teachers. There are also experienced teachers and specialists in pupils' learning problems who can come into the classroom to give support and advice to enable teachers and pupils to understand better the dynamics of situations where disruption occurs. The smallness of schools—most have 400–800 pupils—no doubt assists with the swift identification of problems and enables the resources of the schools and the community to be used effectively. Where it is considered desirable, two teachers can be allocated to all or part of a single class timetable. Most importantly, the class teacher, referred to as the 'father of the class', teaches the same pupils from the ages of 7 to 16, and thus can more easily develop close relationships with both pupils and their families which can be effective in preventing misunderstandings and disaffection. Parents are expected and encouraged to be involved as partners in education and this is ensured by the formal and mandatory framework which schools provide. The exercise of pupils' democratic choices through schools councils goes far beyond tokenism. Pupils' and parents' rights to influence lesson content and presentation, and to decide what subjects a pupil will be examined in, are acknowledged (Danish Ministry of Education, 1977b).

For pupils who persist in disruption despite preventive strategies, there is what the Ministry of Education calls 'observation education' (Jorgensen, 1979). In the first stage the pupil receives support and assistance from trained teachers in his own classroom. In addition, every school has an 'observation clinic' where pupils may go for occasional, temporary, and supplementary help for their normal work. 'Observation classes', which separate pupils both from the school and the classroom for periods of between 6 months and 2 years, exist in most municipalities for disturbed or maladjusted pupils 'in crisis', but aim for their eventual reintegration. The nearest UK parallel to the observation class would be an 'off-site' unit via our secondary schools. Some schools, called 'all day schools', specialize in vocational preparation and work experience for pupils in a single municipality. Finally, there are 'observation schools' for children who might benefit from boarding education because of emotional problems or difficulties of adjustment either at home or at school.

The Danish approach to disruption is of particular interest because of its emphasis on preventive strategies (Topping, 1983), and because of its similarities to what in the United States has come to be called a Cascade Model. In such a model, provision ranges from the simplest to the most complex in order to accommodate pupils with differing educational needs (Reinert, 1980), so that none is allowed to slip through the net.

Another approach which teachers in the UK might consider for adoption is to place the young disruptive child at the primary stage into a special class taught by a specially trained teacher who is supported by the schools' medical-psychological service. Similar procedures are to be found in Switzerland and Belgium.

Youth at risk—Holland

Crime prevention in the Netherlands takes into consideration misbehaviour in schools. Educational and vocational programmes (Junger Tas, 1976) embrace three broad approaches.

Special youth care

Children with school or family problems are referred by social agencies (and not by juvenile courts) for special education in boarding schools, which aims to promote the self-realization of the child by 'surrounding him with a pedagogical climate in which he feels secure and accepted'. Here the norms for judging behaviour are the personal circumstances of the child and not dominant cultural norms.

Compensatory programmes

Compensatory programmes aim specifically to correct what are perceived as inefficiencies and injustices of an educational system where a disproportionate number of pupils from lower-class backgrounds fail. Two thousand schools in five geographical areas, and 19 of the 65 guidance services which cover the country, are involved. Unlike 'pure' compensatory programmes they stress:

(1) The extent to which education must emanate from the life and experience of the child.
(2) The need for the systematic involvement of parents in educational activities within a formalized framework.
(3) The need for collaboration with neighbourhood organizations (youth clubs, etc.) and liaison through a field officer with neighbourhood agencies, such as recreation and housing.
(4) The availability of counselling and guidance for both parents and children.

In addition to a teacher education programme not unlike our own, student teachers receive special training in the use of innovative teaching methods, in individualized work with pupils, and in cooperative planning with parents. This latter work also extends to teachers already in service. Programmes are supported by the Ministry of Education and Science and, interestingly, the Ministry of Culture, Recreation, and Social Work (Dutch Ministry of Education, 1972), thus conceptualizing and tackling the problem on a much wider basis.

'Stimulation programmes'

Relevant government stimulation programmes aim to eliminate lags in educational opportunities. They stress the need to modify characteristics of the school—its curriculum and pedagogy—and to train teachers to develop and use home–school links more effectively. Target children are those aged 8–18 with a history of behavioural difficulties such as aggression, unmanageableness, truancy, inability to play, or irritability.

All programmes give the school a central position in delinquency prevention, following the argument that a person who is integrated into or rewarded by conventional society is less likely to break the law.

One prevention programme concerned with aggressive delinquents (Buikhuisen *et al.*, 1972) suggests the need to change the name 'school' to 'community centre', thus emphasizing the embeddedness of education in the social and recreational activities of the neighbourhood in which both adults and children are engaged, and its extension into activities which are not exclusively intellectual.

Other research on aggression (Wiegman *et al.*, 1983), using data on the effects on young children of aggressive and prosocial stimuli in television film, suggests that negative school experiences may generate deviant behaviour. The study by Junger Tas (1976) of Belgian youth shows a relationship between the number of offences committed and the variables 'liking for school' and 'having a good relationship with the teacher'. Police and justice departments conclude that, in preventing crime and delinquency, the creation of a satisfactory school climate is paramount.

Solutions to the problem of youth at risk described above all aim to intervene at an early stage and, where possible, to keep children away from the legal authorities so as to diminish the risk of stigma. Whilst much can be done to equip young people with appropriate social and practical skills to enable them to cope better and be more acceptable to society (Jongman, 1978), still more solutions (not specified by Jongman) lie in the schools adapting themselves to the needs of alienated youth. Consideration of Dutch and Danish responses to pupil misbehaviour suggests the importance of the school setting, and lend support to reviews of school organization, curriculum, and classroom practices as a means of minimizing pupil disruption (Hargreaves, 1984).

Disruptive behaviour and delinquency: research by Schaber and Hausman (Belgium)

There is a well-established link between troublesomeness at school and delinquency: numerous different studies of delinquency (self-reported and official) show that many delinquents have histories of misbehaviour at school. British research substantiating and exploring the relationship includes that of Hargreaves (1967), Rutter *et al.* (1979), and West and his colleagues (1969, 1973, 1977). Therefore it is perhaps opportune for teachers in the UK to look at a European examination of this issue.

In a new study, Schaber and Hausman (1982) have again explored the relationship, but in a different way, using a self-report questionnaire administered to 2032 pupils (mean age 15½ years) in the Province of Luxembourg. The data were subjected to a path analysis. Although they admit that they have simply established relationships which only longitudinal studies can translate into causes and effects (unfortunately, they do not refer to West's work, which used precisely such an approach), they make out the strongest possible case for regarding delinquency and misbehaviour in schools not just as related, but as the same process. In reply to the question, 'Is it necessary to distinguish misbehaviour in school from delinquency?' they state: 'There is no room for distinguishing these two types of behaviour and fundamentally they belong to one and the same universe. This means that it is now possible to fuse these two types of behaviour, both in respect of definition and measurement' (Schaber and Hausman, 1982, p. 66). On delinquency reduction they say, 'If . . . misbehaviour in school is an important precursor of delinquency, misbehaviour in school would also have repercussions upon the level of involvement in delinquency' (p. 94).

It is likely that Schaber *et al.*'s latter statement is an oversimplification of the relationship, since clearly it can show either disruptive behaviour followed by delinquency, or delinquency followed by disruptive behaviour, or the two developing concurrently. However, what is of interest is their strong restatement of the finding of West and his colleagues (1969, 1973, 1977) that the most significant single factor predictive of later delinquency is troublesomeness at school at the age of 8. This finding needs, particularly in the light of the Belgian study, to be valued for what it implies, namely, increased links between education and penology. We believe this to be true, in spite of some divergence in the study by Rutter *et al.* (1979) from the predictive value for delinquency of teachers' behaviour ratings. (Rutter found that, indeed, these ratings were the best predictor up to the age of 14, that for older girls they were still an excellent predictor, but that their predictive power for older boys was rather poor.)

If we attempt to give full value to West's and to Schaber and Hausman's findings, we engage in important questions of educational philosophy concerning the desirability of a rapprochement between education and penology, over and above that implicit in schools' systems of sanctions and rewards. Three points are worth making here. Firstly, in considering the balance between penal and educational solutions to the problem of disruptive pupils, the popularity in the UK of autonomous off-site units suggests that there may be pressures which currently favour a penal model, pressures increased by the much favoured emphasis upon school effect-iveness. Schools must now publish information about their examination results for parents, who can thus put pressure on schools to maintain behavioural and other standards.

Secondly, the extent to which schools are prepared to accept the disruptive behaviour–delinquency link will be critical, since it will relate to their notions of 'boundary'. There are likely to be resistances to its acceptance where this affects significantly a school's concept of its pupils, and more so in schools where there is already a broad pastoral base and strong community links.

Thirdly, the recent proliferation in Britain—uniquely among West European countries—of off-site units might, it seems to us, provide a bridging area in which criminologists and teachers can carry out collaborative research.

An Austrian scheme for in-service teacher education

In his 'Praxisnahe Fortbildung von Berufschullehrern mit schwierigen Schülern' ('Practical training of technical teachers for work with difficult pupils'), Professor Volker Krumm (1979) gives an account of a training project in behavioural techniques for teachers who were working with vocational preparation courses (14+ age range) attended by pupils who were often difficult and had learning problems. These vocational preparation courses had just become compulsory in Nordrhein-Westfalen for secondary school students, and included many who had been unsuccessful at school and some who had attended special schools. Teachers involved in the scheme felt that they lacked training for work with youngsters with learning difficulties and problem behaviour, so the project Krumm describes started with 1 day of theoretical instruction, including case illustrations. The teachers then decided whether to go beyond the theoretical instruction to a further 2 days of seminars on theory.

The course focussed on practical training, the teachers supplying examples of their current problems—perhaps with an individual child, or with a class—which they then worked through. The approach is a modification of Tharp and Wetzel's (1969) methods. The teacher's 'educational counsellor' (another teacher) intervenes with advice, when invited, the teacher cannot go any further by himself. Two teachers working in the same school act as 'counsellors' for each other. If they experience problems they can also call on the staff of the course team for help. At the end of the casework the teachers write up their findings for all the course members to read. The course team consists of two senior teachers with counselling training, plus two advanced student-teachers. Members of the course team only intervene with guidance when the teachers ask them to. If the teachers wish it, one of the team comes into the school to observe them, or to watch a video of them, etc. Several courses have now been run, and are being evaluated. One or two problems have arisen, e.g. inadequate record-keeping by teachers, and timetabling difficulties making lesson observation difficult to arrange. Positive features are that teacher motivation is very good, as are relationships between teachers and supervisors. The pairing of colleagues has worked well, but observation of each other's lessons has caused some problems. Training sessions on the school site have been more problematic than those held off-site.

Regarding the most important outcome, relationships between the teachers and their difficult pupils *may* have changed for the better, but this is based on the subjective judgement of teachers.

Krumm does not stop at the design of the course described above, but draws implications from it for a model of pre-service and in-service teacher education. This education is seen as being centred on teaching/learning problems which the teacher encounters in his school, and which may refer to an individual pupil or to a group or a whole class. Its value is seen as being greater than that of training through lectures or seminars, since teachers are actively involved, and hopefully attitudes and actions are modified through the project.

His scheme would seem to be well worth exploring in relation to disruptive behaviour in schools, as it seems to us that the in-service teacher education side of this problem has, with rare exceptions (Upton and Gobell, 1980), not been well explored. There is, of course, no need for projects to limit themselves to behavioural approaches: group dynamic strategies, for example, could provide equally viable courses. In a number of current education management programmes in England the issue of peer (i.e. teacher) counselling has received attention and, as in pastoral care programmes for teachers, may be a way forward that could be more widely used.

Conclusion

It is clear that there is a strong community of concern and identity of interest among colleagues across Europe, relating to disruptive behaviour. It is extremely unfortunate that linguistic barriers impede the sharing of insights into, and solutions to, serious socio-educational problems. In spite of the hazards involved in extrapolating from one cultural setting to others, it is apparent, even from the limited data presented here, that European colleagues have ideas which would be worth exploring in our own country—for example, the French Groupes d'Aide Psychopédagogique offer a scheme for preventive work, Krumm's model of teacher training could well be tried out, and the implications of Schaber and Hausman's work on the delinquency–disruption link, reinforcing British findings as it does, could lead to a joint research approach, for instance between criminologists and educationalists.

For practising teachers each cameo offers suggestions. The work of Lurçat points to the need for teachers to teach moral behaviour, whether through being good 'models' for their pupils, or by taking opportunities in the classroom for raising and discussing points of morality as they occur in classroom relationships. For example, the work of GAPPs shows the teacher the importance of spotting and treating incipient behaviour problems early, and of preventive work which will impede their full development. The Austrian scheme suggests the value for teachers of in-service training in behavioural techniques.

All the 'cameos' illustrate both a general concern among leading educationalists and their agreement that, whatever the causes of disruption, solutions need to be explored within the school system. The range of suggestions will be of interest to teachers and administrators in the UK as they seek to prepare their defences against further cut-backs in expenditure from central government and calls for greater public accountability. The greatest source of encouragement from these examples may be that most of these suggestions need not necessarily involve massive public expenditure, but that improvements will come as schools and teachers become more sensitive and responsive to changes in society. The risks attached to ignoring school disruption or responding inappropriately, however, are made very clear in the links which Dutch and Belgian commentators claim to establish with subsequent delinquent patterns.

References

AMMA (1984) What are our infants turning into? *Report,* **7** (1).

Buikhuisen, W., Jongman, R. W., Schilt, T., and Schilt-Drost, T. (1972) *Onder Zoek Agressieve Kriminaliteit in Limberg.* Discussienota Krimin. Instit. Rijksuniv. Groningen. In Junger Tas (1976).

Danish Ministry of Education (1977a) *The Education Act on the Folkeskole.* DME, Copenhagen.

Danish Ministry of Education (1977b) *The School, the pupil, and the parents.* DME, Copenhagen.

Danish Ministry of Education (1978) *The Upper Secondary School Curriculum: General Principles.* DME, Copenhagen.

Dutch Ministry of Education (1972) *Vejledning om Folkeskolens Observations-undervisning.* Folkeskolelovens Circulære af 4.2.72. DME.

Hargreaves, D. H. (1967) *Social Relations in a Secondary School.* Routledge & Kegan Paul, London.

Hargreaves, D. H. (1984) *Improving Secondary Schools.* ILEA, London.

Jongman, R. W. (1978) Klasse Elementen in die Rechtsgang. Groningen Criminologisch Institut. In Wiegman *et al.*

Jorgensen, I. Skov (1979) *Special Education in Denmark.* Der Danske Selskab, Copenhagen.

Junger Tas (1976) *Delinquency Prevention in Dutch Educational Programmes.* Ministry of Justice, WODC.

Krumm, V. (1979) Praxisnahe Fortbildung von Berufschullehrern mit schwierigen Schülern in Sommer. KH ed. *Brennpunkte der Berufsbildung.* I. J. Holland u. Josenhaus Verlag, West Germany, pp. 21-35.

Lawrence, J., Steed, D. M., and Young, P. (1984) The disruptive pupil in Europe, Part I, 17 August; Part II, 24 August. *Education.*

Lawrence, J., Steed, D. M., and Young, P. (1985) European opinions on disruptive behaviour in schools: provision and facilities, causes and cures. *Cambridge Journal of Education,* Lent Issue.

Lurçat, L. (1980) La Violence à l'école maternelle, *Petite Enfance,* October–December (42-43). France.

Reinert, H. R. (1980) *Children in Conflict.* C. V. Mosby, St Louis, Mo.

Rutter, M., Maugham, B., Mortimore, P., and Ouston, J. (1979) *Fifteen Thousand Hours.* Open Books, London.

Schaber, G., Hausman, P., *et al.* (1982) *Le Poids de l'inadaptation au mileau scolaire dans le processus délinquentiel,* vols 1 and 2. Centre Luxembourgeois de Recherches Sociales et Pédagogiques.

Steed, D. M. (1982) Tired of school: Danish disruptive pupils and ours, *Cambridge Journal of Education,* **13** (1), 20-25.

Tharp, R. G., and Wetzel, R. J. (1969) *Behaviour Modification in the Natural Environment,* 2nd edn. Urban Schwarzenberg, London and Vienna.

Topping, K. (1983) *Educational Systems for Disruptive Adolescents.* Croom Helm, London.

Upton, G., and Gobell, A. (1980) *Behaviour Problems in the Comprehensive School.* Faculty of Education, Cardiff University, Cardiff.

West, D. (1969) *Present Conduct and Future Delinquency.* Heinemann Educational Books, London.

West, D. J., and Farrington, D. P. (1973) *Who Becomes Delinquent?* Heinemann Educational Books, London.

West, D. J., and Farrington, D. P. (1977) *The Delinquent Way of Life.* Heinemann Educational Books, London.

Wiegman, O., Baarda, B., and Seydel, E. R. (1983) Aggression: a Dutch contribution. In Goldstein, A. P., and Segall, M. H. (eds), *Aggression in Global Perspective.* Pergamon, New York.

Subject Index